Studying Classroom Teaching as a Medium for Professional Development

Proceedings of a U.S.-Japan Workshop

Hyman Bass, Zalman P. Usiskin, and Gail Burrill, Editors

Mathematical Sciences Education Board/Center for Education/
Division of Behavioral and Social Sciences and Education

U.S. National Commission on Mathematics Instruction/
Board on International Scientific Organizations/Policy and Global Affairs Division

National Research Council

NATIONAL ACADEMY PRESS
Washington, DC

NATIONAL ACADEMY PRESS • 2101 Constitution Avenue, N.W. • Washington, DC 20418

NOTICE: The project that is the subject of this report was approved by the Governing Board of the National Research Council, whose members are drawn from the councils of the National Academy of Sciences, the National Academy of Engineering, and the Institute of Medicine. The members of the committee responsible for the report were chosen for their special competences and with regard for appropriate balance.

This study was supported by the National Science Foundation (ESI-0001439), The Spencer Foundation, and the MCI WorldCom Foundation. Any opinions, findings, conclusions, or recommendations expressed in this publication are those of the author(s) and do not necessarily reflect the views of the organizations or agencies that provided support for the project.

Library of Congress Cataloging-in-Publication Data

Studying classroom teaching as a medium for professional development : proceedings of a U.S.-Japan workshop / Hyman Bass, Zalman Usiskin, and Gail Burrill, editors.
  p. cm.
"Mathematical Sciences Education Board/Center for Education/Division of Behavioral and Social Sciences and Education, U.S. National Commission on Mathematics Instruction/Board on International Scientific Organizations/Policy and Global Affairs Division, National Research Council."
Workshop hosted by Mathematical Sciences Education Board and United States National Commission on Mathematics Instruction, August 2000, Makuhari, Japan.
Includes bibliographical references.
  ISBN 0-309-08252-8 (pbk.)
 1. Mathematics–Study and teaching (Elementary)–Japan–Congresses.
2. Mathematics–Study and teaching (Elementary)–United States–Congresses. I. Bass, Hyman, 1932- II. Usiskin, Zalman. III. Burrill, Gail. IV. National Research Council (U.S.). Mathematical Sciences Education Board. V. United States National Commission on Mathematics Instruction.
 QA135.6 .S78 2002
 372.7'0952–dc21

                          2001007273

Suggested Citation: National Research Council. (2002). *Studying classroom teaching as a medium for professional development. Proceedings of a U.S.-Japan workshop.* Hyman Bass, Zalman P. Usiskin, and Gail Burrill (Eds). Mathematical Sciences Education Board, Division of Behavioral and Social Sciences and Education, and U.S. National Commission on Mathematics Instruction, International Organizations Board. Washington, DC: National Academy Press.

Additional copies of this report are available from National Academy Press, 2101 Constitution Avenue, N.W., Lockbox 285, Washington, D.C. 20055; (800) 624-6242 or (202) 334-3313 (in the Washington metropolitan area); Internet, http://www.nap.edu.

THE NATIONAL ACADEMIES

National Academy of Sciences
National Academy of Engineering
Institute of Medicine
National Research Council

The **National Academy of Sciences** is a private, nonprofit, self-perpetuating society of distinguished scholars engaged in scientific and engineering research, dedicated to the furtherance of science and technology and to their use for the general welfare. Upon the authority of the charter granted to it by the Congress in 1863, the Academy has a mandate that requires it to advise the federal government on scientific and technical matters. Dr. Bruce M. Alberts is president of the National Academy of Sciences.

The **National Academy of Engineering** was established in 1964, under the charter of the National Academy of Sciences, as a parallel organization of outstanding engineers. It is autonomous in its administration and in the selection of its members, sharing with the National Academy of Sciences the responsibility for advising the federal government. The National Academy of Engineering also sponsors engineering programs aimed at meeting national needs, encourages education and research, and recognizes the superior achievements of engineers. Dr. Wm. A. Wulf is president of the National Academy of Engineering.

The **Institute of Medicine** was established in 1970 by the National Academy of Sciences to secure the services of eminent members of appropriate professions in the examination of policy matters pertaining to the health of the public. The Institute acts under the responsibility given to the National Academy of Sciences by its congressional charter to be an adviser to the federal government and, upon its own initiative, to identify issues of medical care, research, and education. Dr. Kenneth I. Shine is president of the Institute of Medicine.

The **National Research Council** was organized by the National Academy of Sciences in 1916 to associate the broad community of science and technology with the Academy's purposes of furthering knowledge and advising the federal government. Functioning in accordance with general policies determined by the Academy, the Council has become the principal operating agency of both the National Academy of Sciences and the National Academy of Engineering in providing services to the government, the public, and the scientific and engineering communities. The Council is administered jointly by both Academies and the Institute of Medicine. Dr. Bruce M. Alberts and Dr. Wm. A. Wulf are chairman and vice chairman, respectively, of the National Research Council.

U.S.- JAPAN TEACHER DEVELOPMENT
WORKSHOP STEERING COMMITTEE

Hyman Bass, *Cochair*, University of Michigan
Zalman P. Usiskin, *Cochair*, University of Chicago
Deborah Loewenberg Ball, University of Michigan
Toshiakira Fujii, Tokyo Gakugei University
Jacqueline Goodloe, Burrville Elementary School, Washington, DC
Daniel Goroff, Harvard University
Keiko Hino, Nara University of Education
Haruo Ishigaki, Waseda University
Hajime Yamashita, Waseda University

Jerry Becker, (Ex Officio) Southern Illinois University
Frances Curcio, (Ex Officio) New York University
Hiroshi Fujita, (Ex Officio) Tokai University

Gail Burrill, Director, Mathematical Sciences Education Board (MSEB)
Tamae Maeda Wong, Program Director, U.S. National Commission on Mathematics Instruction (USNCMI)
Brian McQuillan, Senior Project Assistant, MSEB
Mariza Silva, Senior Project Assistant, USNCMI
Kara Suzuka, Consultant
Makoto Yoshida, Consultant

Acknowledgments

The Mathematical Sciences Education Board and the U.S. National Commission on Mathematics Instruction gratefully acknowledge the National Science Foundation, The Spencer Foundation, and the MCI WorldCom Foundation for their financial support of *Studying Classroom Teaching as a Medium for Professional Development: Proceedings of a U.S.-Japan Workshop.*

We would like to acknowledge the staff at the Center for Education and International Organizations Board for their efforts in putting the workshop together, and the subsequent proceedings. In particular, Danna Brennan and Myrna McKinnon were instrumental for overseeing logistical arrangements for the workshop. Yuri Maeda provided on-site support along with Saitou Harumichi, Yoshimichi Kanemoto, Eri Matsuda, Tatsuhiko Seino, Kaori Tabeta, and Yoshihisa Tanaka from Tokyo Gakugei University. We also are grateful to Professor Hiroshi Fujita, Chair of the Ninth International Congress on Mathematical Education (ICME-9), for his cooperation and support of the workshop, to those who made the classroom visit to Setagaya School possible, and to Hiroshi Nakano and Shunji Kurosawa for sharing their lessons with us. In addition, Tad Wantanabe helped facilitate the arrangements and did on-site translation during the workshop. Special acknowledgment goes to Makoto Yoshida for his help in setting up the workshop, translating materials, and serving as an interpreter for both the Japanese and the U.S. participants during and after the workshop. Brian McQuillan was responsible for preparing this report for publication. Mariza Silva served as the website manager who prepared the on-line version of the workshop proceedings, which is available on the project home page at http://www4.nationalacademies.org/pga/math.nsf.

We also are grateful to the members of the steering committee for their oversight in planning the program for the workshop. In addition we wish to acknowledge the speakers and in particular the discussion group leaders for their contributions and leadership that gave substance to the discussion.

This report has been reviewed in draft form by individuals chosen for their diverse perspectives and technical expertise, in accordance with procedures approved by the National Research Council's (NRC) Report Review Committee. The purpose of this independent review is to provide candid and critical comments that will assist the institution in making its published report as sound as possible and to ensure that the report meets institutional standards for objectivity, evidence, and responsiveness to the study charge. The review comments and draft manuscript remain confidential to protect the integrity of the deliberative process. We wish to thank the following individuals for their review of this report: Hilda Borko, University of Colorado; Clea Fernandez, Columbia University; Roger Howe, Yale University; Jean Krusi, Ames Middle School, Ames, Iowa; Catherine Lewis, Mills College; Nanette Seago, VideoCases for Mathematics Professional Development, Riverside, California; and Akihiko Takahashi, University of Illinois at Urbana-Champaign.

Although the reviewers listed above have provided many constructive comments and suggestions, they were not asked to endorse the conclusions or recommendations nor did they see the final draft of the report before its release. The review of this report was overseen by Gilbert J. Cuevas, University of Miami. Appointed by the NRC, he was responsible for making certain that an independent examination of this report was carried out in accordance with institutional procedures and that all review comments were carefully considered. Responsibility for the final content of this report rests entirely with the authoring committee and the institution.

Preface

The Ninth International Congress on Mathematics Education (ICME-9) held in Makuhari, Japan, in August 2000 provided a unique opportunity for the Mathematical Sciences Education Board and the U.S. National Commission on Mathematics Instruction. Together with educators from the Japanese mathematical community, they hosted a workshop on teacher development immediately following the Congress. The aim of the workshop was to draw upon the expertise of participants from the two countries to work on developing a better understanding of the knowledge that is needed to teach mathematics well and how to help teachers gain this knowledge. The workshop focused on using the study of classroom events to help elementary mathematics teachers improve their teaching. In the first part of the workshop, participants considered a professional development approach that the Japanese refer to as *jugyokenkyu* or "lesson study." In the second part of the workshop, participants considered the use of classroom documentation and written cases, highlighting some of the work performed in the United States.

The workshop consisted of large group plenary sessions, panel discussions, activity-based sessions, and small group discussion. Interactions between the two cultures were made possible by simultaneous translation. *Studying Classroom Teaching as a Medium for Professional Development* is a record of what took place at the workshop. The first section consists of papers written after the workshop by two participants reflecting on their experiences during the workshop. The body of the proceedings consists of edited transcriptions of the talks presented in plenary sessions and of the remarks given by panel members on various topics. The final section of the document contains the summaries of small group discussions describing the group response to one or two focused questions.

A videotape accompanies the book and includes video selections of classroom lessons and a Japanese postlesson discussion that were shown at the workshop. These segments—along with written cases describing mathematics classes—were used to engage participants in observing and discussing classroom practices, allowing them to consider how such materials might be used in professional development contexts. Supporting print materials, such as transcripts and lesson plans, are in the appendixes.

Studying Classroom Teaching as a Medium for Professional Development is intended for people interested in ways that teachers might work on their teaching, opportunities for teacher learning, or for investigating what it might mean to use teaching and learning as a place to study and improve it. The videos shown at the workshop and the plenary sessions played vital roles in stimulating and grounding the conversations of the participants. This document might be used in the same way—to stimulate conversation among teacher educators, helping them shape their work. As you engage with these materials, you might consider questions such as the following: What do teachers in these two countries do that enables them to develop their teaching practice—to become increasingly more adept at designing lessons, carrying out those lessons with their students, and all the time observing how the lesson is working with those students? What do teachers need to learn to engage in the practice of mathematics teaching? How do educators from the two countries talk about and make records of teaching that inform their conversations? How do teachers in Japan and the United States use practice to work on their teaching?

It is as important to note what these materials are *not* designed to do. These materials are *not* appropriate for comparing U.S. and Japanese teaching—the lessons were not chosen to represent typical teaching in either country. Neither have these materials been designed for use in professional development; they constitute fragments of teaching, without context, or tasks from which teachers might learn. These materials are also not designed to show exemplary practice. What these materials are designed for is to create opportunities to explore what it might mean to use teaching practice as a medium for professional development.

The workshop was a meeting of two very different cultures: people trying to solve in their own ways common problems of mathematics education and the education of teachers. The U.S.- Japan workshop was one attempt to move forward in building a collective understanding about the possibilities and challenges of such work. We personally found it a rich and rewarding experience and hope that through these proceedings, you will be able to share in the discussions and deliberations in ways that will make it a fruitful experience for you.

Sincerely,

Hyman Bass, *Co-chair*
U.S.- Japan Teacher Development
Workshop Steering Committee

Zalman P. Usiskin, *Co-chair*
U.S.- Japan Teacher Development
Workshop Steering Committee

Contents

INTRODUCTION   **1**

REFLECTIONS ON THE WORKSHOP   **3**

Observations from the Study of Teaching Practice as a Medium for
Professional Development   **5**
    Henry S. Kepner, Jr.

Building an International Community: Sharing Knowledge and
Experiences in Professional Development for Mathematics Education   *10*
    Carol E. Malloy

BACKGROUND CONTEXT FOR TEACHER PREPARATION IN THE UNITED
STATES AND IN JAPAN   **19**

Elementary Mathematics Education in the United States   **21**
    Deborah Schifter

Mathematics Teacher Education in Grades 7–12 in the United States   **28**
    Zalman P. Usiskin

A Study of Teacher Change Through Inservice Mathematics Education
Programs in Graduate School   **35**
    Keiko Hino and Keiichi Shigematsu

Recurrent Education in Japan: Waseda University Education Research
and Development Center   **44**
    Toru Handa

Recurrent Education in Japan: Kanagawa Prefectural Education
Center   **46**
    Mamoru Takezawa

LESSON STUDY AS PROFESSIONAL DEVELOPMENT   47

Setting the Stage   49
Deborah Loewenberg Ball

Lesson Study: What, Why, and How?   53
Yoshinori Shimizu

Framing Lesson Study for U.S. Participants   58
Makoto Yoshida

Lesson Study from the Perspective of a Fourth-Grade Teacher   65
Hiroshi Nakano

Studying Classroom Teaching as a Medium for Professional Development: Video Component   67

Reflections on Videos: Panel   68
Jacqueline Goodloe   69
Jerry Becker   70
Ichiei Hirabayashi   72

PROFESSIONAL DEVELOPMENT THROUGH THE USE OF RECORDS OF PRACTICE   77

Professional Development Through Records of Instruction   79
Deborah Loewenberg Ball and Hyman Bass

Professional Development Through Written Cases   90
Margaret S. Smith

MATHEMATICAL KNOWLEDGE OF TEACHERS PANEL   99

Zalman P. Usiskin   101
Deborah Schifter   104
Haruo Ishigaki   107
Miho Ueno   108

SMALL GROUP DISCUSSION   111

Group I,   *Michelle Manes*   113
Group II,   *Denisse Thompson*   118
Group III,   *Susan Beal*   124
Group IV,   *Ramesh Gangolli*   128
Group V,   *Susan Wood*   134

APPENDIXES

Appendix A:	Workshop Agenda	139
Appendix B:	Participant List	144
Appendix C:	Steering Committee Biographical Information	149
Appendix D:	A Plan for the Lesson on Division by a Two-Digit Number	154
Appendix E:	A Demonstration Lesson: Function Thinking at Sixth Grade	157
Appendix F:	A Study Lesson: Large Numbers at Fourth Grade	177
Appendix G:	Records of Instruction: Reasoning About Three Coins at Third Grade	215
Appendix H:	Transcript of Excerpts from Small Group Discussions	227
Appendix I:	A Written Case: Pattern Trains at Sixth Grade	231
Appendix J:	To Become a Mathematics Teacher	248
Appendix K:	Glossary	252
Appendix L:	Workshop Reading List	254
Appendix M:	References	255

STUDYING CLASSROOM TEACHING AS A MEDIUM FOR PROFESSIONAL DEVELOPMENT: VIDEO COMPONENT

[Total Time: 90 minutes]

(1) A Demonstration Lesson: Function Thinking at Sixth Grade
Shunji Kurosawa
Setagaya Elementary School
Tokyo Gakugei University, Japan
August 3, 2000
Approximately 21 minutes

(2) Sixth-Grade Postlesson Discussion
Facilitator: Takashi Nakamura
Teacher: Shunji Kurosawa
August 3, 2000
Approximately 22 minutes

(3) A Study Lesson: Large Numbers at Fourth Grade
Hiroshi Nakano
Setagaya Elementary School
Tokyo Gakugei University, Japan
December 7, 1999
Approximately 22 minutes

(4) Records of Instruction: Reasoning about Three Coins at Third Grade
Deborah Loewenberg Ball
Spartan Village Elementary School, East Lansing, MI
September 18, 1989
Approximately 13.5 minutes

(5) Excerpts from Small Group Discussions
August 7, 2000
Approximately 8.5 minutes

Introduction

What teachers do in their classroom makes a difference in what students learn. Many experts agree with this statement and suggest that professional development of teachers is central to sustaining and deepening efforts to provide quality mathematics education for all students (National Research Council [NRC], 1996; National Science Foundation, 1998). However, much professional development provides teachers with knowledge and skill but leaves them to make their own connections with their daily practice in the classroom. As the nation undertakes improvement of instruction in mathematics classrooms, there is a need to access the best information available and to create opportunities to learn to use this information universally to help teachers improve their practice. Learning from other countries can be a valuable source in efforts to develop a more coherent approach to mathematics teacher education issues in the United States.

The release of the Third International Mathematics and Science Study has heightened interest in the Japanese educational system as a resource for those thinking deeply about teacher preparation in the United States (Stigler and Hiebert, 1999). Results from international studies (Beaton et al., 1996; Husen, 1967; McKnight et al., 1987; Stevenson et al., 1986) consistently show that Japanese students outperform those in the United States in most content areas. Evidence from research (Lewis and Tsuchida, 1997, 1998; National Center for Education Statistics, 1996; Shimaihara and Sakai, 1995; Stevenson and Stigler, 1992; Stigler et al., 1999; Yoshida, 1999) indicates that the Japanese have a highly developed teaching culture where the acquisition of knowledge of teaching is significantly unlike that in the United States. One factor in Japanese teacher development programs seems to revolve around careful design of lessons where teachers learn content and teaching in the process of developing a common lesson done through a community of professionals in a coordinated and deliberate effort to improve instruction. This approach also serves as a way to mentor those new to the profession. Recent work in the United States by researchers in professional development in mathematics education (Ball and Cohen, 1999; NRC, 2001; Schifter et al., 1999; Shulman, 1992; Stein et al., 2000;) has begun to build experience and expertise with tools for professional development based on tasks of teaching such as video, case studies, teacher reflection on practice, analysis of student work, and mathematicians' commentary. Mathematics educators from the United States and Japan have much to learn from each other by sharing their work and current thinking on the professional development of teachers.

The Mathematical Sciences Education Board (MSEB) and the U.S. National Commission on Mathematics Instruction (USNCMI) recognized and took advantage of a unique opportunity to bring these educators together. Following the Ninth International Congress on Mathematics Education (ICME-9) held July 31-August 6, 2000, in Makuhari, Japan, MSEB and USNCMI held a two- and a half-day workshop on the professional development of mathematics teachers. The workshop was able to capitalize on the presence of mathematics educators from the United States and Japan attending ICME-9, using the expertise of the participants from the two countries to develop a better, more flexible, and more

useful understanding of the knowledge that is needed to teach well and of how to help teachers obtain this knowledge.

The workshop provided an opportunity to learn about the structure of Japanese lesson study and enabled mathematics educators from the United States to share with Japanese colleagues their recent thinking about some promising approaches to teacher development in the United States. Thus, a major focus of the workshop was to discuss teachers' opportunities to learn in both societies, using teaching practice as a medium for professional development. The first part of the workshop addressed practice by studying the preparation for and enactment of an actual lesson. The second part of the workshop addressed practice by considering the study of records of teaching, including videos of classroom lessons and cases describing teachers and their work. These proceedings reflect the activities and discussion of the workshop using both print and video to enable others to share in the workshop experiences.

Reflections on the Workshop

The two-and a half-day workshop—The Study of Teaching Practice as a Medium for Professional Development—focused on the use of teaching practice as a way to study what elementary mathematics teachers need to know to teach well. The opening sessions were designed to share background information about the education of mathematics teachers in the two countries. The first whole day of the workshop addressed practice by studying the preparation for and enactment of an actual lesson, through an investigation and analysis of Japanese Lesson Study. On the second day, participants considered records of teaching that included a video of a classroom lesson and an analysis of a case describing teachers and their work.

After the workshop, two of the participants wrote papers describing the events from their perspective as mathematics educators. The following two papers reflect their overviews of the workshop, their sense of what they learned, and how the workshop experience related to their own background and work as mathematics teacher educators.

Observations from the Study of Teaching Practice as a Medium for Professional Development
 Henry S. Kepner, Jr., University of Wisconsin-Milwaukee

Building an International Community: Sharing Knowledge and Experiences in Professional Development for Mathematics Education
 Carol E. Malloy, University of North Carolina-Chapel Hill

Observations from the Study of Teaching Practice as a Medium for Professional Development

Henry S. Kepner, Jr., University of Wisconsin-Milwaukee

The workshop considered the study of teaching practices as a medium for professional development. Three main approaches were identified and discussed at length during the conference: the lesson study—a frequent practice in Japan, and two evolving practices using records of study in the United States—classroom video and written case study.

The overall workshop activities represented a clear difference in approach to professional development priorities and background. First, the Japanese participants reflected an almost unanimous awareness and acceptance of content and its placement in the national curriculum. When a mathematical topic was identified, they responded by knowing the grade level of its presentation and what students should already know at that time. This clear and consistent assumption of student mathematical content background was not evident among the U.S. participants. As Deborah Schifter and others noted, in the United States the local control of schools combined with diverse teaching strategies and curricula often supports professional development that focuses on isolated topics that may not be closely related to the mathematics in the curriculum such as group work, use of manipulatives, or problem solving.

Second, throughout the workshop, Japanese participants focused more consistently on the mathematical structure and clear student performance expectations in a lesson. Each move made by the teacher was first addressed with regard to the mathematical goal of a lesson. Again, this single purpose was not as evident among the U.S. participants. Often, other issues related to the observations, such as a teacher's skill in eliciting student ideas, arose first before the attention to the mathematics and its structure.

This study of teacher development as advocated in two countries brought together different perspectives on what teachers could learn from two different, yet similar, sets of evidence with a focus on teacher planning, instructional materials, classroom activity, and student work—both through videos or observations and written work. The positions, presented by several members of Japanese and U.S. mathematics educators, teachers, and mathematicians, showed both perspectives.

The lesson study format, with slight variations, is conducted by a group of teachers, often with a university educator, who develop a lesson in great detail for self-study and sharing among colleagues who come to observe the lesson taught by a member of the group. The lesson study has an accepted place as professional development in the elementary schools and to a lesser extent in the middle schools. It is not accepted as needed by most secondary teachers of mathematics. In both plenary and small group discussions, the Japanese university participants repeatedly saw the lesson study as a way to help elementary teachers improve their reportedly minimal mathematical background.

The lesson study team makeup and purpose vary depending on the primary reason for a lesson study. The activity may be for the professional growth of the teachers at a school or district or for a focus group of teachers where the activity is primarily a demonstration lesson for the engagement and growth of those participating—the team and observers on that day. It was reported that a university person was often invited to be a team member or a reactor for a local lesson study. University participants at the workshop noted that a university person who does not contribute significantly to the team or review process would not be invited back to future lesson study efforts.

Lesson study is constructed to do research on the feasibility or effectiveness of a lesson. The lesson might be necessary for a new mathematical topic inserted in the curriculum, a different lesson approach or structure for a standard topic, or a new approach for a topic that is perceived as difficult to teach. Such lessons are often done at demonstration schools associated with universities and less often at other schools.

In the lesson study process, teachers from the host school and frequently from surrounding schools and universities observe the class and participate in professional discussion following the lesson. Although there was substantive professional discussion along with challenge or disagreement among the teacher, lesson study team, and observers, for the most part there was a politeness and cautious consideration for the teacher and team-developed lesson. When pressed, several of the Japanese participants indicated that the actual conclusion of a lesson study process was "a party" at which there might arise substantive criticism of, or disagreement about, the lesson and/or its delivery.

When participants viewed or read descriptions of lessons and student responses, there was a marked difference in U.S. and Japanese reactions about the students' content background. While U.S. participants often had varying perspectives on student mathematical background, the Japanese participants reflected apparent uniformity about where that content would be presented in the school curriculum and the background students would have experienced. This difference, attributed to a national curriculum by Japanese participants, made an educational discussion much more focused by the Japanese. Although the lesson study activities experienced and discussed at the workshop encouraged each observer to bring their own professional perspective, the presentations and discussions indicated that the Japanese teachers had a common set of expectations and points of reference.

For the Japanese, there was an overriding concern for the mathematics, its structure, and attempts to motivate students to learn it. This was critiqued within the lesson plan and the way the lesson was implemented. Most questions started with issues of mathematical purpose along with effectiveness of student motivation.

In small group and follow-up discussions, the function of a lesson study as a device for professional development was probed in depth. Conference participants reported the development of both a set of observation criteria and a language of discussion useful in the professional conversation. This was a means of communicating the criteria or expectations of the observers and the lesson study team, including the classroom instructor. Examples of pedagogical jargon, in the English translation provided by Toshiakira Fujii and other Japanese participants, led to implied observation criteria. The criteria, also associated with the development of the lesson plan, included

- the opening problem setting with its motivational focus;
- the teacher's questioning, both the sequence of questions and attention to *hatsumon,* "thought-provoking questions" important to mathematical development and connections;
- *kikan-shido,* "between desk walking" or "purposeful scanning" referred to the teacher's purposeful observations and interactions while "walking among the desks" observing student work;
- the teacher's skill in anticipating student thinking;
- *bansho*, or "blackboard writing," stressed the organization of student work and key mathematical statements or results recorded by the teacher on the blackboard;
- *neriage,* "raising the level of the whole class discussion," through the orchestration and probing of student solutions, usually in the whole class format; and
- *matome*, the teacher's mathematical summary of the lesson for the whole class, with attention to students' ideas and contributions.

The extensive discussion of such criteria was seen by all participants as important

to help both preservice and experienced teachers to be productive observers of classroom practice. Participants from both countries indicated that training individuals to be effective observers of the content development was a difficult task that occurs over time. In particular, Deborah Ball noted the difficulty experienced in helping teachers observe what the demonstration teacher is really doing to develop the mathematics.

From the Japanese participants, there was a non-deviating focus on the correctness of the mathematics during the lesson and teacher summaries. It was frequently noted that an underlying purpose of lesson studies was to assist preservice and professional teachers to increase their mathematical knowledge—which university participants reported as weak. This purpose for lesson study presented a challenge with respect to lesson study team composition. While the team typically included a group of teachers in the host school, in some cases there was a reference to the involvement of a university mathematics educator or mathematician on the team. It would that if seem this member is not an integral member of the team, the lesson might lack the mathematical precision and development expected. Such team makeup is often an area of concern in U.S. professional development when it is school based.

The Japanese educational process demonstrated in the lesson study examples stressed the challenge to the teacher of motivating the students about the mathematical topic without forcing the teacher's view on the students in the developmental portion of the lesson. Although this position had similarities to the lessons illustrated at the workshop, it was noted that this was in contrast to the most common mode of U.S. instruction, variations on a direct instruction format.

The teacher's intent to bring multiple student presentations together controlled the conclusion of a Japanese lesson. However, in contrast to constructivist lessons where student summaries often are encouraged, the Japanese participants adamantly stated that the final summary of the mathematical conclusion must be made by the teacher to ensure that students heard correct mathematics correctly stated.

A perspective of both approaches centered on observing and reflecting upon student work in the learning of mathematics. In the lesson study process, the teacher observers were intent on observing what students did during the observed class. Frequently each observer would take responsibility for looking at the seat work of a particular student and even asking questions quietly during the period, gathering information about students' reactions to the lesson. Observers are careful not to become teacher's aids. In the case study approach, reflections of videotapes and samples of student work were used for a similar goal.

The professional development culture of lesson study provides a real-time observation and discussion for the observers, a portfolio notebook kept at the host school, and perhaps a short article on the lesson in a local Japanese education periodical. The best of these lessons becomes part of the teaching resources for others to use in teacher preparation or professional development.

Although there was an educational history of lesson study as an ongoing activity, participants noted that the use and involvement were uneven. Discussion indicated that schools attached to universities do many lesson studies while public schools do far less. Several participants from public schools indicated that lesson studies were often omitted due to other

priorities of the school staff or administration. Workshop participants indicated that many teachers serve as the lesson study teacher only once or a few times *in a career*. The impact of lesson study is primarily on the teacher team that created the lesson. They spend considerable time outside of their daily practice preparing the lesson and postlesson reflection and documentation. For observers, this is an opportunity to establish and continue professional communication and take away ideas for implementation or refinement. For preservice teachers, this can have a powerful impact on learning from the demonstration of more experienced teacher teams. For experienced teachers, a lesson may present a new curriculum piece or a new pedagogical strategy.

During the workshop, discussions in small groups and individual conversations considered the merits of using the different forms of studying practice. The live observation of a teacher and class in action around a focused lesson plan brings a strong cultural component to lesson study for the Japanese participants. Their continual reference to "seeing with the eyes" is the essence of professional growth. The use of videos of lessons along with samples of student work and an opportunity to have reflections from the classroom teacher seemed to make a classroom video a possibility for reflection on a lesson. However, the written case approach was not seen as valuable by the Japanese because of the lack of an authentic teacher and students. Also, the participants were concerned that the perspective of the writer limited the opportunity of each participant to bring their own perspective to the discussion.

Lesson study requires the actual enactment of the lesson study process for preservice or professional development for a set of individuals. In contrast, the video and written case study records of practice, organized and packaged for on-demand use, could be used at the instructor's choice in settings across time and geography. That is, a collection of records of practice could be used semester after semester in a teacher preparation program for preservice teachers. Or a record of practice could be used for professional development in school districts across the country.

One comparative strength of the records of practice approach is the opportunity to develop these records over time with the same children or different children. How does their mathematical communication grow over a year, or even over years? Records of practice (videos, written student work, transcripts) could be collected and organized for such study. When used for research or professional development, the records could be revisited repeatedly for purposes of argument or clarification of a classroom act by student or teacher. The real-time observation in a lesson study would not have this opportunity to "see it again."

Lesson study has its roots in the lesson on the day of observation, although lesson study is about much more than a single lesson. Japanese educators are concerned about students' growth in mathematics and communication, how lessons are sequenced and how ideas are built across lessons and grades despite the existence of a national curriculum.

The workshop clearly presented two approaches to professional development through the study of teaching practice. Two models of records of practice, video and written case studies, were identified as providing tools that multiple audiences could use at convenient times and locations. The need to develop a package that could be used by those distant from the teaching being recorded and with varying leaders was an important consideration in effective use of these tools for professional development. Lesson study was conducted with primary attention to professional development by those present at the lesson. The resulting lesson plan and indications of student responses might be written for a local or national professional journal to give teachers a plan determined effective by the observers and those who conducted the lesson study.

Building an International Community: Sharing Knowledge and Experiences in Professional Development for Mathematics Education

Carol E. Malloy, University of North Carolina-Chapel Hill

Mathematics educators in the United States and in Japan are working to provide preservice and practicing teachers with exemplary professional development in mathematics teaching. However, situations confronting the United States and Japan in mathematics education are quite different. The United States is faced with a teacher shortage in mathematics education (Riley, 2000), and numerous mathematics classes at the elementary and middle grade levels are taught by teachers without substantial mathematics training (Dossey and Usiskin, 2000). Additionally, over 30 percent of U.S. students at grade 4, 6, and 12 perform below the basic level of achievement on the National Assessment of Educational Progress (Dossey, 2000).

In Japan, students have historically achieved at high levels in mathematics; however, the results of the Third International Mathematics and Science Study show that 47 percent of Japanese students do not like mathematics (Hashimoto, 1999). In response to the national concern that schooling should respond to the needs of children, "in 1998, the Ministry of Education, Culture, Sports, Science and Technology reformed the Course of Study for K-12 to emphasize the well-being of human development of the child in a changing international society" (National Science Foundation, 2000). This plan reduces the number of days students are in school and the mathematics content hours that they experience. The plan also mandated changes in university teacher preparation programs that reduce the preservice content course credits while increasing the pedagogy course credits. These changes in philosophy and programs come to Japan at a time when there is a surplus of mathematics teachers and a decline in the population of school-age children.

GOALS OF THE WORKSHOP

Both the United States and Japan are faced with challenges in the mathematics education of their students. One strategy is to address the challenges through a dialogue of mathematics educators about the delivery of professional development to teachers. To promote this dialogue, the National Research Council (NRC) held a U.S. - Japan Workshop on Professional Development in Makuhari, Japan, centered on the questions: What knowledge of both content and pedagogy do teachers need to teach well and how can teachers come to acquire this knowledge in ways that are usable in practice? The major goal of the workshop was to use the expertise of the participants to investigate these questions to develop ideas and insights that could address the issues surrounding the preparation of mathematics teachers.

This workshop used an accessible medium, teaching practice, as a tool to address professional development of mathematics teachers in both countries. Before the conference, participants received papers that explained and demonstrated three forms of professional development using teaching practice: (a) lesson study, or *jugyokenkyu* as it is practiced in Japan, and (b) two types of records of practice—cases and fairly complete records of instruction including classroom video called record study, from the United States.

In this paper, I chronicle the events of the conference through my experiences as a mathematics teacher and teacher educator from the United States. I begin by explaining my position and the approach to professional development and teacher preparation coming into the workshop. Next I share my journey through the workshop, the insight I gained, the confusion I felt, and how this experience reshaped my view of teacher preparation.

MY POSITION AS A TEACHER EDUCATOR

In teacher education, as in many disciplines, teaching and learning are intertwined. We learn our disciplines— pedagogy and content—and we learn more about teaching as we practice our discipline. To foster this type of teaching and learning within the methods and mathematics classes I teach and the professional development I offer to

practicing teachers, I use a "community of learners" approach where the participants and I interchange the roles of the teacher and the learner. The tools that I use are case discussion with narratives of teaching and learning, lesson records through the medium of video and student work, reflection, and study groups. My goals are to help preservice and practicing teachers learn strategies to understand how their students' learn, to develop strategies to enhance student learning, and to have a strong foundation in and conceptual understanding of the mathematics they are teaching. As a community, students in classes and teachers in professional development sessions explore educational topics and issues through inquiry and critique, striving to find answers to questions and formulate positions. We use inquiry to explore the mathematics content and related issues. We develop and model what we think are appropriate pedagogy strategies for teaching mathematics and content for middle and high school students. The most important phase is our reflection. Each of us personally reflects on our teaching to assess how we are doing our work to improve our practice and achieve the goals we have individually set for ourselves. Over the past 30 years I have isolated three essential components that support this method of professional development:

1. love of and passion for teaching and learning;
2. knowledge of content with the necessary pedagogical skills and ability to assemble, synthesize, and convey course content to students; and
3. continuous reflection that guides learning and teaching.

These three components were central

in the three forms of professional development discussed at the workshop.

JOURNEY THROUGH THE WORKSHOP

The workshop was planned to promote a collaborative atmosphere between the participants from the United States and Japan who were teachers, teacher educators, and researchers from both countries. We were assigned to seats so that we could form small discussion groups that would include people from both countries and with varied backgrounds and careers. The format for most workshop sessions started with presenters sharing information about key topics followed with participants reacting to and discussing what was shared in a group as a whole, in small prearranged groups, or in clusters based on seating assignment.

The first session was designed to give us an understanding of the educational systems, teacher preparation, and professional development in the United States and Japan. There are clear similarities in the structures that support mathematics education in both countries. Neither country has a nationally organized system of professional development, although professional development does exist at the school, district, university, regional, and national levels. At the elementary level teachers are generalists teaching all academic subjects, and at the high school level teachers are specialists teaching in only one curricular area. The textbook selection process is similar in both countries. In the United States individual states or school districts authorize textbooks that match the curriculum guidelines of states and districts. In Japan the Minister of Education, Science and Culture authorizes

textbooks that he deems suitable to be used in schools, which match the Japanese national curriculum (Japan Society of Mathematical Education, 2000). With guidance from principals and district (prefecture) administration, schools are then allowed to select from the list of approved texts for students.

Differences in structured programs far exceed the similarities. The most obvious difference is that Japan has a national curriculum in mathematics, and the United States does not. In the United States individual states or districts control educational programs for students, resulting in varied educational curricula; whereas in Japan the Minister of Education, Science and Culture controls educational programs, ensuring uniformity throughout the country. Certification requirements are different. Mathematics teachers for the middle grades in the United States are not always certified in a content area, while those teachers in Japan are certified in mathematics only. This enables Japanese preservice teachers for the middle grades to take more mathematics content courses. Most certification programs in the United States require that teachers participate in professional development programs to retain their certification. A typical requirement is six credit hours every five years in education courses—not necessarily mathematics courses (Dossey and Usiskin, 2000). However, Japanese teachers obtain a lifetime certification and are not required to take additional courses during their teaching careers. Requirements for initial teacher preparation are different. Teacher preparation programs in the United States require 12 to 15 weeks of student teaching under the supervision of a classroom teacher where teacher preparation students observe and independently teach the full schedule of their supervising teacher for at least 6 to 8 weeks. It is expected that new teachers have gained the necessary skills to be independent in their first years of teaching, but many school districts have induction programs where new teachers have mentors who are available for support. In Japan the system is slightly reversed. Japan requires approximately three weeks of student teaching where they observe other prospective teachers, and then they teach alone and in teams with a master teacher. When most new teachers are hired, they are paired with experienced teachers for a year so that they can team teach with the master teacher as they develop their skills as teachers. They also are required to attend professional development sessions throughout the year.

The forms and goals of professional development in the United States and Japan reflect the needs of teachers to improve their practice, the needs of their students, and the structure of each country's teacher preparation programs and certification requirements. Professional development in the United States is structured to help teachers grow in a variety of ways. Some may address change in classroom practice to be more inclusive of all students, or focus on helping teachers understand the mathematics they teach, while others may help teachers with pedagogical decisions and strategies for effective instruction. Generally professional development is structured to support the accumulation of continuing practice credits for certification. Fried et al. (1998) provide a list of professional development strategies used in the United States, from teacher-led learning within schools or classrooms such as action research, study groups, coaching, and mentoring to formal opportunities outside the classroom such

as workshops, institutes, courses, and seminars. The most commonly used strategies include short sessions at meetings of professional organizations, school-based workshops on specific topics, or two- to three-week grant-supported workshops in the summers with follow-up sessions during the academic year. In many cases teachers who participate in these forms of professional development are not offered indepth follow-up sessions to reflect on their practice. None of these strategies include avenues for teachers to use observation of colleagues' teaching as a tool for learning. Teachers in the United States are solitary practitioners, coming together to learn about teaching but working in isolation in their classrooms (Lewis, 2000).

Similar to teachers in the United States, Japanese teachers use professional development to improve their practice, to learn more mathematics and pedagogical strategies, and to make better pedagogical decisions in their instruction. However, teachers in Japan use observation and collaboration as the core of their professional development called *konaikenshu* through lesson study. Lesson study is an in-school teacher education strategy where teachers are engaged in action research about teaching (Yoshida, 1999). Lesson studies are held to educate preservice teachers, mentor and instruct novice teachers, improve the skills of all teachers, maintain collaboration among teachers, and share ideas and new approaches. Shimizu (2000) explained that lesson study consists of precollaborative work among teachers, lesson observation, and postcollaborative work. This cycle is repeated over time in an iterative process. Professional development also has other forms in Japan. Teachers participate in workshops at the university and in school-based study groups where they study a variety of topics (Yoshida, 1999). Japan's large-scale meetings of mathematics educators may be focused around demonstration lessons.

ELEMENTS OF PROFESSIONAL DEVELOPMENT IN THE THREE RECORDS OF PRACTICE

Lesson Study

The first full day of the workshop was dedicated to lesson study and reflection. The day began with an optional viewing of a videotape of a sixth-grade lesson for those who had not been able to attend the actual lesson. The day's schedule included presentations, small group discussions, and group viewing of a second videotaped lesson. The workshop then became a postconference for the lesson study where we reflected on the lesson with the teacher and lesson team. As the presentations and conversations in small groups progressed, the U.S. participants learned that there are several forms of lesson study. Because of language differences and translations from Japanese to English, there was some confusion about the definition for lesson study. What follows is my understanding of the two forms of study. Lesson study is a school-based strategy primarily used at the elementary level directed by teachers within a school. Teachers decide on the content of the lesson study and proceed through a process that generally has five components: (1) teachers plan the lesson collaboratively; (2) the lesson is taught by one teacher and observed by other teachers; (3) the team of teachers meet to reflect on the lesson and improve it; (4) the lesson is taught again, usually by another teacher, with refinement; and (5) the lesson is discussed again and made into a booklet that is available to other teachers. Lesson

study is an accepted part of teaching in Japan at the elementary levels, although the workshop participants indicated that in some schools teachers had fewer than two lesson studies a year. Teachers interviewed by Lewis (2000) said that if they did not do research lessons, that they would not be teachers.

Teachers also participate in a public lesson study, called *jugyokenkyu*, which is open to teachers and educators from outside of the school and the prefecture (district). Most elementary and lower secondary schools conduct lesson study, but the universities and national schools generally conduct public lesson study. Also, when schools receive grants to develop their educational programs, it is expected that they will conduct a lesson study to present their products and findings. Study lessons—the lesson itself—at conferences become a method of transferring or transmitting good teaching ideas from one teacher to another throughout the country. With a national curriculum and textbooks authorized by the Minister of Education, Science and Culture, lesson study seems to offer an efficient form of professional development for teachers. Lewis (2000) indicated that Japanese teachers credit lesson study as the primary method they used to learn to teach.

Toshiakira Fujii, in his comments at the beginning of the day, said, "The lesson is the battlefield of teaching. And the teacher is evaluated by the quality of the lesson." Lesson studies are works in progress where teachers strive for perfection through the iterative process of demonstration and reflection. Thus the function of lesson study is twofold: a method of research and a place to present new approaches. The teacher's aim is to ask colleagues to identify flaws in teaching through their eyes and to identify the causes of the failure of the lesson (Hirabayashi, 2000). For this process to be productive, the teacher has to prepare a carefully planned and detailed lesson that includes the purpose, topic, teaching process, student activities, and intended results. Hirabayashi (2000) describes lesson study as the "method of research in mathematics education that is the way to grasp the true state of affairs of the problem in its whole and bring the synthetic, totally recognized interpretation about it, being aware of many factors which are subtly interacting to each other as if it were in one organism" (p. 1). He believes that because lessons are complicated processes and their results on student learning are too subtle to express in writing, lessons can only be evaluated through close observation. You have to see what actually occurred in the lessons—both teaching and learning.

In this, my first observation of lesson study through a videotape of the lesson and a discussion of the participants in the process, I was amazed and pleased with the detail of the lesson and the reflection of the participants. The teacher's ability to pose the problem precisely, the functional thinking of the students, the questioning that required each student to think of multiple ways to solve the problem, the varied representations of solutions and the students' interpretations of the different forms were impressive. The teaching of mathematics content dominated the lesson and the post-lesson reflection session continued the focus, with the teachers having a lengthy conversation of the different meanings of 4×48 and 48×4. Although I was surprised with the length of this conversation, it demonstrated the importance given by the Japanese teachers to teacher and student content knowledge.

After a few hours of learning about lesson study, we understood that the work required to prepare a lesson for observation and review was extensive. Most of the U.S. participants wondered how teachers could take so much time with planning. When we inquired, we were told that lesson studies are not the norm for instruction. The Japanese teachers explained that most of their lesson plans were in the teacher's editions of the textbooks. Lesson studies were tools to improve instruction, not to develop daily lesson plans. The concept of lesson study is an effective tool to create a community of learners throughout Japan because of the capacity to share research and approaches to teaching within schools, prefectures, and the national education community. Knowing this, we were surprised to learn that even though many elementary and some lower secondary teachers participate in research lessons, it rarely occurs in the upper secondary schools.

Records and Practice

In Deborah Ball's opening comments on the first day of the workshop, she questioned how teachers in Japan and the United States use practice to work on their teaching. She expanded the battlefield concept expressed by Toshiakira Fujii to the use of record study and case study as tools to analyze and learn the practice of teaching. Deborah Ball believes that practice is not learned by just doing it, nor is it learned by just acquiring knowledge or watching expert performances. To learn a practice teachers have to progress through the steps of studying, trying, analyzing, improving, and developing new knowledge, as is the case with lesson study and record study.

In the second day of the workshop, we learned about professional development through records of instruction. Records of instruction used in the United States include videotapes of classroom instruction, written cases that describe actual classroom situations and issues that arise, student's written work, transcripts of lessons, teachers notes, and lesson plans. Record study is useful for many reasons. Records are used to provide a context for learning and place professional development in the context of practice. The ability to select records to be studied ensures that the knowledge generated is useful and usable in practice. Specifically, the use of record study allows teachers to select particular problems of mathematics teaching and learning to be studied and can provide exposure to practices that teachers have not seen or do not know. Most importantly for U.S. teachers, the use of records for analysis allows teachers to critique practice in a safe environment where they are not asked to criticize each other's teaching. Record study can be problematic because not all records are worthy of study. It is difficult to design a good task for learning that will help develop norms for the professional study of teaching. Additionally there are challenges as teachers move from evaluation and judging to the analysis of teaching and in balancing the analytic work with practical outcomes (Ball and Bass, 2000).

The challenges of the use of record study can be addressed through the appropriate design and enactment of record study. For instance, video records and case records accompanied by focused questions about the records provide teachers with an opportunity to develop the ability to analyze and reflect on their practice. Record study can enable teachers to understand and improve their pedagogical content knowledge. "Pedagogical knowledge is a special form of knowledge that bundles mathematical knowledge with knowledge of learners, learning, and pedagogy" (Ball and Bass, 2000). Records can expand the pedagogical content knowledge that teachers possess because records afford teachers the opportunity to view, understand, analyze, and reflect on situations that they have not experienced in their classrooms. Margaret Smith explained, in the session on case studies, that records "create generalities that teachers can use to think about their own teaching." They allow teachers to investigate instruction through records to develop generalities that might be applied to their practice. Moreover, record study can help teachers learn (a) how to pay attention to and teach every student in the class, (b) how to know and use mathematical knowledge to help students learn, and (c) how to work with others on developing knowledge for teaching (Ball, 2000).

In my practice I use case and video records, thus I was not surprised with the information shared at the workshop. I was pleased that the readings and the presentations on record study stressed the need for pedagogical content knowledge. I believe that questions asked of the participants both at the beginning of the workshop and in our small groups could not be answered without a foundation in pedagogy, content knowledge, and pedagogical content knowledge. It was clear to me that the three forms of professional development on teaching practice (lesson study, video records, and cases) could be part of the answer, but we were just beginning a long journey.

Reflection

At the end of the workshop we realized that we had only scratched the surface of developing answers to the questions that focused the workshop: What knowledge of both content and pedagogy do teachers need to teach well and how can teachers come to acquire this knowledge in ways that are usable in practice? Questions and comments were shared at the end of each day as participants from each country reflected on what they had observed, heard, and learned. Ichiei Hirabayashi explained that curriculum development is composed of technology and humanity, and we had only addressed the technology. He said that the humanity of the teacher was evident in the way students were attentive throughout the entire period. But he said, "Lesson study is not enough. We need good experienced teachers to guide us. I videotape myself every day as the mentor teachers instructed me." He challenged us by saying, "In the United States you have to determine how to incorporate lesson study into your school. What are you going to do and what problems do you anticipate when you return?"

Deborah Schifter suggested some needs that teachers might have before they participate in lesson study, including understanding that mathematics is more than being able to apply a single algorithm and that understanding alternate forms of mathematical procedures is the basis of mathematical reasoning and valid thinking. Haruo Ishigaki explained that teachers learn in the same ways that students learn. He commented that excellent teachers do not have perfect knowledge, "They are 80 percent confidence and 20 percent doubt. Their knowledge has to be updated and restructured often." He stated that students see extraordinary things but may make mistakes. These mistakes, however, are valuable and should be treated as a resource by the teacher.

As I listened and reflected on my experience, I was thinking, is it possible for us, in the United States, to use what we have learned to improve professional development for our preservice and practicing teachers? First I had to think about what I had learned. My overwhelming realization was that mathematics educators from different parts of the world, with different spoken languages and cultures, spoke in unison as we discussed our goals and needs to improve mathematics education. Our strategies and tools of delivery were different, but we were seeking similar outcomes. The most exciting new knowledge was my personal understanding of the organization and execution of lesson study and the power of lesson study to improve content knowledge and pedagogy of teachers and the delivery of content to students. My beliefs about the importance of teacher collaboration and observation of each other's teaching to improve practice and the use of record study to help teachers construct new pedagogical, content, and pedagogical content knowledge were reinforced.

Second, I had to personalize the questions for my own practice. How could I use all that I had learned in my practice as a teacher educator? How could my students benefit from my experience?

PUTTING IT TOGETHER IN PRACTICE

Clearly, the most important experience from the workshop to me was being part of a community of learners from the United States and Japan coming together to begin to answer questions regarding professional development. Just as we had extended our community to include each other, I decided to try to broaden my preservice students' community of learners to include all of the mentor teachers and students using a modified lesson study approach. Normally each student interacts with and learns from one mentor teacher in a full year practicum. In the fall semester the students observe their mentor teacher in all classes, tutor students, help in the classroom, and discuss lesson planning and teach a trial lesson. During the second semester they do their formal student teaching. I will only have three preservice students in mathematics this year, and I plan to place them all in the same school for their practicum.

All mentor teachers agreed to participate in a modified lesson study with the mentor as the teacher. The mentor teacher and student teacher will select a class that the three students and I will observe. Prior to the observation we will meet with the teacher to learn about the class and the lesson she plans to present—to learn her rationale for the pedagogy and content and what she expects from the class. Next we observe the class, taking notes on what we see. After the observation we will meet with the teacher to discuss and critique the lesson. These discussions are beneficial for the teachers because they can see how to improve the lesson and they are beneficial for the students because they learn how the teacher implements what she had

planned and begin to think as a teacher, reflecting on what worked, what did not, and why.

Another change in my practice this year will be the cooperative planning process for student demonstration lessons. Students will be required to teach one lesson in their mentor teacher's class. In prior years each student would plan and teach a lesson. The mentor teacher and I would observe and critique the lesson. Now, instead of having the students plan their lesson independently, my three students and I will act as a team to plan three different lessons—one for each student. Our team and the mentor teacher will observe and critique the lesson. Our goal this year is to build a community of learners that can depend upon one another for knowledge and support. We are trying to remove the myth, through our modeling, that teachers in the United States have to be solitary professionals. I hope that through these two modifications of lesson study, my students and their mentors will learn not only more pedagogy, mathematics content, and pedagogical content knowledge but also the importance of peer observation, collaboration, and group planning.

Background Context for Teacher Preparation in the United States and in Japan

The opening session of the workshop included presentations designed to give participants some sense of mathematics education and teacher preparation and development programs in the two countries. Deborah Schifter and Zalman Usiskin gave a broad overview of elementary and secondary teacher preparation and development programs in the United States. Keiichi Shigematsu and Keiko Hino described a case study of a middle-grades teacher who had taken a part in a graduate teacher education program in one Japanese university, while Toru Handa and Mamoru Takezawa spoke of other examples of professional development efforts in Japan at the secondary level.

Elementary Mathematics Education in the United States
Deborah Schifter, Senior Scientist, Education Development Center

Mathematics Teacher Education in Grades 7–12 in the United States
Zalman P. Usiskin, Professor of Education and Director of the University of Chicago School Mathematics Project, University of Chicago

A Study of Teacher Change Through Inservice Mathematics Education Programs in Graduate School
Keiko Hino, Associate Professor, Nara University of Education
Keiichi Shigematsu, Professor, Nara University of Education

Recurrent Education in Japan: Waseda University Education Research and Development Center
Toru Handa, Mathematics Teacher, Waseda University Honjo Senior High School

Recurrent Education in Japan: Kanagawa Prefectural Education Center
Mamoru Takezawa, Mathematics Educator, Kanagawa Prefectural Education Center

Elementary Mathematics Education in the United States

Deborah Schifter, Education Development Center

I have been asked to provide some background for this workshop on elementary-level mathematics instruction in the United States. I will be touching on four main themes: (1) the tradition of local control of education policy in the United States, (2) the fragmentation of teacher education, (3) current efforts to improve education, and (4) challenges to this improvement.

WHO CONTROLS U.S. EDUCATION?

First, and this is not specific to elementary education, is the question of who controls U.S. education policy. The federal government has limited power over our schools; it does not establish a national curriculum. Nor is teacher education or assessment a matter of national policy. Instead, each of the 50 states has its own policies in such matters as teacher certification and curriculum, and in some states, curriculum decisions are actually left to local school districts or even individual schools. In spite of the extreme fragmentation of authority over U.S. education, there is considerable uniformity in what is taught—largely attributable to the way textbooks are produced, marketed, and adopted.

A second mechanism for ensuring a degree of uniformity is the concern that students are prepared for college entrance exams. Although this directly affects only secondary school instruction, this concern exerts indirect pressure on instruction in the lower grades. With such decentralized control over education policy, along with the tendency of all institutions to maintain the status quo, it is difficult to make fundamental changes in our schools. However, two arms of the federal government, the National Science Foundation and the U.S. Department of Education, do provide grants for projects that appear to promise improvement in educational practice. Through this mechanism, the federal government can exert some influence on policy decisions.

FRAGMENTATION OF TEACHER EDUCATION

I now consider fragmentation of teacher education and, specifically, implications at the elementary level. In the United States, it is widely believed that a stable school environment better serves young children. This is accomplished by keeping one teacher with the same class for the full school day. In most schools, teachers are responsible for teaching all subjects to their students—mathematics, reading and writing, science, and social studies. From the background reading for this workshop (Appendix L), I understand this situation is the same as in Japan. In U.S. undergraduate teacher preparation and inservice professional development programs, there is pressure to learn about instruction in all of these subjects. As a consequence, most teacher preparation programs—determined by state certification requirements—generally offer one or two courses in the teaching of mathematics (National Center for Education Statistics, 1995; America Federation of Teachers, 1997; Ingersoll, 1998). Some also require that prospective elementary teachers take at least one mathematics course, while others have no such requirement. On the other hand, there are some states like Georgia that now require undergraduate students to take several mathematics courses to become certified as elementary teachers. However, it is unusual for the mathematics courses to be coordinated with the education programs at the university.

In many states, teachers must spend a certain number of hours in professional development settings to maintain their certification. However, once again, there is no uniform system of professional development. Some workshops are organized by the school or the school system, and these may be led by district personnel or by consultants who are hired from outside to work with teachers for a single day. The content might involve a new teaching technique or assessment procedure, student behavior or some such social issue, classroom discipline, or time management. They rarely deal with mathematics or how children learn (Garet et al., 1999; Shields et al., 1999). It is unusual for teachers to come together regularly to discuss substantive or problematic issues in their practice—although there are exceptions. Some teachers on their own initiative seek out courses at universities or summer programs, which again vary greatly from one another (McLaughlin, 2000). And there are some schools or school districts that have organized and coordinated substantive, professional development programs.

CURRENT EFFORT TO IMPROVE ELEMENTARY EDUCATION

Perhaps the most significant point in our discussion at this workshop is that until recently, the principal goal of elementary mathematics instruction in the United States has been computational proficiency (National Council of Teachers of Mathematics, [NCTM] 1989). The emphasis has been on remembering facts and algorithms and being able to produce correct answers with speed. The curriculum also included learning the names of particular shapes, the use of a ruler, the formulas for the area and perimeter of a rectangle, and sometimes the volume of a rectangular solid. Like the rest of the mathematics content, word problems have been treated mechanically.

This emphasis on memorization rather than sense-making activity is evident in such errors commonly seen in the elementary classrooms as shown in Box 1. In these examples, the children are applying single-digit math facts but are not remembering the computational procedures. Because they are not thinking about the size of the numbers they start with or what the operations do, they form no reasonable estimate of the outcomes. If neither the children nor their teachers have learned to approach such problems with the expectation that they should make sense, it is difficult to correct the misconceptions at the base of these errors.

This brings us to efforts to improve elementary mathematics in the United States. For many years, going back at least as far as the work of John Dewey, there have been educators devoted to rethinking K-12 mathematics, designing materials, working with teachers, and producing policy statements. The most dramatic recent change came just a decade or so ago when some of these people came together under the auspices of the NCTM to produce a set of standards documents. NCTM is a professional organization of mathematics educators whose work is mainly conducted by volunteers and supported by a full-time staff.

The first three NCTM documents set out standards for curriculum, teaching, and assessment respectively: *Curriculum and Evaluation Standards for School Mathematics,*1989; *Professional Standards for Teaching Mathematics*, 1991; *Assessment Standards for School Mathematics*, 1995. The fourth, *Principles and Standards for School Mathematics*, 2000, was

intended to update, refine, and elaborate on the issues presented in the first three. The main principles guiding these documents are that mathematics is about reasoning; that children be recognized as mathematical thinkers; and that eliciting, assessing, and building upon their thinking should be at the heart of instructional practice. In particular, the documents argued that children should be encouraged to use a variety of methods for representing and solving problems and then present their work to their classmates for further analysis. These documents also emphasize that mathematics is more than arithmetic. Geometry and data should be made significant components of the curriculum beginning in kindergarten.

The federal government does not set a national curriculum. These standards are offered as recommendations, without any requirement that people should follow them. However, at the federal level, the National Science Foundation and the U.S. Department of Education have supported these reforms. They have funded research centers and professional development programs and provided grants to produce curriculum materials at the elementary, middle, and secondary levels. These materials started to become available around 1996 and 1997.

To provide an idea of what the standards support and the kinds of activities included in the new curricula, I offer two examples taken from the newest NCTM document (2000). A vignette is presented of a fifth-grade class that had been given the homework problem 728 divided by 34. One child, Henry, presented his solution method (Box 2). Henry explained to the class, "twenty 34s plus one more is 21. I knew I was pretty close. I didn't think I could add anymore 34s, so I subtracted 714 from 728, and got 14. Then I had 21 remainder 14."

Another child, Michaela, presented her solution (Box 3). Michaela described the steps of the conventional division algorithm. "34 goes into 72 two times, and that's 68. You've got to minus that, bring down the 8, and then 34 goes into 48 one time."

Apparently, their teacher had not shown the conventional division algorithm to her students, and Michaela's classmates said they did not understand her method. Asked to explain, Michaela took the class through the steps again but with the same response. Then the teacher asked the class to identify the similarities in the two

procedures and assisted them by inserting a 0 so that the children could more easily see where Henry's 680 shows up in Michaela's process. Through the discussion that followed, using Henry's solution as a point of reference, some of Michaela's classmates could begin to see the logic of the steps she had taken.

Another example is also taken from *Principles and Standards for School Mathematics*. In this fifth-grade class, the students had been given a word problem that involved adding 1.14, 0.089 and 0.3. They were asked to work in groups to come up with an answer. Although they had done preparatory work on decimals, adding them was a new topic. One group presented this solution (Box 4).

They explained that you change all the decimals into regular numbers. Then you add them all up and get 206. When challenged by their teacher to consider whether a number that size makes sense, they restored the decimal point. And their final answer was 2.06.

The second group, which had done the calculation correctly, explained, "The reason we didn't line up all the numbers was because we had to line up tenths with tenths, and the hundredths with the hundredths to make it come out right, and," they added, "the thousandths with the thousandths." However, when the class came together to discuss their solution methods, neither group was convinced by the other's explanation. Both answers could not be correct, but as a class, they could not resolve the stalemate before the lesson ended that day.

The next day, the teacher suggested that some of the students work on this problem with base 10 blocks. Their representation is shown in Box 5. The children in the class were convinced by this demonstration. Not only did it help them determine that 1.529 is indeed the correct answer, but it also helped them interpret the argument the second group had given—you add tenths with tenths, etc.

These examples illustrate the spirit of the mathematics education reforms in the United States. In the past, accepted practice would have required the children to memorize the steps of the division

algorithm as presented by Michaela, with no attempt to explore the reasoning behind it; or in the past, children would have had to have memorized two different rules for adding numbers: For whole numbers, line them up at the right, but for decimals, line them up at the decimal point. In the vignettes, we see children sorting out the logic of the calculation procedures. It is noteworthy that in both examples, the children have been given responsibility for explaining their reasoning to themselves and to their classmates. Their teacher posed a question or offered a suggestion that helped them find the sense in the procedures they were learning.

CHALLENGES TO THE IMPROVEMENT OF MATHEMATICS EDUCATION

One of the most difficult issues that the United States faces in improving elementary mathematics education is that most

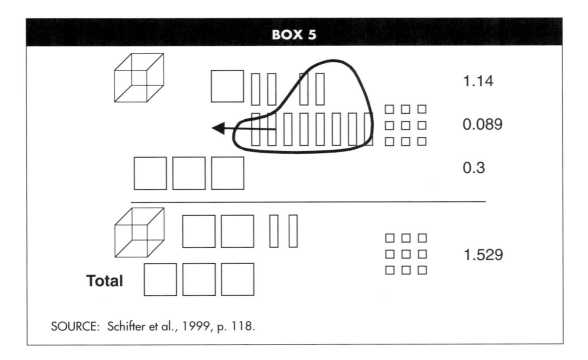

BOX 5

1.14

0.089

0.3

1.529

Total

SOURCE: Schifter et al., 1999, p. 118.

teachers do not understand the mathematics they teach very well (Ball and Wilson, 1990; Ma, 1999; National Center for Education Statistics, 1995; National Research Council, 2001). In the past 15 years, there have been many studies that have documented this problem, which has become an increasing concern to many U.S. educators and policy makers. In my first example about division, the teacher herself understood the comparable reasoning behind the two methods presented by her students, and so she could draw their attention to it. In the second, the teacher understood the principle that underlies addition of whole numbers and decimals and so could suggest a representation that would help her students see it too. However, such teachers are, at this time, more the exception than the rule in the United States. Most, having been educated in mathematics restricted to memorization of procedures, have not learned how to make sense of mathematics. In general, U.S. teachers have not had opportunities to learn mathematics from a conceptual perspective.

The examples I have given come from the most recent *Standards* document published in spring 2000. When the first *Standards* document appeared in 1989, there were few instances of curriculum materials that laid out a coherent mathematics program. By the early 1990s, it became apparent there were serious problems with the way teachers were interpreting the *Standards* documents. These were largely rooted in a failure to appreciate that the core idea of the reform was making sense of mathematics. For example, one interpretation held that the standards were about teaching essentially the same mathematics content, but now the children were sometimes to work in small groups, or were to use manipulatives, as well as paper and pencil (Weiss et al.,

1994). So there were many professional development workshops devoted to these teaching strategies. However, when the children were put into groups, they were not necessarily given problems that required real thinking. And when they were given blocks to use, they were merely shown yet another set of steps to remember.

Another interpretation was that the new practice was to emphasize problem solving. So some teachers committed one day each week to it. Although many of these problems did require some hard thinking, they were not necessarily related to a coherent conception of the content that the children needed to learn. In one very disturbing interpretation of the *Standards*, some teachers agreed on the importance of eliciting ideas from their students but did not understand that they had a further responsibility to critically analyze those ideas for mathematical soundness. Indeed, having themselves been taught that mathematics is memorization, many teachers have never developed the skills required for assessing the logic of a mathematical argument. Nor do they even realize that this is something that they, much less their students, should be doing.

There was some research in the early 1990s that alerted us to these problems of practice in the name of the *Standards* (NCTM, 1991). And there were some programs for college students preparing to become teachers, and for teachers already practicing, working to address them. As a result of these programs, and with support from new curriculum materials, there are now a greater number of classrooms in which the new vision of mathematics teaching practice has successfully taken hold (Briars and Resnick, 2000).

However, since 1995, a movement has emerged to put a stop to these reform efforts. This movement has arisen out of several concerns. Some people became justifiably alarmed when they saw some of the problematic practices I have just described. And even where the mathematics was being taught well, some parents were made uneasy by the unfamiliar look of the mathematics their children were bringing home. Others felt that the new practices would interfere with children learning basic arithmetic and algebraic skills, without which they believe mathematical understanding cannot develop. Still others were distrustful of teachers who now aspire to a more complex, intellectually, and demanding practice. In any case, some reformers now confront groups of parents supported by some professional mathematicians and backed by wealthy funding sources who have succeeded in blocking local and state reform efforts (Battista, 1999; Becker and Jacobs, 2000; Grossman and Stodulsky, 1995). Although this conflict has made its way into the media, society at large—including the journalists covering the conflict— is unaware that the questions concerning how learning takes place or how children put mathematics concepts together are complex and profound.

The one mathematical specific that seems to come up regularly in the debate is the role of conventional computation algorithms. In the public arena it is posed baldly: Should teachers encourage children to devise procedures that make sense to them—for example, to add 45 + 36, children will often find the sum of 40 and 30 first, then add 5 and 6, and then total the partial sums: 70 + 11 = 81—or should teachers demonstrate conventional algorithms? As my earlier example suggested, the dichotomy is a false one.

Nonstandard procedures can render the meanings of the operations transparent and the reasoning behind the standard algorithms accessible. However, as the debates get played out in public, sensible and deep discussion of such issues becomes increasingly difficult.

To summarize the context in which we are working to educate teachers and support their professional development, many teachers have yet to be introduced to the idea that mathematics is about reasoning, that children, and they themselves, have mathematical ideas and the capacity to explore and critically assess them. Once they come to appreciate that doing mathematics is a sense-making activity, there is much mathematics content for them to learn. Then they must create a teaching practice that is different from the practice they know, that helps their students understand the mathematics too. Finally, they must do all this while keeping up with comparable developments in the teaching of literacy, science, and social studies. And yet there exists no coherent teacher education and professional development infrastructure to support these efforts.

Furthermore, we are trying to do this work in a period in which basic directions in education policy are the subject of contentious political debate. Wanting to do the best for their students, teachers are caught in the middle, attacked for their students' failures, held accountable for an impossibly difficult task. However, as I and my colleagues have discovered, once teachers begin to learn mathematics in settings that support the development of their own powers of reasoning, they become eager to learn more mathematics for themselves and to provide their students with opportunities they missed out on as children.

Mathematics Teacher Education in Grades 7–12 in the United States

Zalman P. Usiskin, University of Chicago

Good afternoon. It is a pleasure and an honor to present this overview of secondary mathematics teacher education in the United States.

At least since the 1960s, when the results of the International Study of Mathematics were announced and Japan scored at the top and the United States at the bottom, Japan has been seen as a place to which we might turn to improve mathematics education in the United States. In the early 1980s, at the University of Chicago, we had the opportunity to translate Soviet and Japanese high school texts, and we were able to see the algebra and geometry taught in junior high school and how virtually an entire population can be brought to higher mathematical performance. The recent Third International Mathematics and Sciences Study suggests that we may be able to learn not only how to raise student performance but also instructional techniques from Japan (National Center for Education Statistics [NCES], 1996).

In turn, the size of the United States and the length of time we have been working to improve mathematics education has led to numerous studies and projects in the United States. We hope that some of the ideas we have been working on will be informative and stimulating, and we look forward to sharing them.

In the workshop materials, we presented data regarding mathematics teacher education in the United States. These are pages 31–34 of a longer document that was distributed at the Ninth International Congress on Mathematics Education (Dossey and Usiskin, 2000). Rather than repeating what is there, I will elaborate on the picture the data present with regard to mathematics teacher education for those who teach mathematics in grades 7–12.

With respect to the first two questions considered in Deborah Schifter's remarks, the situation is the same at grades 7–12 as at grades K–6. Decisions are left to states and schools, and education is fragmented.

To understand the picture of mathematics teacher education, it helps to have knowledge of the mathematics curriculum at the secondary school level. There has never been a national curriculum in the United States. But at a given time, most schools follow much the same curriculum. This is because, among the most-used textbooks, there is a strong tendency to have the same content and approach.

I begin with a typical curriculum of 50 years ago for high school and the first year of college for well-prepared students

(Table 1). At that time, algebra and geometry were avoided almost entirely until ninth and tenth grades. Only a minority of students took mathematics beyond tenth grade (National Advisory Committee on Mathematical Education [NACOME], 1975).

The most-used and most influential of the new math curricula, the School Mathematics Study Group (SMSG) curriculum, and the demands for increased performance in mathematics and science modified the 1950s curriculum in a number of ways. Some content was moved into lower grades, and other content was compressed and integrated. Also, many schools maintained a second curriculum for slower students. As a result, by 1975 a typical curriculum was bifurcated as shown in Table 2 (NACOME, 1975).

In this 1970s curriculum, there was some algebra and geometry in eighth-

TABLE 1 Typical Curriculum for High School and First Year of College, 1950

Grade	Content
7th	Arithmetic
8th	Arithmetic
9th	First-year algebra
10th	Geometry
11th	Second-year algebra
12th	Solid geometry; trigonometry with logarithms
College	Analytic geometry; first-semester calculus

SOURCE: NACOME, 1975.

TABLE 2 Typical Curriculum, 1975

Grade	Most Students	Slower Students
7th	7th-grade mathematics	7th-grade mathematics
8th	8th-grade mathematics	8th-grade mathematics
9th	First-year algebra	General mathematics (arithmetic)
10th	Geometry	Consumer mathematics (financial arithmetic)
11th	Second-year algebra with functions	
12th	Functions and trigonometry	
College	Calculus	

SOURCE: NACOME, 1975.

grade mathematics textbooks, although these topics were often skipped to review arithmetic. At the high school level, solid geometry had disappeared. Functions became a stronger theme in second-year algebra, and logarithms were studied there rather than in trigonometry. For better students—perhaps 5 to 10 percent of the age cohort—the typical curriculum was moved down a grade, and trigonometry was taught with second-year algebra so that these students could take calculus in the 12th grade.

Although I listed "calculus" as the first college course, it must be noted that virtually every college had some sort of placement exam that had to be passed before students were allowed to take calculus, and most students did not pass that exam. Except for those in college who majored in mathematics, engineering, the physical sciences, or were very good students, it was very common for students to have to take a year of mathematics in college before calculus. This is still the case.

Notice that the slower students studied little or no geometry and little or no algebra except formulas and the simplest of equation solving. As a result, in most high schools some mathematics teachers taught nothing of what we consider today to be high school mathematics. In many schools, these teachers were certified in other subjects and had little interest and not much background in mathematics.

Today the situation is more complex (Table 3). The textbooks for sixth and seventh grade are still mostly arithmetic, but some newer middle school curricula have strong strands in algebra and geometry. Most high schools still teach full years of algebra and geometry, but some schools follow integrated curricula in which algebra, geometry, functions, and statistics receive attention every year. Some schools put almost all of their students in the same curriculum. But 20–25 percent of students take these courses at least a year earlier, and perhaps another 25 percent take these courses at least a year later. A small percent of schools offer statistics at the 12th-grade level. Currently about two-thirds of all high school graduates complete the equivalent of 11th-grade mathematics

TABLE 3 Typical Curriculum, 2000

Grade	Content
6th	Arithmetic or first-year middle school mathematics
7th	Arithmetic or second-year middle school mathematics
8th	Prealgebra or third-year middle school mathematics
9th	First-year algebra or first-year integrated mathematics
10th	Geometry or second-year integrated mathematics
11th	Second-year algebra or third-year integrated mathematics
12th	Precalculus
College	Calculus

(Campbell et al., 1997), just about the same percent as attend some college (U.S. Department of Education, 2000).

However, any national percentages hide the extraordinary diversity that occurs in the United States, even within relatively small geographic regions. The public schools serving some affluent suburban areas surrounding cities seem to provide an education as fine as that found in the schools of the top-performing countries of the world (Kimmelman et al., 1999). From these schools, well over 90 percent of students go to college, and almost all will graduate from college. It is not unusual for 15 percent or more of the graduates in these schools to have completed a year of calculus by the end of 12th grade (Campbell et al., 1997). From ninth grade, they have often taken four years of each of the "big 5" subject areas: English writing and literature, mathematics, science, social studies, and language, in addition to participating in school-sponsored sports teams and clubs. Students are generally well-behaved, and their teachers tend to be older and more experienced.

In contrast, some of the public schools serving students in poorer areas seem to provide more childcare than education. From these schools less than half of the age cohort graduate from high school on time (12 years after they began first grade) (World Almanac, 2000), and only in recent years has half the age cohort attended some college by the age of 25 (NCES, 2000). The students who remain in these schools are in an environment in which school does not have the importance that most of society would give to it. Calculus is not offered in these high schools, and even precalculus is taken only by a few students. Teachers tend to be younger, and they are often paid less even though their job may be more difficult.

Adding to the diversity, courses with the same name can be quite different. For instance, in the city of Chicago at the present time all students are required to study first-year algebra in ninth grade. The students have come from a curriculum that is almost entirely arithmetic in grades K-8 and they are not ready for the algebra courses of today, which assume that some algebra has been learned in earlier grades. So an algebra teacher has two choices: teach a standard algebra course and have the majority of students fail, or teach a simplified algebra course aimed directly at the end-of-year test that counts for a major part of a student's grade. Most teach a simplified algebra course, with content very much like the content students in better schools learn in their prealgebra course.

I provide this background because I believe it is needed in order to understand teacher education in mathematics. In the United States, requirements for a certificate to teach are set by each state. A generation ago, a mathematics teacher in grades 6–8 needed to know little more than arithmetic in order to teach the curriculum that was there. In virtually all states, a teacher with elementary school certification was considered to have enough mathematics background to teach the mathematics in these grades.

A generation ago at grades 9–12, even in fine high schools there were mathematics teachers who taught nothing beyond first-year algebra. A high school with a few mathematics teachers who had taken little more than calculus was not considered to have a problem because these teachers would be teaching students who would probably never get to algebra, let alone get to calculus.

The situation is quite different today. Some algebra and some geometry are in all years of the newer middle school curricula, and if schools are to teach these curricula and others in line with the recommendations of the National Council of Teachers of Mathematics [NCTM] *Standards* (NCTM, 1989, 2000), they need teachers of mathematics in grades 6–8 with stronger backgrounds in mathematics than they might have needed even a decade ago. General and consumer mathematics are being taught to far fewer students in grades 9–12, and the majority of students are taking mathematics through the 11th grade (Campbell et al., 1997). As a result, a high school that wishes to upgrade its curriculum no longer has the luxury of carrying a few teachers on its faculty who are relatively untrained in mathematics. There is consequently great pressure to increase the mathematics backgrounds of teachers at both the middle and high school levels.

What backgrounds do teachers have? Public schools are usually required to use certified teachers whenever possible, and private schools are also under some pressure to have their teachers certified. The usual certification at the elementary school level is to teach all subjects, while certification at the secondary school level is to teach specific subjects such as mathematics, or English, or biology. Each of the 50 states in the United States sets requirements to become a certified teacher in that state. In all 50 states, there is elementary school certification, usually for grades K–8, and secondary school certification requirements, usually for grades 7–12 or 6–12. In 30 of the states, there is a special certification to become a middle school mathematics teacher, always covering grades 7 and 8 and usually covering other grades, sometimes going down to grade 5 or up to grade 9 (Blank and Langesen, 1999).

In 1996, about half (49 percent) of all eighth-grade students were taught mathematics by teachers with an undergraduate major in mathematics or mathematics education.

The best data that I could find show that in 1998, 88 percent of high school mathematics teachers in the United States were certified in mathematics (Blank and Langesen, 1999). To become certified to teach high school mathematics, a prospective teacher typically needs 30 semester hours in mathematics, equivalent to 8–10 semester courses, about equivalent to a major in mathematics or mathematics education. These courses are normally taken from the following list: calculus (two semester courses), differential equations, advanced calculus or real analysis, linear or matrix algebra, college-level geometry, higher or abstract algebra, computer programming, elementary statistics, history of mathematics, probability, and discrete mathematics. Except for calculus, which might be taught by graduate students, these courses tend to be taught by faculty who have little or no experience teaching precollege mathematics, and the same courses are taught to those who wish to teach as to those who wish to do graduate work in mathematics. Realizing that high school teachers need to know some mathematics that graduate students in mathematics do not need—for instance, a deeper knowledge of Euclidean geometry or of number theory—a college may offer these courses or a course in topics in mathematics with content appropriate for enrichment in high schools.

In all states, in addition to mathematics content courses, many education courses are required for certification to be a mathematics teacher. Most of these courses are general education courses, taken by students regardless of subject interest, such as educational psychology and philosophy and history of education. In all states, a course in methods of teaching is required for certification. This course discusses various techniques for teaching and testing students. In large colleges, this course is separated by subject area; there are special sections for mathematics. The most important part of the training is classroom observation followed by teaching actual classes in a school under the guidance of the normal teacher of those classes. This "student teaching" or "practice teaching" experience usually occupies a student full time for a period of 8–15 weeks, depending on college and state requirements. Some states have a further requirement of passing a test in general education principles and in mathematics; in my state, the prospective teacher also must pass a test on the Illinois and U.S. constitutions.

To maintain certification in 44 of the states, teachers are required to participate in inservice programs every few years (Council of Chief State School Officers, 1998). Activities that qualify for inservice may range from full university courses to attendance in a local professional meeting. There is almost no control over the substance or quality of these programs, and many teachers try to satisfy these requirements with the least amount of work required.

On the other hand, most school districts provide more pay to teachers who have substantial numbers of semester hours beyond the bachelor's degree (American Federation of Teachers, 2000). This provides an incentive for a teacher to take university courses. A master's degree typically requires one year's work beyond the bachelor's. The median teacher has taught for about 15 years, and that teacher is likely to have a master's degree and perhaps 15–30 additional semester hours of credit. This graduate work may be in education or in counseling or in psychology or in mathematics

education or in any number of other areas. Thus, many and perhaps most experienced mathematics teachers have strengthened their backgrounds with some courses designed for experienced mathematics teachers, or filled in their backgrounds with courses in mathematics, statistics, or computer science no more difficult than undergraduate mathematics courses. But most teachers have not taken what a mathematician would call graduate work in mathematics.

Can I describe what is typical in a mathematics methods course, or in a mathematics course for secondary school teachers? No. There is no canonical form. As far as I can tell, there is no textbook in common use in these courses. Professors generally teach what they feel is most important. In the 1980s, mathematics methods courses would probably devote some time to discussions of problem solving á la Pólya, but there might be little else in common. In the 1990s, there would usually be some discussion of the NCTM *Standards*. But because these courses have so little in common, there is very little in the history of mathematics education, or in mathematics education research that is common knowledge among mathematics teachers in the United States. This is not merely true in mathematics but in all subjects, and it makes teachers and schools susceptible to the latest education fads.

Many leaders ask teachers to take full advantage of technology while there are those who think that calculators have already ruined a generation of students. The *Standards* ask teachers to teach using discussion and discourse among students (NCTM, 1991), yet there are those who think that these methods promote chaos and are not nearly as efficient as direct instruction. The *Standards* recommend that teachers use a variety of assessment techniques (NCTM, 1995), while high-stakes tests are often entirely multiple choice. The high-stakes tests given by states are often in conflict with national standardized tests and with the textbooks that have been adopted by the school district. There are those who wish to place all students at a grade level in the same mathematics courses and those who wish to continue the practice of differentiating students based on previous performance and perceptions of ability. These conflicting voices are heard by the teacher at a time when a greater variety of curriculum choices exist than perhaps ever before: integrated curricula and traditional curricula, curricula that emphasize skills and curricula that emphasize applications and modeling, curricula that assume students are self-motivated and curricula designed as if only a few students are self-motivated. Consequently, the mathematics teacher in the United States is beleaguered, under pressure to do everything for everyone.

Perhaps some of these same issues exist in Japan. Such an environment produces many challenges for teacher education in mathematics, and perhaps some opportunities. I look forward to our work here as suggesting ideas for helping to improve mathematics teacher education and helping to meet the challenges of teaching mathematics in a new century.

A Study of Teacher Change Through Inservice Mathematics Education Programs in Graduate School

Keiko Hino and Keiichi Shigematsu, Nara University of Education

Our topic is on Japanese teacher preparation for inservice preparation in graduate school. Rather than an overview on this topic, however, we present a more microscopic outlook. In Japan, few jobs are available for young teachers; therefore, teacher inservice and the reeducation of teachers is now taking place in graduate schools. Teachers can take time off from their jobs for two years to go to graduate school. Another option is to spend one year in graduate school and return to the teaching profession during their second year. Taking night courses also has recently become an option. Thus, while working as a teacher, teachers can get a master's degree in two years. Various courses that are being discussed at universities include a new graduate school program, a one-year course, a long-term course lasting more than two years, and correspondence courses.

In this workshop, lesson study is one of the central themes. When teachers receive training in graduate school, lesson study is very significant. One example is a program at Nara University of Education for junior high school teachers. Elementary school teachers also can develop in their profession through similar graduate programs. The inservice education needs at graduate schools have increased, and there is a greater demand for this type of course.

Figure 1 provides a framework for the inservice education program at the Nara University of Education. The center illustrates what kind of skills teachers acquire in the two years in the area of self-expression, the ability to express themselves. We want them to develop the power to explain the power of mathematics. This is one kind of self-expression. The other kind of self-expression is whether teachers can convey and communicate their own practice to other teachers. Certain facets that are included in this self-expression category can be viewed from two perspectives. One is toward the left-hand side in Figure 1. The professionalism of the teachers can evolve if teachers further cultivate their profession and study mathematics, mathematics education issues, or children's issues in learning. Japanese teachers are required to have counseling capabilities, so they have to enrich their specialty areas. Another viewpoint is the arrow coming from the right-hand side of Figure 1 to the center. This information exchange is not limited to within the Nara University of Education but includes elementary schools and high

FIGURE 1 Framework of inservice mathematics education program at the graduate school of the Nara University of Education.

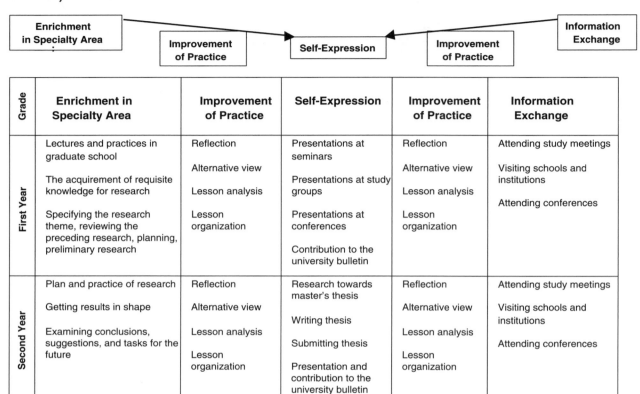

Grade	Enrichment in Specialty Area	Improvement of Practice	Self-Expression	Improvement of Practice	Information Exchange
First Year	Lectures and practices in graduate school The acquirement of requisite knowledge for research Specifying the research theme, reviewing the preceding research, planning, preliminary research	Reflection Alternative view Lesson analysis Lesson organization	Presentations at seminars Presentations at study groups Presentations at conferences Contribution to the university bulletin	Reflection Alternative view Lesson analysis Lesson organization	Attending study meetings Visiting schools and institutions Attending conferences
Second Year	Plan and practice of research Getting results in shape Examining conclusions, suggestions, and tasks for the future	Reflection Alternative view Lesson analysis Lesson organization	Research towards master's thesis Writing thesis Submitting thesis Presentation and contribution to the university bulletin	Reflection Alternative view Lesson analysis Lesson organization	Attending study meetings Visiting schools and institutions Attending conferences

schools, not only in our prefecture but the neighboring prefectures and teachers in those prefectures. Through such exchange and participation in academic meetings, teachers can further cultivate their professional skills.

Figure 1 does not show lesson study, but teachers aggressively participate in a lesson study program. In the two-year program, the first year takes place at the graduate school level. However, in the second year teachers go back to their original school for further training or further education.

With respect to the second purpose of our research characterizing the school teacher's change, we found that a teacher's growth in mathematics takes place in four phases. Phase one is consideration of their own teaching practice; teachers have to be aware of the framework for their own teaching practice. In other words, they have to be aware of the issues in their own view of their teaching. Unless they are aware of their problems or issues, it is very difficult to motivate them to improve their teaching ability. Second, a clear understanding of their issues, however, will not be sufficient to move to the next step. They need to think about what they should do. So they must search for another implicit framework (phase two). In phase three, that framework is internalized, and finally through that process an improved framework should be developed (phase four). These four phases show that improvement in professional ability, for example, having more students come to enjoy mathematics, happens only when teachers construct their own framework for mathematics teaching. An explicit diagram is advantageous (Box 1). In our research we found that if a teacher can notice improvement, the teacher will continue to further improve his or her professional ability.

Now we go into more detail about our research concerning the teacher's

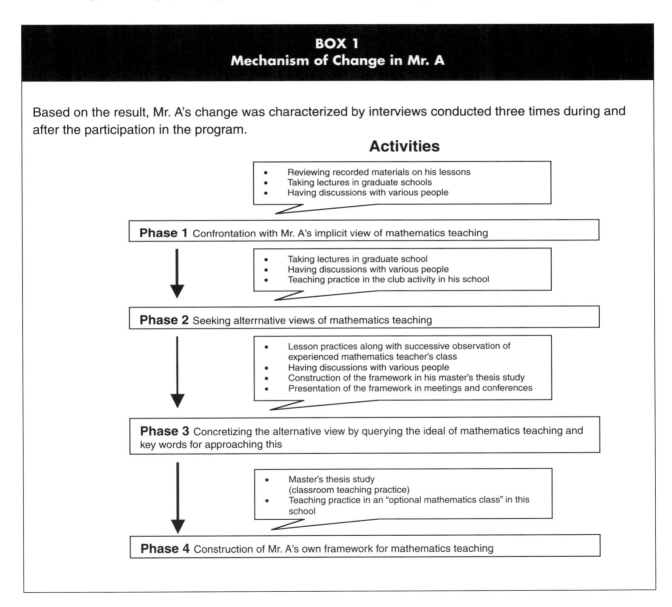

BOX 1
Mechanism of Change in Mr. A

Based on the result, Mr. A's change was characterized by interviews conducted three times during and after the participation in the program.

Activities

- Reviewing recorded materials on his lessons
- Taking lectures in graduate schools
- Having discussions with various people

Phase 1 Confrontation with Mr. A's implicit view of mathematics teaching

- Taking lectures in graduate school
- Having discussions with various people
- Teaching practice in the club activity in his school

Phase 2 Seeking alterrnative views of mathematics teaching

- Lesson practices along with successive observation of experienced mathematics teacher's class
- Having discussions with various people
- Construction of the framework in his master's thesis study
- Presentation of the framework in meetings and conferences

Phase 3 Concretizing the alternative view by querying the ideal of mathematics teaching and key words for approaching this

- Master's thesis study (classroom teaching practice)
- Teaching practice in an "optional mathematics class" in this school

Phase 4 Construction of Mr. A's own framework for mathematics teaching change. Improvements in the teacher's teaching practice has been mentioned several times, but what do we mean by teaching practice? There are three perspectives from which we looked at the teaching practice (Box 2). One is the class program itself. In other words, preparing for the class—organizing the class—is one practice. Another is during the class, the kind of practice the teacher carries out. And the third aspect is after the class, making improvements in the practice the teacher has just finished. In other words, prelesson, midlesson, and postlesson are the three different aspects pertaining to the teaching practice.

In our study we surveyed teachers, interviewed teachers, and collected class observation cards from the participants of the class. Using these different methods, we tried to analyze the improvement in these three different levels of teaching

practice of the teacher. Mr. A is a junior high school teacher, who admitted that he had very little interest in mathematics education (Box 3). He was more interested in guiding his students in the extracurricular activities of rugby games. After 15 years of experience, Mr. A wanted to improve his skills and his performance as a school teacher. How did his teaching practice actually change? The improvement of Mr. A's teaching practice and his professional development was initially assessed by observing his class before he took this graduate course. Then we went back to his class, after he took this two-year course at the graduate school. The contents of the two classes that were observed were almost identical. We tried to compare what we noticed had changed over the two-year period (Box 3). We analyzed these observations from three perspectives. First, we analyzed

---

BOX 2
Purpose of the Research

1. To characterize a school teacher's change through participation in mathematics education program at the graduate level.
2. To assess the change of the teacher from the perspective of teaching practice in their mathematics class.

Mathematics teachers' teaching practices are construed as the ability that enables teachers to conduct activities such as:

- Prelesson: To organize and transform content knowledge along with the purpose. To have the "eyes" to evaluate the result of such a process.
- Midlesson: To execute the plan. To create activities that lead to the goal, taking notice of a student's situation all the time, sometimes by applying various routines and other times by inventing them promptly.
- Postlesson: To reflect on the lesson using as a basis information about the attainment of a teacher's goal. To work out instructions concretely for the next lesson.

BOX 3
Method

The teaching practice of a teacher was assessed twice, before and after the participation in the graduate school program offered by Nara University of Education.

Mr. A's Profile
- A junior high school teacher working at a public secondary school.
- In addition to teaching mathematics, he arranges student club activities every day after school and also on the weekend.
- He does not participate in any mathematical study groups.
- "I have been teaching for 15 years. To keep up the times, I want to study how to make use computers toward mathematics education in new ages. I also need to develop my teaching practice in class through this program. When I return to my school, I need to show my improved teaching practice to my colleagues."

Lesson Observation Dates and Participants
Before: February 17, 1998, at a junior high school first-graders' class (seventh-grade) and a second-graders' (eighth-grade) class.
- Observers: 5 persons (2 university instructors, 1 high school mathematics teacher, 2 graduate students).
- Target students: 6 first graders and 6 second graders.
After: February 15, 2000, at a junior high school first-graders' class.
- Observers: 5 persons (2 university instructors, 1 high school mathematics teacher, 2 graduate students).
- Target students: 5 first graders.

Data Collection
Prelesson
- To teacher: interview questions on mathematics and learning.
- To target students: interview on their belief and interest of mathematics.
Lesson Observation
- Recording of the lesson by videotape recorder and microphones.
- Observation by a script form from two aspects: the flow of lesson and students' activities.
Postlesson
- To teacher: interview on self-assessment of the lesson.
- To target students: interview on their interest and motivation toward the content they learned in the lesson.

from the observer's viewpoint. Observers were fellow graduate students, the teachers who had already finished the graduate school program, and ourselves, the researchers.

We made three findings. We did not see any dramatic change; however, Mr. A's attitude with respect to the students had clearly changed. There are some specific data to indicate this change in attitude, which is shown in Figure 2. This figure shows the rate of correspondence among different observers before, during, and after this graduate course.

Before Mr. A took the graduate course, most observers agreed that Mr. A was just teaching with a one-way method, teacher to students. This is shown by the overall high rate of correspondence among the observers. After the two-year course, this approach changed dramatically to become more interactive (Box 4). Notice the decrease in the rate of correspondence in most items. Mr. A's teacher-directed way of teaching eased a little. That was a unanimous observation.

The second perspective is the observation made by the students themselves (Table 1). Here again, dependence on textbooks has changed. (In a different research study, we found that the Japanese teachers who do not like mathematics would inevitably depend on the textbooks in teaching the mathematics classes.). But as you can see, after this two-year course, Mr. A depended less on textbooks, which meant that he was trying to cater to the actual needs of the students in his class, and students noticed the difference.

And the third perspective is the self-assessment by Mr. A (Table 2). Throughout the graduate course, Mr. A learned that what is most important is for the students to learn mathematics, not for the teacher to learn mathematics. What is most important in organizing the math-

FIGURE 2 In the eyes of the observers.

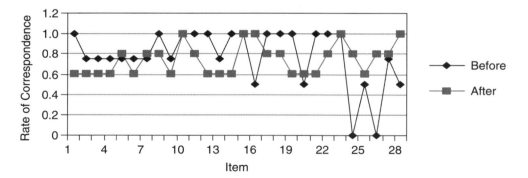

NOTES:
Mr. A's teacher-directed ways of teaching eased a little. Communication with students was brought into the class. The time for students' activities was put in the lesson. Rate of correspondence among the observers on each item, or what was the percent of observers who agreed that the item was oberved in the lesson. (1) items No. 1 to 14 concern of the teacher, (2) items No. 16 and 17 concern of the classroom atmosphere and (3) items No. 19 to 28 concern students in the class.

BOX 4
Features of the Lesson That Are Commonly Recognized by All Observers

Before 1998
- The teacher does not suggest students try various approaches to solve a problem.
- The teacher does not relate mathematics with other subjects or daily life.
- The teacher does not instruct to develop individually.
- The teacher teaches the content exactly as it is in the textbook.
- The teacher gives a teacher-centered telling of the lesson.
- Many students do not volunteer to state their opinions.
- Many students do not think in various ways.
- None of the students in the class chat among themselves.
- All of the students in the class put their textbooks and notebooks on their desks.

After 2000
- The teacher doesn't relate mathematics with other subjects or daily life.
- Communication with students is seen.
- Communication among students is not seen.
- Some students in the class have private chatter.
- Many students tackle to compute, draw figures and graphs, or use compasses and rulers.

TABLE 1 In the Eyes of Students

Items Recognized By Students	Before (%)	After (%)
Many of his lessons go with textbooks	100	80
Materials are often used in his lessons	0	20
I ask him questions frequently	67	40
Pace of his lessons seems fast	83	20
Frequently students attempt to first solve the problem by themselves	100	100
We often have a discussion	17	60
Two teachers have taught me a lesson	0	0
I write the lesson summary with my own words	25	60

NOTES:
Fewer students feel that the pace of his lessons is fast. More students think they have discussions in the class.

TABLE 2 In the Eyes of the Teacher

Items for the Interview	Before 1998		After 2000
	First Year of Junior High School	Second Year of Junior High School	First Year of Junior High School
Aims of the lesson	To understand how to construct figures. To learn how to use the compass.	To understand the Midpoint Connection theorem and to use it.	To promote students' exploratory activities.
Special attention	To make all students learn the proper use of a compass.	To make students understand the theorem.	To value students' voluntary statement. Not to force teachers' views. To give comments on contents that require direct explanations.
Did you value students' discussion?	No	No	Yes
Did you arrange time for students to solve problems by themselves?	No	No	Yes
Did you give teacher-centered lesson?	Yes	Yes	No
Did you communicate with the students?	Sometimes	Sometimes	Yes
Did you consider connecting the subject with daily life examples?	No	No	No
Did you conjecture possible questions the students may have prior to the lesson?	Yes	Yes	Yes
Did you make use of wrong answers provided by students?	No	No	Yes

NOTES:
He gave a better evaluation to his "after" lesson than "before" lesson. The aims of the lesson focused on students' thinking and attitude. Special attention to teaching instructions can be seen in the "after" lesson, while they were restricted solely to the teaching contents in the "before" lesson.

ematics class is to make sure that the students learn, that the class is more student focused, and student oriented. And through his self-assessment and through interviews, we can see that he has actually learned that difference. The biggest change within Mr. A was that he learned that he needs to communicate with the students (Box 5). He learned that what is often termed the mathematical activities of the students need to be supported. And to do this, you have to provide enough time for the students to engage in mathematical activities. Mr. A learned that as well. As we saw at the beginning of this discussion, these changes did not take place at once. Rather, the changes were supported by Mr. A's long-term investigation into his own framework of mathematics classroom practice characterized by the four phases of growth.

While this is a case study involving just one teacher, we are continuing our research involving elementary school teachers and senior high school teachers. Our preliminary findings indicate that we can see similar improvements in teaching practices and professional development based on the fact that the teachers need to have an open mind, identify and recognize their shortcomings and areas for improvement and be willing to try to cope with the changes. The responsibility of the graduate school is to help teachers tackle those issues and challenges.

BOX 5

Conclusions
- Change in the teacher's teaching practice in mathematics class was mainly observed in two aspects.
  — The teacher came to communicate with his students with respect to mathematics.
  — The teacher came to have more time for the students to work on his or her own.
- The emergence of this "pedagogical reasoning" was supported by his long-term investigation into his own framework of mathematics classroom practice. The process of investigation was characterized by four phases.
- The graduate program influenced his change by providing opportunities in observing, practicing, and discussing mathematics classes in junior high school and in planning and conducting a research study for the purpose of writing a master's thesis.

Tasks for the Future
- By accumulating the information from more cases, the process of teacher change needs to be clarified further.
- Construction and modification of the classes and the program that enhance the smooth shift along the four phases need to be investigated from different angles.

Recurrent Education in Japan: Waseda University Education Research and Development Center

Toru Handa, Waseda University, Honjo Senior High School

Waseda University has an annual summer seminar for inservice teachers at what we call recurrent education centers. In 1996, Waseda University Education Research and Development Center launched this program. Since then, four or five days in August are dedicated to this seminar, with about ten courses. The basic course is for beginning users of personal computers. There is a class management and an attainment management course; a course of English with personal computers; a course of Japanese language with personal computers; courses in mathematics, social studies, and sciences; a course to make computers; and a course on networks in schools. This seminar is for inservice teachers. We now have information technology everywhere, but teachers need to use the technology and information media to make their classes more interesting and easy to understand by students. Therefore, for each subject, teachers must first improve their computer literacy; however, Japanese teachers are busy in daily routines. From early in the morning to late in the evening, they have to manage extracurricular courses. Before classes and after classes, there are teachers' meetings. So they do not have enough time for studying information technology.

So how can teachers change their classroom teaching to use technology and the information media? First, how can they get information that will be useful in their teaching? How can they introduce the technologies and information media into the classrooms? How can they create self-made successful classes? To achieve these things, they need the basic knowledge and expertise for the new technologies and information processing media.

Specifically, some of my remarks focus on how to improve and change the mathematics classes. The two mathematics courses I selected are an introduction to MATHEMATICA, a software package that processes numerical formulas and does mathematical integration, and how to make a web page. A web page is a future textbook, and that means the teacher must be able to use HTML.

On the first day of the seminar, basic MATHEMATICA and the basics of HTML are presented exclusively for the real beginners. So these are really the basics. And on the second and third days they use MATHEMATICA to process formulas and to enjoy the program. At the end of the third day they learn about software other than MATHEMATICA. On the fourth day they create a web page using MATHEMATICA and then develop the teaching materials for their own classes. Finally they make presentations and have a discussion about their work.

Word processing software in Japan for information technology literacy is Excel and Ajitalo. Our participants vary in skill level. We had one person who had never touched the keyboard of a computer, 72 percent of the participants didn't know about MATHEMATICA at all, and about 83 percent had no web page experiences. Despite this, the participants finish the seminar with some achievements. The computer beginners in last year's seminar created a spiral structure of shells and used formulas to make simulations. By changing the value of a constant, one participant created different types of shells. Some showed a tangent of the function as an example of simulation. Last year we had a three-day seminar, and after completing the three days, participants could create such simulations.

Finally, I would like to address some of the problems or the challenges that we have now. The budget for the education center is limited. We do not receive many grants, so the participants have to pay approximately $100 for four days. Maybe this is too expensive. A second problem is that the number of trainee teachers does not increase in the way we would like to see. There could be several reasons. First we do not have a preparation initiative tied to promotion. In Japan this kind of recurrent training is not so popular, and it is not generally accepted. Also in Japan, once teachers get a teaching certificate, they can stay there without studying or learning anything new until retirement age. In addition, even during the summer holidays, Japanese teachers are very busy because they have to take care of extra-curricular activities. Teachers also have to ask for permission of the principal or head teachers to participate in this kind of a seminar, which introduces all sorts of procedures. Another possible reason is that there are some people who take this course every year, many of whom are very experienced teachers. We probably need to prepare several different levels of the courses and a follow-up service. We have to develop the mailing list of the participants and make a database system so that we can continue to provide information about teaching and education to the teachers. For these reasons, it is difficult to motivate the teachers to participate in this kind of seminar. The important thing is considering how we can create new ideas and how we can create a good image about participation in the seminar. Demonstration lessons may be an effective method in this respect.

Recurrent Education in Japan: Kanagawa Prefectural Education Center

Mamoru Takezawa, Kanagawa Prefectural Education Center

The Kanagawa Prefecture, the local government, carries out programs for the inservice programs for teachers. The education center is located in the middle of the prefecture so teachers in Kanagawa Prefecture can come to it easily. This is where teachers receive training, both during summer vacation and during the school terms. They also come for training as a long-term researcher or student for one or two years. We provide training for between 40,000 to 50,000 teachers from 1,644 schools. The center has a staff of 50. I belong to the information technology and education department.

The education center is organized into four divisions: Japanese art, social science or social studies, and foreign languages for English and Spanish (Kanagawa has a relationship with Peru and Brazil in South America, and we have many children from Peru and Brazil); mathematics; information technology and education department; and principal and vice principal school management. The basic programs in information technology and education start with general seminars, followed by specialized seminars like networks, multimedia, robot programming. For example, Logo or Mindstorms can be used. We also have a leader seminar to create information technology coordinators, and we nurture leaders throughout the year. There is a license seminar for the new evaluation of the national curriculum. We also act as a help desk for supporting other departments such as science, social studies, and Japanese language in how they can utilize information technology.

What is the license seminar? In 2003, Japan will have a new national curriculum. The subject of information or informatics will be added to the high schools' programs in the new curriculum. However, we have no teachers to teach that subject. So for the next three years, we have to train or develop teachers in informatics. The program is targeted at math and natural science teachers and is a three-week summer seminar to give them the license to get ready for the new curriculum in 2003. One of the issues is that many of the better mathematics teachers are using computers. They will receive a license for information technology, and when they are ready to teach it, the number of good mathematics teachers will be depleted.

Lesson Study as Professional Development

The first full day of the workshop began with a presentation by Deborah Ball designed to set the stage for the use of teaching practice as a medium for professional development. She framed a central question for workshop participants to consider: "How do teachers in Japan and the United States use practice to work on their teaching?" The rest of the workshop was spent exploring three different examples of the use of teaching practice as a medium for professional development: lesson study, video records of a class, and two cases describing mathematics classes.

The sessions that focused on lesson study included general descriptions of the design and enactment of a lesson and postlesson reflection by the instructor and observers. Yoshinori Shimizu provided background on the nature of lesson study, and Makoto Yoshida extended that background and described one project on the implementation of lesson study in a U.S. school. Participants viewed two classroom lessons and the follow-up postlesson discussions. Hiroshi Nakano, the teacher in the fourth-grade lesson, gave a brief description of how lesson study was carried out at his school and his thoughts about the value of lesson study for his own professional growth. Video excerpts from the lesson and a printed version of the postlesson discussion are included in the following section as part of the proceedings. The day ended with three panelists reflecting on lesson study, the lessons they had observed, and how the day's experiences related to their own backgrounds as mathematics educators.

Setting the Stage
Deborah Loewenberg Ball, Professor, University of Michigan

- What can be learned from using practice as a means of developing teachers' knowledge of mathematical content and how to teach that mathematics?
- What questions should frame our thinking?

Lesson Study: What, Why, and How?
Yoshinori Shimizu, Associate Professor, Tokyo Gakugei University

- How does lesson study work and what is its role in developing teachers' content knowledge and understanding of how to teach?

Framing Lesson Study for U.S. Participants
Makoto Yoshida, Professor, Columbia University Teachers College

Lesson Study from the Perspective of a Fourth-Grade Teacher
Hiroshi Nakano, Elementary Teacher, Setagaya Elementary School and Tokyo Gakugei University

Setting the Stage

Deborah Loewenberg Ball, University of Michigan

The question we want to work on together is, "How do teachers in Japan and the United States use practice to work on their teaching?" Why are we so interested in learning how teachers in both countries use the practice of teaching itself to work on their teaching? Let us think about other practices for a moment, for example, singing opera, writing poetry, playing soccer, cooking, or the practice that we are interested in here, teaching. It is important to notice three things about learning practices. First, you do not learn a practice simply by doing it. For example, poets do not become good at poetry simply by sitting with paper and pencil and writing. You do not learn to cook simply by taking pans out of the cupboard and putting a pan on the stove with some food. Practices also are not learned simply by acquiring knowledge. No one becomes a good soccer player by reading books about soccer. Finally, practices are not learned only by watching experts do them. If you attend a concert and listen to an opera singer perform opera, it is not likely that you will be able to perform opera yourself. Each of these can help. It can help to watch experts engage in a practice. It can help to acquire knowledge about the practice. And it can

help to do the practice. But none of these is enough.

LEARNING PRACTICES

Let me make some points about how practices are learned. First, learning a practice requires study. It requires trying things, and it requires analyzing how the things that you tried work. Such analyses enable improvements. You develop new ideas of things to try. This is true for playing soccer. It is true for writing poetry. It is true for many practices. We are interested in how the practice of teaching is learned, and all of these things are important to learning the practice of teaching.

Second, there are practices involved in learning a practice; for example, watching teaching is not common sense. If you bring someone into a classroom and ask them to watch a lesson, they may not know what to watch. They may not notice what the children are doing. They may not know how to listen to the very specific way a teacher asks a question. There are things to learn about how to watch teaching carefully. There are things to learn about how to discuss teaching with colleagues.

There are things to learn about how to make records of one's teaching so that later one can examine one's own work and the work of the students, show these records to other people, and discuss them. None of these things are automatically known. These are the things I mean by practices important to learning a practice; and if we talked about opera or cooking or soccer, we could make a list of practices important to learning those practices as well.

In the workshop, we want to learn what practices teachers in Japan and the United States use to learn the practice of teaching. What do teachers in these two countries do that enables them to develop their teaching practice?

MATHEMATICS TEACHERS' PRACTICE

Keiko Hino and Keiichi Shigematsu gave a definition of teaching practice in their paper. They said that mathematics teachers' practice can be construed as a set of abilities grouped into three parts: prelesson, midlesson, and postlesson.

Prelesson. The mathematics teachers' practice is construed as the ability to first, in the prelesson, organize and transform mathematical knowledge according to the goals and purposes of the lesson. Second, the prelesson requires teachers to have what they call the "eyes" to evaluate how that organization of the mathematics works for the students.

Midlesson. Next, they talked about the midlesson. They mentioned several things that teachers must do while enacting the lesson in class. First, teachers must execute the plan they have made. They must move from the piece of paper with the design and use it with the students in their class. This means they must create

activities that lead to their goal, and they must take notice of students' current situations all the time. In the sixth-grade classroom we visited at Tokyo Gakugei University Elementary School the other day, we noticed that the teacher was constantly looking at the students, watching, trying to figure out how the lesson was being received and experienced. Do the students understand? Do they know what I am asking them to do? Do they understand each other? Sometimes teachers apply routines they already know, but they must make judgments; they must decide that this moment is the moment for that routine. Sometimes situations arise in teaching for which teachers have no routine, and at those times, as Professors Hino and Shigematsu suggest, teachers must promptly invent new actions to manage what they see happening in their class. This is very complicated work.

Postlesson. In the postlesson, teachers reflect on what happened in the lesson. They analyze how the design worked with their students, and they develop concrete plans for the next lesson on the basis of what happened in that lesson.

Summary. This is a cycle of design: generating designs, using the design with students, analyzing how it works, revising the design for the next step. How do teachers learn to do this well? What activities and practices do teachers in Japan and the United States use to develop their abilities to carry out this practice of teaching? Keiko Hino and Keiichi Shigematsu indicated that there are several abilities that are important in a mathematics teacher's practice. One is the ability to design lessons, to organize and transform mathematical knowledge and have eyes to evaluate the results of the design. Another is the ability to enact lessons, to carry them out in class. This involves creating activities, taking notice of students, applying routines, and inventing actions depending on how students understand the content.

Finally, this indicates the need for yet another ability: the ability to analyze lessons. Through such analyses, teachers develop knowledge about teaching and work out concrete plans for next lessons. How do teachers develop knowledge about teaching so that each day, each year, with each class of students they become more skillful, more able to do these things? What practices enable them to become increasingly more adept at designing lessons, carrying out those lessons with their students, and all the time observing how the lesson is working with their students?

WHAT DO TEACHERS NEED TO LEARN?

So I offer a short but difficult list. What do teachers need to learn to engage in this practice of mathematics teaching? One thing that repeatedly came through in their discussion of practice was how to pay attention to and teach every student in the class. We were impressed that with a class of 33 students the teacher was watching and looking around, trying to understand what the students were learning. This is not an easy thing to do. How do you figure out what the students understand, whether they are paying attention, whether they are following, if the examples make sense, if they are interested, and if they are learning? Students are different from one another. This requires great skill to do what sounds like a very simple thing.

Second, teachers need to know how to know mathematics and to use it to help their students learn. This is not the same thing as knowing mathematics to do mathematics by yourself. How do teachers learn to know mathematics in ways that enable them to organize the content, create activities, and adjust the activities to address the goals of the lesson as well

as particular students' interests, needs, problems, difficulties, and so on? This is another big area. In the presentations from the United States, we heard that we face serious problems of teachers not knowing mathematics well enough to help each of their students learn mathematics. Teachers' mathematical knowledge equips them to teach all students, so the first and second points are very related.

Third, and perhaps a little different, is that teachers need to learn how to work with others on developing knowledge for teaching. Some of us watched a group of Japanese teachers discuss a lesson last week, and today we will learn about lesson study. One important practice for developing teaching is to work with others on teaching, to learn to do the kinds of things that I have been talking about. One interesting point in Professors Hino and Shigematsu's study was how frequently a note was made that Mr. A engaged in discussions with others about his teaching. We are interested in what Mr. A did in these discussions, what he talked about, what he learned. How do teachers learn to work together with others to develop their teaching?

QUESTIONS FOR CONSIDERATION

I want to end by suggesting some simple questions that we should ask ourselves as we learn about what Japanese and U.S. teachers are doing to work on their practice. As we learn about lesson study, for example, we want to know what the teachers actually do as they engage in the practices of lesson study. What do they work on? What do they use to work on this? Do they look at students' work? Do they look at mathematics books? Do they read articles? Do they bring in other people with whom to talk? What do they use to enable this work? Who works with teachers? Do teachers do this alone? Do others work with them? What do teachers seem to learn and how do they learn these things?

We want to ask these same questions tomorrow when we examine some of the practices of teachers in the United States who also work on practice to develop their teaching. We hope to leave here with more knowledge about what it takes to use practice as the site for working on something that cannot be learned only through study, only through watching experts, or only by working alone and just doing it. What does it take to use practice as a site for developing practice?

Lesson Study: What, Why, and How?

Yoshinori Shimizu, Tokyo Gakugei University

Lesson study is a common element in Japanese educational practices. At the outset, however, there are differences in cultural background that should be considered as we discuss lesson study at the elementary level. Professor Usiskin indicated, for example, that student teachers in the United States usually have eight to ten weeks for training in the classroom, but the Japanese student teachers spend three or four weeks or in some cases just two weeks in classroom work. Also, in Japan in elementary schools and junior high schools there is a very large teachers' room where every teacher has his or her own desk. Those teachers who are not giving lessons spend their time in this room. Most U.S. teachers have their own room where they spend their time when they are not teaching. Consider one other example. About ten years ago, I visited a middle school in San Francisco. When the lesson started, a boy began to eat an apple during the lesson. "Why was this boy eating?" I asked the teacher after the lesson. She said, "He must have been hungry." What I wanted to ask was why he had to eat an apple in his class during a lesson, because it would never happen in a Japanese classroom. So things that we take for granted in our own culture may be some things that are not natural at all on the other side of the ocean. We have to keep that in mind when we consider any cultural activity like teaching.

What follows is a brief outline of lesson study with a special focus on the role of lesson plans. Sometimes this is called the agenda or schedule, but whatever its name, for Japanese teachers it is something that is taken for granted, although they do not always prepare the lesson plan.

Lesson studies are held at different levels, and there are different types as well. Lesson studies are conducted as part of the preservice teacher training programs for student teachers. There is another type, called intraschool lesson studies, where maybe three times a year lesson studies are held within a particular school. Lesson studies are also held on a prefectural level, city level, or a school district level, and consequently organizations and programs vary, which is an important consideration to remember. Finally, lesson studies are held at the national level, open to outsiders. I just listed four different types, but this, of course, is not an exhaustive list. There may be some other types as well.

Generally a lesson study consists of the following: the actual classes taught to pupils, observation by others, immediately followed by intensive discussion called the study discussion. Designing, enacting, and analyzing are the three stages that evolve before, during, and after the lesson, in other words preparation, implementation, and analysis (Box 1). There is extensive preparation made before the class, and there will be extensive work done after the lesson study as well, which will be used as a follow-up and as a preparation for the next lesson studied. These events form a cycle.

Lesson studies also have different objectives and aims. One is to educate student teachers, and a second is to monitor and instruct novice teachers. In the late 1980s, a new system of teacher education programs was introduced in Japan for new or novice teachers. Newly hired teachers are closely supervised for a one-year period by the deputy school

---

BOX 1
How Lesson Studies Are Structured and Delivered

Before
- Deciding a "theme" (and organizing a team)
- Selecting a particular topic for the study
- Writing a lesson plan (analyzing the topic to be taught, assessing students' learning, examining the task to be posed, thinking teacher's roles, etc.)
- Discussing and revising the lesson plan(s)
- Tried by other teachers, or in another class
- Reflecting on the lesson and re-revising the plan

During
Teaching/observing the lesson
- Recording what the teacher and students said, how students worked on the task during their seat work, and what was written on the chalkboard
Extensive discussion on the lesson
- A self-reflection by the teacher
- Discussion on the task, students' responses, teacher's roles, and so on
Comments and suggestions by a mathematics educator or an experienced teacher

After
- Ideas are used in the following lessons
- Next theme may be identified
- A report of the lesson is sometimes shared with outside people

principal or by well-experienced teachers. As part of the program, novice teachers have to take various classes, and the contents of these courses are well defined, and often lesson study is a part of these courses. Another objective for all teachers is to improve teaching skills, which is what counts most of all. All teachers also need to learn the roles of maintaining and managing the school, and therefore collaborations among teachers are needed. Lesson studies are conducted to maintain such collaborations. Lesson study can be used to improve teacher content knowledge. In addition, the national-level study programs that are organized by a group of teachers or by a school are sometimes used to share new ideas, new methods, test new materials, or new approaches, as well as to demonstrate those new approaches.

Usually lesson studies begin by choosing a specific theme. For example, a focus in the current movement of educational reform is on helping children develop their own thinking ability. This focus may guide the selection of the theme. More general themes may also be chosen, such as "teaching pupils how to live." A team of teachers is organized as part of the process. When the size of the school is small, the entire school will often be involved in the team. A particular topic is selected for the study, and the lesson plan is written by the team. One thing to be emphasized here is that by writing and revising a lesson plan, we work on the lesson plan, refining it in an iterative manner. The content knowledge, the pupil's learning level, the specific tasks to be presented to that pupil are part of the lesson plan. "Are you going to use the number 10 or 12 for this particular task of multiplication?" It can make a big difference, and such minute details are well planned before the class is given. Usually the class duration is 45 minutes long, but hours of preparations are made beforehand. Sometimes the same topic is taught by other teachers in other classrooms for trial purposes. Then you revisit and reflect on the lesson to rerevise the lesson plan.

The activities above occur before the class. During the study lesson in class, the observers will take very detailed notes. What are the responses of the pupils to the given task and what did the teacher say? What were the questions raised by the pupils? What the teacher wrote on the blackboard is recorded as well. In other words, many things happen during the observation phase.

During the postlesson discussion that follows the study lesson, the teacher who taught the class would share his or her own impression or reflection about the class with the observers. This is followed by intensive discussions on the tasks, students' response, teacher's role, and on and on. An invited principal, mathematics educator, or experienced teacher may give comments and suggestions about the class as well.

After the study lesson, the feedback from this class would be used for the next class, and the theme for the next class will be identified as well. Sometimes a report is put together, the ideas from a lesson study are presented in journals, or the materials are distributed within the school or within the school district to be shared by fellow teachers.

That is the basic outline of lesson study, but I would like to say a few words about the lesson plan. Throughout the lesson studies, the lesson plan serves as a medium for communication among teachers (Box 2). Lesson plans have various purposes or objectives as well. Box 3 shows the common framework for lesson plans. The matrix shows the steps that should be followed during a 45-

BOX 2
Lesson Plan as a Medium for Communication Among Teachers Throughout the Lesson Study

- Sharing ideas
- Discussing various aspects of the lesson
- Used as a frame of reference for the lessons
- Shaping the lesson flow (script)

BOX 3
A Common Framework for Lesson Plans

Steps	Main Learning Activities	Anticipated Students' Responses	Remarks on Teaching
Posing a problem			
Students' problem solving on their own			
Whole-class discussion			
Summing up			
(Exercise/Extension)			

minute class. These give the teacher a certain image of how the class is going to move forward. Sometimes an exercise or an extension will be provided as the final step.

Keeping the common framework for lesson study in mind, we can interpret some of the findings of the Third International Mathematics and Science Study videotape classroom study conducted by Stigler and his colleagues that compared eighth-grade mathematics lessons in Germany, the United States, and Japan. One of the biggest differences among the three countries was, for example, the alternative solutions presented by the teachers and by the students during one class (Figure 1).

As Figure 1 indicates, more alternative solutions are presented by students in Japan than in Germany and the United States. This is naturally interpreted as closely related to the lesson plan because it is reflected in considering the antici-

FIGURE 1 Lessons that included alternative solution methods.

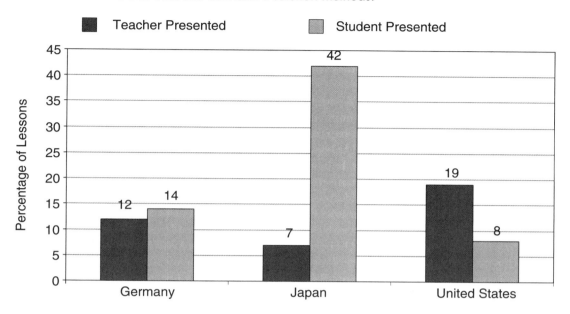

SOURCE: Data adapted from Stigler, 1999.

pated response of the children and in the course of discussing and revisiting the lesson plan. In fact, the anticipated students' responses make up a large part of the lesson plan (Appendix D).

Finally, throughout the discussion on lesson study, the teacher's content knowledge and understanding of teaching practice will improve, and through the entire lesson study this will be further refined (Box 4).

As was mentioned above, lesson study is a common element in Japanese educational practices. Also it is a necessary element for improving teachers' content knowledge and understanding of how to teach.

BOX 4
Teachers' Content Knowledge and Understanding of How to Teach

- Interwoven in a certain way
- Reflected on his/her anticipation of students' response to the task to be posted
- Developed through examining and discussing lesson plans and by observing and reflecting on the lesson
- Elaborated in the process of lesson studies

Framing Lesson Study for U.S. Participants

Makoto Yoshida, Columbia University Teachers College

First of all, I would like to quote from the book *The Teaching Gap,* written by James Stigler and Jim Heibert (1999).

> Our goal is to convince the reader that something like lesson study deserves to be tested seriously in the United States. It is our hypothesis that if our educational system can find a way to use lesson study for building professional knowledge, teaching and learning will improve.

This became a popular book that talks about lesson study and implementing professional development programs that are similar to Japanese lesson study in the United States.

My presentation is in three parts. In the first I talk about Japanese lesson study; in the second part I discuss the lesson study project in which I am involved in the United States; and in the third part I provide some insights from these projects and discussion of the challenges we face implementing lesson study in the United States.

Establishing a lesson study goal is the first thing that teachers in Japan usually do. One example of such a goal is "Promoting Students' Ability to Think on Their Own Autonomously, Invent, and Learn from Each Other: Focusing on Problem-Solving-Like-Learning in Mathematics."

As you can see, the goal is not "improving basic mathematics calculation skills" or something like that but is broader and more general and created for all teachers in all subjects in the school.

Lesson study continues over a period of several years, and usually that one goal is used the entire time. During the first year, the teachers may investigate what is lacking in students' abilities, find out what they can do to foster students' skills in that area, and create a tentative goal. This process helps the teachers develop a focused lesson study goal for the school. For the second and third year they continue the lesson study activities, testing to see if the skills they have focused on are improving. Usually during the final year, they have an open-house study lesson, called *kokaijugyo* in Japanese. The teachers organize and plan lesson study activities, including setting up a lesson study promotion committee to do the scheduling and monitor their progress. In addition, they often have an outside adviser to assist them in conducting lesson study so they can receive some knowledge from experts.

The short version of a lesson study cycle is planning, implementing the lesson, and discussion of the lesson. This lesson study cycle is carried out by a small group of teachers that consists of about four to six teachers. Sometimes a discussion on how to improve the lesson will be held, and other members of the group will try out the newer version of the lesson in a different classroom. The lesson plan is used as a base for discussion about the lesson. Therefore teachers in Japan produce a very detailed lesson plan that contains a description of the lesson, goals, relationship between the lesson and the unit, and the process of the lesson, i.e.– how the lesson will be taught, in screen-play-like format. During a study lesson, one of the teachers then teaches the lesson, while the other teachers observe. These observers keep a record of the student work and what is presented on the blackboard, and this is then used to discuss the lesson. The outside examiner also gives advice.

School in Japan starts in April and has three trimesters. Time is devoted during the beginning of the year to setting up the lesson organization. For example the teachers at a school may decide to have three different groups within the school, the first- and second-grade teachers in the lower grade level, third- and fourth-grade teachers in the middle grade level, and fifth- and sixth-grade teachers at the upper grade level. A typical one-year schedule is provided below (Figure 1). A group might spend about 20 hours within a 3-week period, with meetings devoted to planning, teaching a lesson, and the ensuing discussion. One example of time spent by a group during a lesson study cycle is shown in Figure 2.

What did the teachers discuss throughout this lesson study cycle? They consider the goal and focus of the lesson and

FIGURE 1 A typical one-year lesson study schedule.

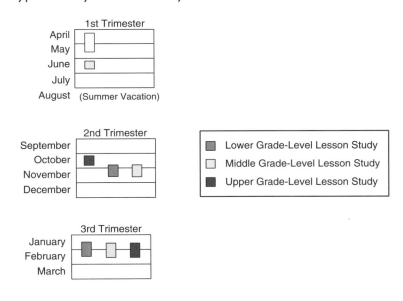

FIGURE 2 A lesson study cycle and time.

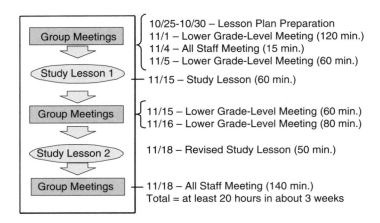

the relationship between the lesson and the unit. In one lesson they might focus on manipulatives, solutions anticipated from students and teachers' responses to these, planning questions that provoke students' thinking (which the Japanese teachers usually call *hatsumon*), and how to use the blackboard during the lesson. They also discuss time allocation, handling individual differences, how to end the lesson, and very abstract issues, such as the students' skills and knowledge about mathematics.

For example, consider a first-grade lesson on a simple subtraction, two-digit number minus a one-digit number. "Akira collected 12 Ginkgo leaves. Then he drew 7 faces of his family on the leaves. How many leaves are left over?" Calculating 12 minus 7 involves borrowing. In the first phase of planning the lesson, the teachers talked about anticipated students' responses (Box 1).

The examples in Box 1 are some of the anticipated students' solutions the teachers suggested. Then the teachers looked at available manipulatives and

discussed whether those manipulatives could help them identify students' solutions if they ask the students to use them when they solve the problem. The discussions led the teachers to think about criteria for constructing good manipulatives: relate to potential student thought processes, easy for students to understand how to use them, easy for students to explain their solutions using them, easy to put them back into their

---

BOX 1

Counting-Subtraction Method:
    Taking away 7 from 12 by counting
Subtraction-Addition Method:
    12 consists of 10 and 2
    $10 - 7 = 3$ $3 + 2 = 5$
Subtraction-Subtraction Method:
    12 consists of 10 and 2
    7 consists of 5 and 2
    $12 - 2 = 10$ $10 - 5 = 5$

original position or shape so that the students can rethink their thought processes. For the first lesson, the teachers decided to use tiles, made on drawing paper covered with spray glue (Figure 3).

This makes it possible to put student work on the blackboard, and the tiles won't fall off. This manipulative made the record easy to present. However, what the teachers found after teaching the lesson was that these individual tiles made it difficult to understand the students' solution processes. Each tile represents one, and even though it seems like subtracting seven at once, when students actually do the subtraction, they are moving tiles one by one. The students had trouble explaining what they did using the manipulative as well. So the teachers devised a model using ten tiles, gave the students some scissors, and asked them to cut (Figure 4). If students cut as shown in Figure 4, they took away seven tiles as a chunk and then added those remaining numbers 3 and 2 together to get the answer 5 (using an addition-subtraction method). Another student might cut each individual tile one by one and move them one by one to do the subtraction (using a counting-subtraction method). In this way the teachers could identify the solutions that the students used.

After the open-house study lesson, teachers often prepare something like a research report. The report probably will contain all lesson plans that they created and their reflection of their lesson study activity at the school.

For the second part of this presentation, I discuss one of the projects I am working on in the United States, a project centered on trying out lesson study in a U.S. setting. This lesson study project involves the Patterson Public School No. 2 (PPS2), in Patterson, New Jersey, and the

FIGURE 3 A manipulative developed by the teachers for subtracting "12–7."

Step 1: All 12 pieces of paper are face up.

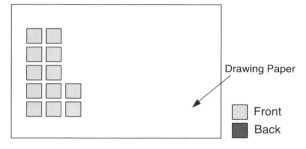

Step 2: 7 pieces of paper are turned over to show the subtraction of 7 from 12.

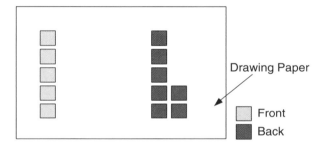

FIGURE 4 A manipulative developed by the teachers for the second implementation of the lesson.

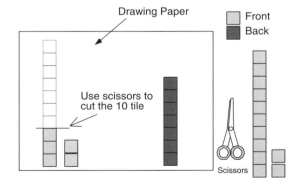

Greenwich Japanese School, an all-day Japanese School in Greenwich, Connecticut. The project is directed by Professor Clea Fernandez from Teachers College, Columbia University, and myself.

PPS2 is an inner-city public school, primarily minority students, with almost 98 percent of the students on the free lunch program. Within that school there is a group called the math study group, 14 teachers, the principal, and the vice principal. They decided to meet every Monday from one to three. The principal juggled the school schedule to make sure that those teachers actually had time together to carry out lesson study. The principal used student teachers; however, she did not use any extra funding to cover the cost to make this possible. The Greenwich Japanese School is actually a Japanese public school, and the teachers are rotated from Japan every three years. Teachers also conduct lesson study regularly in Japan.

The PPS2 teachers had a preliminary planning meeting. At first they were hesitant to open up their classrooms, even though they were convinced that lesson study is cooperative work. We decided to take them to the Japanese school's small lesson study open house to show some lessons developed through lesson study and the teachers' discussion of the lessons. After PPS2 teachers visited the open house, one of the teachers from PPS2 told me that they talked about it and said: "Well, if those Japanese teachers can do something like that, we can too." The Japanese teachers made several trips to PPS2 to help American teachers conduct lesson study. The Japanese principal, Mr. Tanaka, explained how to set up a lesson study goal for the school. He pointed out that the goal should relate to their vision of what kind of students they wanted to produce in the school. The

students come to the school as first graders and then those students gradually grow through the experience gained in the school and graduate, for example after the sixth grade. That means whatever concerns there are about the sixth graders, these may be common concerns found in each grade level. This then is really a school concern. His other comment was that teachers typically teach a particular student only for one year. The impact of one year is not enough to change the student. Other teachers in the school have to get together and set overall goals for how the students should be prepared throughout the entire six years of schooling. In other words it is important for a school to have a consistent instructional goal and that all teachers follow the goal in order to foster student learning.

To learn about creating a lesson plan to use for lesson study, the PPS2 teachers decided to learn the Japanese way first and then decide if that process could be adopted in their work. PPS2 teachers then taught some lessons that were developed through lesson study and were closely supported by the Japanese teachers. The Japanese teachers observed these lessons. The Japanese teachers offered the following comments as important points for improving those lessons: clarifying the goal of the lesson, planning all activities within the lesson in order to achieve the goal, organizing students' presented work, and clarifying the purpose for assigning a second problem. There are some important points here. If you give a second problem, you have to have a purpose. Is it to vary what the students learned in the first place or is it something that is challenging students based on what they have learned? Another point is design of the introduction to the lesson. You cannot just put the central problem at the beginning of the lesson.

You have to have some kind of motivating setting for the students. You must also consider allocation of time.

For the third part of my presentation, I discuss the insights and challenges of doing lesson study in the United States. Although there are difficulties, I think it is possible to do lesson study in the United States. However, lesson study is not just teachers' collaborative work or just planning lessons together or some kind of cultural thing. We need to study lesson study to find out what the Japanese do and then think about what we are going to do in the United States. We need research on lesson studies, and we have to remember that improving teaching takes time. In Japan right after World War II, a majority of the teachers were teaching by telling and giving knowledge. After 50 years, the study of teaching became more student centered, and lessons are more similar to what you observed at Tokyo Gakugei University, Setagaya Elementary School, during the Ninth International Congress in Mathematics Education. Japanese teachers usually say if some major things change in the curriculum, it takes about ten years to settle in. We have to think about change that way, which means we must really be patient.

First, a good mathematics curriculum needs to be developed. This is something that we found with the teachers at PPS2 who were participating in the lesson study. As they did lesson study, they also did curriculum development. So the focus is on two things (thinking about teaching improvement and developing curriculum), but time for lesson study is limited. My suggestion is if there is a good curriculum developed somewhere else, the teacher can test it in the classroom by doing lesson study. We also found out that U.S. teachers often focus on each individual lesson, not thinking about the whole unit.

Maybe that is because teachers are just taking one lesson from this textbook, another lesson from that one, and putting them together to make a unit. So the development of curriculum has to have some kind of design. Then it can be tested during lesson study, and what was found in the classroom can be fed back into the curriculum development.

The last major point I want to make is that mathematical knowledge needs to be fostered. During lesson study there is a lot of discussion about different ways of solving the problem. In that sense teachers are learning many things related to mathematical knowledge. However, within the group there has to be somebody who has a little more content knowledge about something to challenge the others. If that type of person is missing, it is very difficult to foster teachers' content knowledge. In our project, the Japanese teachers actually watched the lesson and gave comments. That helped the U.S. teachers think about the lesson more deeply and learn a lot about mathematics. It is important to find someone who will take this responsibility.

This workshop is a learning process for both countries. Many of the teachers in Japan may think that lesson study is conducted everywhere in the world, especially in the United States. Japanese teachers think that many famous instructional and learning theories from the U.S. are based on research on real practice. They think that lesson study is what is producing all those educational ideas. That is not always true, particularly in the United States. Many theories are not tested through conducting something like lesson study. I think this must be somewhat surprising for the Japanese teachers. So I believe that this kind of workshop can provide an opportunity for the Japanese to rethink lesson study. By learning how educators in the world are interested in the Japanese lesson study, the Japanese teachers can rerealize the importance of lesson study and deeply reflect on how it works, which in turn can help revise lesson study in a more meaningful and powerful way to improve teaching. Japanese educators have learned and adapted much from the U.S. educators. Now is the time to give something back to the U.S. community because they are very interested in lesson study. This is an opportunity to help U.S. educators learn what the Japanese educators know about how to conduct lesson study. I believe by having more occasions to help U.S. educators learn about lesson study, the Japanese teachers also could engage in deeper conversations on teaching that also will help them rethink their own notions of lesson study. It also is important for the Japanese teachers to leave records of lesson study for the future. Although lesson plans are on a piece of paper, I believe that it is very important to have a video record of the lesson. Teachers are very busy, and it is hard to take time to read a document. Unfortunately many good teachers are retired, or will retire, and there is no record or videotape of their lessons. So as we think about the future, I think we should try to develop some kind of system to keep a good record of lesson study in Japan. One possibility might be to build a library for lessons developed through lesson study, so, for example, if teachers want to get a sample of lessons on fractions they could have access to such lessons through the library.

Lesson Study from the Perspective of a Fourth-Grade Teacher

Hiroshi Nakano, Tokyo Gakugei University Setagaya Elementary School

I come from Tokyo Gakugei University Setagaya Elementary School in Shinjuku Ward in Tokyo. I have been a teacher for 18 years, and I moved to my current school two years ago. For my initial 16 years I taught at a public school run by the Tokyo Metropolitan Government. My discussion here is mainly about what is done at the public schools in Japan, because my current school, Tokyo Gakugei University Elementary School, is a sort of research study school. What is done there is different from what is done at the public schools.

At public schools, at least in my case, the study lessons were done once or twice a year. At Tokyo Gakugei University Elementary School, almost on a monthly basis someone is there to observe our class, but at public schools it is usually just once a year or twice a year at the most. During my career I have conducted more than 30 study lessons. My first study lesson was when I was still a university student as part of the preservice training program. I had my first inservice study lesson during my first year as part of the Tokyo Metropolitan Government school district training program. In the case of Tokyo Metropolitan Government, most of the study lessons are on the

school level or on the ward or district level. The school year begins in April in Japan. At the beginning of the school year, the teachers who are interested in mathematics in a school ward will come together and organize a team. They develop a plan for the year, and they decide who is going to give the study lesson. Some people volunteer. Some are strongly urged by others. "This will be a good experience for you." There is some pressure to take part.

Once we decided when to conduct the study lesson, prelessons would be conducted two or three times before the actual study lesson. Usually the schools in the adjacent areas would come together for this prelesson to discuss the lesson plan. On the very day of the study lesson, the lesson would be given, followed by discussion, and then a party. The principal of the school and the research promotion committee chairperson are major players in those lesson studies. I was once a research promotion committee chairperson, but it varies depending on the school. Usually one year or two years is the length of the cycle of the lesson study.

In not-so-motivated schools, there is almost no lesson study. It depends largely on the school. However, in interschool study, each school is required to conduct in-school lesson study. During the prelesson study, the teachers teaching first and second grade form one group, third- and fourth-grade teachers form another group, and the fifth- and sixth-grade teachers form a third group for the discussion. The research promotion committee chairperson sometimes joins those groups, and sometimes we would call in an external adviser to have the discussions. Then we conduct the class and have a discussion afterwards, in which the teachers within the school participate.

I was primarily engaged in ward-initiated lesson studies and school-initiated lesson studies. For me, what is lesson study? It is an indispensable field of training. When I was in the university, I did practice teaching just like lesson study. The teacher responsible for my teaching training told me that it is very important to have lesson study, and that idea has not changed since then.

I would like to make my class be enjoyable for children's thinking. I want the class to operate so that the children's thinking can be recognized by others and also by the teachers. I also like to make the class feel that they can find out about

the similarities and differences of their ideas in relation to others. To realize these wishes means training. That is how I see lesson study. Lesson study is where you can express your ideas and also you can improve your position and status. Through these lesson studies you can make presentations about your teaching within the mathematical education community and establish your own ideas.

What we learn from lesson study changes as we accumulate experiences. When you have little experience, you learn methodology and how to run the class. You are taught by many people through the prelesson studies. As you gain experience, rather than learning how to conduct the class, in prelesson study you can get to know the value of mathematics and the value of the materials. Accumulating such experiences was a great asset for me. Through the prelesson study I am taught by others. Having others point out my weaknesses, I understand what they are. This leads to motivation to improve for the next occasion. However, lesson study is rather difficult even if you plan ahead very well. Even though you think you did well, others might point out what went wrong. So lesson study is both difficult and rewarding.

Studying Classroom Teaching as a Medium for Professional Development: Video Component
(see the accompanying videotape)

LESSON STUDY

Workshop participants viewed two elementary classes and the follow-up or postlesson discussion for each lesson. As part of the Ninth International Congress on Mathematics Education (ICME-9) that preceded the workshop, workshop participants had the opportunity to visit a sixth-grade class during an introductory lesson on functions. Makoto Yoshida translated the lesson and the postlesson discussion for those in attendance. The lesson plan and transcripts of the selected portions of the lesson and postlesson discussion are available in Appendix E. During the workshop itself, participants viewed a video of a fourth-grade lesson on place value along with a video of the postlesson discussion by the observers. The lesson plan, a description of the content, and a summary of the postlesson discussion held by the Japanese, both translated by Makoto Yoshida, and a transcript of the selected portions from the actual lesson and discussion can be found in Appendix F.

VIDEO SELECTIONS

A Demonstration Lesson: Function Thinking at Sixth Grade taught by Shunji Kurosawa, Tokyo Gakugei University Setagaya Elementary School

Lesson and Postlesson Discussion among Sixth-Grade Lesson Observers

A Study Lesson: Large Numbers at Fourth Grade taught by Hiroshi Nakano, Tokyo Gakugei University Setagaya Elementary School

Reflections on Videos: Panel

A panel addressed the following questions related to the fourth- and sixth-grade lesson:

- How do the two lessons compare?
- What are the differences and the similarities?
- What was the mathematical content and how did the lessons develop student understanding?

Panel Moderator: Keiichi Shigematsu, Nara University of Education

Jacqueline Goodloe, Resource Teacher, Burrville Elementary School, Washington, DC
Jerry Becker, Professor, Southern Illinois University
Ichiei Hirabayashi, Professor Emeritus, Hiroshima University

COMPARISON OF THE TWO LESSONS

Jacqueline Goodloe, Burrville Elementary School

First I would like to say that this has been a very rewarding experience, both the Ninth International Congress on Mathematics Education (ICME-9) and this workshop. I am an elementary mathematics resource teacher. A mathematics resource teacher in the District of Columbia public schools does not have responsibility for one classroom but services all the teachers in that building in mathematics. Our school has about 360 students, a relatively small enrollment with classes from all day prekindergarten through sixth grade.

I want to point out some of the similarities that I saw in the two lessons. Both lessons addressed important mathematical ideas, getting a sense of large numbers, posing questions, finding functional relationships. Most elementary classroom teachers do not often discuss these mathematical ideas. The teachers in the videos often related the task to concepts with which the students were familiar. Time was allowed for students to talk and explain their thinking. In both examples, class size was large, between 30 and 40. That is large for some U.S. classrooms. The planning was evident. Another similarity that is familiar to some of us was the teachers' genuine delight in student learning and student understanding.

The strength I see in lesson study is the growth that develops through the collaboration and discussions with other teachers. This is not always evident in U.S. schools—thinking about "why we do what we do." Reflecting on practice is an area in which I would like to see some improvement by teachers in the United States.

In both videos we saw the teachers moving around in the classes. However, we did not discuss a lot today about what specifically the teachers were looking for that was going to help them assess the student learning. They were moving throughout getting an understanding of what the students were thinking, but what were the teachers thinking as they watched the students?

Much of the lesson study in the preplanning deals with anticipated student responses, the student results. I would like to know more about how much time is spent developing that part of the lesson and the source of that information. Is it all from the teacher's experiences? Is it all from the study group's experiences? Where do we get the notions of how students will respond and how can that benefit teachers? As we look at the videotapes and sit in discussion groups, something else about lesson study emerges. There are implications about what "teacher talk" is about. The last discussion about new teachers, preservice teachers, and those that are new to lesson study and how they must know the curriculum, the textbook, and the mathematics was important. When does this happen and over how long a period of time are we talking about? If lesson study is such a powerful tool, I am wondering if videotaping of the sessions should be done so that other teachers can get the benefit of the experience. There are other questions as well. For example, what does lesson study look like at the high school level? Do skilled teachers, inexperienced teachers, and preservice teachers all have different perspectives on the lesson study?

This past week I have heard more and more about the Japanese intent to engage students in interesting and motivating activities and, in fact, one of the speakers talked about developing a sense of wonder and a new approach for mathematical thinking. I would like to know, if lesson study is so powerful a resource for professional development, why aren't more lesson studies done in all the public schools as much as is done in schools attached to a university? It would seem that the public school teachers could benefit from this powerful resource as well. The workshop has opened my eyes to some wonderful and powerful ways of looking at mathematics and of looking at mathematics teaching. Teaching is hard, and thinking about teaching is even harder.

FOURTH GRADE AND SIXTH GRADE: OBSERVATIONS OF THE TWO LESSONS

Jerry Becker, Southern Illinois University

I feel very fortunate to have had the opportunity to see Mr. Kurosawa's lesson, the film of Mr. Nakano's lesson, and to have had the benefit of the discussion of these lessons. If I put both of these lessons together for a moment, that is, if I just speak in aggregate of some of the observations I made, the first thing I would say is this, Teaching mathematics is really a big job! Overall I thought the tasks in both of the lessons were very good. To begin with I was not so sure about the task around which Mr. Nakano developed his lesson plan, but eventually through the discussion I came to see that it was also a very good task. One of the things I noticed is that the productions and the observations of the students during the lesson are written on the board for everyone to see. They are left there so they can be referred to and so students

have enough time to write them down in their notebooks and to refer to them. We saw in each of the lessons that the teachers wrote down a number of important observations made by the students.

In the sixth-grade lesson I think the number of observations on the part of the students was nine or ten, and none were suggested by the teacher. The teacher rather skillfully set the learning situation and then provided time for the students to use their own natural thinking abilities. So the lesson proceeded on the basis of the productions of the students, which I think is significant. Another thing I noticed is that in both of the lessons not only did the students seem to be enjoying them and sometimes getting excited about what was going on, but they felt perfectly comfortable in sharing their observations. The significance of this to me is that the classroom situation has all the makings of a community of scholars. These young people feel perfectly comfortable once the learning task is set, and they are given time to make their observations, to share them, and to get reactions from the other students. It was also very clear to me that the teachers were experts on the problem task and in handling and managing the lesson so that when various responses were given by the students the teacher knew how to respond to those and how to deal with them. Clearly they were very knowledgeable about what was going on.

I think the students had time to work on the tasks, to use their own natural thinking abilities. The teacher took time to view the work the students were doing so that the responses that fit the objective of the teacher could be written up on the board for everyone to see, where it could form the basis for a discussion. There was also encouragement to the students to write down their observations, writing out their observations in words as well as writing down what they were thinking in mathematical symbols.

I saw a very nice contrast with what we commonly see in the United States. There is a difference between verbalizing observations and verbalizations. Verbalizations come as a consequence of learning mechanical procedures, but here in the lessons we saw the students commenting on and explaining the reasons for the observations that they made. The teacher asked for clarifications. Students were asked to verbalize their thinking. To me this forms the basis for developing the language of mathematics in the classroom, and I think this is very important. At the end of the lessons, the teacher asked students, for example, to think of a general expression for a given number of minutes later. The common approach is to go right to that expression, but here the focus was on all of the processes that lead up to that. Also, we found the teachers making a conscious attempt to put the problem situation into the reality of the students, and I thought that was very good.

In discussing the lessons, it occurred to me that what we are talking about here is the assessment of lessons. During ICME-9 I heard several talks in which the points were made that good problems are crucial in assessment, the assessment of lessons as well as the assessment of individual learning. It is the case that the teacher can get whatever the teacher asks for, and that means the richer and the more open the problems, then the more potential they have for revealing students' understandings and abilities. For example, at the beginning of Mr. Nakano's lesson, I thought he was going to engage in direct teaching, and I wondered why he was going to do that. It took me a while to realize that was not the case. In fact, he was seeking to find out what the students'

understandings and abilities were, and he had a systematic way of approaching the situation so he could get some insight. We saw that insight also in the discussion of the lesson. So there was time given to the students to show what they could do with these learning tasks, and in so doing we could get some insight into the difficulties they had, the ability that they seemed to be able to demonstrate, and so on.

Since my first visit to Japan many years ago when I talked about the things I thought I had learned from observing numerous class lessons, my colleagues back in the United States commented, "But, Jerry, you have to remember that is Japan. The culture is very different from ours. You cannot import what goes on in another culture." I didn't believe that then, and I don't believe it now. I think we can look at the tasks, for example, what was on the blackboard (Appendix F). We can have very good insight, regardless of culture, about the problem the students are given and the different ways the students approach it. While we watch the students and listen to them develop their own ways of dealing with the problem situation, we can see that they exhibit responses that are qualitatively different. The students generate a situation where they can discuss, in a mathematical way, many responses and perhaps even come to a consensus about which are the better ones from a mathematical point of view. I don't think that is specific to any one culture. What that is specific to in my judgment is mathematics, and teaching and learning mathematics.

Finally, in our small group discussion we were considering the question: How do skilled teachers learn about and make use of their students' knowledge and capabilities to help them to learn mathematics? We have seen during the discussions here that the skilled teacher poses a problem situation and lets the students show what they can do. That is a good way to get insight. We also discussed or had described to us the importance of and the meaning of a detailed lesson plan. So before the lesson is ever taught, the teachers sit down and discuss the problem situation and try to list all of the anticipated responses of the students. If the three of us are the team that is getting ready to develop a lesson, then I am going to learn quite a lot about that problem situation from my colleagues, and perhaps they will learn something from my insights on the problem too. While the lesson is in progress, the teacher has the option of purposefully scanning the work of the students. By looking at their work, the teacher can decide which responses everyone should see. The teacher knows which responses should be shared on the board and why they should be discussed. The reason, of course, is because the discussion will tie in with the objective of the lesson that the teacher has in mind.

LESSON AS A DRAMA AND LESSON AS ANOTHER FORM OF THESIS PRESENTATION

Ichiei Hirabayashi, Hiroshima University

Prelude

I remember it was around 1975 that I happened to be visited by two American professors: one of them was in science education whose name I have forgotten, and the other was in mathematics education named M. Vere Devault. I had seen his name in the *32nd Yearbook of the National Council of Teachers of Mathematics* and other publications, but it was my first time to meet him. At that time I

was a young professor at Hiroshima University, and it was very impressive to hear from him that there were two features in the research on curriculum in mathematics education: technology and humanity. I think the same two features would be in lesson study.

Since then, in Japan, and perhaps in America, the research on technological features has developed remarkably, but not much attention has been paid to the humanistic feature. This feature is far more important than the technological one because of its external effect on children's future life. There also are the same two features in the lesson, and I would guess in a workshop on lesson study as a method of research about mathematics teaching, the technological feature would also be emphasized far more than the other. In this atmosphere of research, it is important to stress the humanistic feature of the lesson, and this is the very reason that I wrote this short paper.

A Reminiscence: Complexity of a Lesson

I wish to start with a reminiscence of my own when I was mathematics teacher in the lower secondary school soon after the graduation from university. In this school I had the same two courses for two classes in the same grade. I taught them the same topics almost every time in the same way in each class. But in the final examination, I was surprised to find that the achievement of the class taught in the second lesson was far better than the first, although each class was equally divided according to their ability at the start of the term. The reason seemed evident: The teaching ability of the teacher (me) had progressed from the first lesson to the second. But at that time it was difficult, and still is, for me to analyze this reason clearly and persuasively. The lesson is a very complicated phenomenon with many subtle factors interrelating with each other: the teacher's ways of speaking, asking, responding, and time, place, gestures, and so on. Among these factors, there may be some vital importance in deciding the success or failure of the teaching. Lesson is a complex phenomenon in a "classroom culture," as pointed out by Heinrich Bauersfeld (Bauersfeld, 1996).

The advantage of lesson study as a method of research in mathematics education is that it is the way to grasp the true state of affairs of the problem in its whole and to bring a synthetic, totally recognized interpretation to it, being aware of many factors that are subtly interacting with each other as if it were in one organism. The lesson, as I mentioned above, is a very complicated process, and its effect on students' learning is too subtle to express in a simple literal thesis. It can be evaluated only through close observation about what is actually going on; a mere written report is not only unable to describe the actual state of affairs but often overlooks the kernel and essential points of the lesson.

Lesson Demonstration in Conference

Before War World II, we had two or three normal schools for the education of primary school teachers in each 47 prefectures of the country and several higher normal schools for the education of the secondary school teachers in some districts of the country. One or two primary or secondary schools were attached to these teacher training schools for the training of student teachers and the practical research of education. In each attached school it was a custom to have a conference usually once or twice a year to present educational ideas to the teachers of the district. It also was a custom to have a session of lesson observ-

ing, where an expert teacher from this school showed a lesson, which was a model for the participating teachers. During a renowned teacher's lesson, the class might be surrounded by many attending teachers occasionally numbering more than the pupils in the class. There was one thing to be noticed here: The observing teachers seemed to believe that a unique best teaching method was embodied in this expert teacher's demonstration of teaching and could be learned only through observing this model lesson directly.

At that time we had a national curriculum (as is still the case), and in primary school, textbooks were exclusively edited by the Ministry of Education. Under these educational-political circumstances, it was natural that teachers at that time believed in the existence of a best method of teaching and seriously wished to acquire it. Certainly it would be an obvious falsehood that there is a unique best teaching method. However, there is a profound implication in believing that a teaching method, whether good or bad, is embodied in a teacher's performances or even embedded deeply in the teacher's character. The only way to know is to see the lesson.

This tradition of lesson observing during a conference has been maintained over a long period of time in every school attached to a university or its department of education. And even more than this, custom has spread to almost every regional educational conference of teachers. Most teachers in Japan, in transmitting their educational ideas to others, seem to prefer demonstrating an actual lesson to a formal oral or written presentation. To show their beliefs through an actual lesson is far easier than to express them on paper. I think this may be the reason we see the "demonstration lessons" in many conferences of teachers.

But recently I began to feel some anxieties: Has "lesson observing" become something like a mere ritual of the conference without any reflections on its function as a method of studying the problem of mathematics education?

Functions of Lesson Study

I think we can notice two functions for lessons open to other teachers in an educational meeting:

1. as a method of research and
2. as a place for presenting new ideas or findings.

In the first, the lesson is open to colleague-teachers in a school or in a regional conference, and the analysis is divided according to its aim:

- to ask fellow teachers to see a typical lesson to become aware of the teaching problems through the many eyes of the participants and
- to find causes of failure or success of the lesson or to focus attention on some particular problematic factors.

In both cases it would be better to prepare a written lesson plan for the participants' reference.

The second function should be a carefully planned lesson. Observers should be informed about its aim, topic, teaching process, supposed pupils' activities, and intended results beforehand.

Traditionally in research in mathematics education, we present the results of our research in a paper, but I think there is another way of presentation. The demonstration lesson as in the second function, I would like to say, is a form of research

report that can be compared to the thesis in a paper. Our findings during lesson studies could be ones that are difficult to inform others about using the usual form of thesis in a paper. They may be transmitted best through the demonstration lesson. Such a lesson, I think, should qualify as a written paper. These lessons are different only in form and have the same values as the written thesis. They have the same quality as the performance of a musician or the masterwork of an artist, which should be considered as a whole, not broken into pieces.

Conclusion and Additional Comments

Lesson study is a synthetic method of research in teaching and learning. We should regard this method as legitimate as the usual analytic method of science. As mentioned above, lesson study is a very complicated phenomenon and not easily studied by a strict analytic method of investigation. The natural complexity of this originates in our thinking or learning activities. An analytic method is difficult to use in treating such a complex phenomenon and often overlooks some subtle and essential factors.

The demonstration lesson is another form of thesis presentation, and we should consider how such a lesson should be undertaken. Among many things to be considered, the most important is how to make a lesson plan. Here I give some of my ideas about how to write lesson plans as I am not satisfied with the current ways of doing so:

- The anticipated process of teaching may be a mere outline of the lesson, but the teacher's intention should be clearly described. In Japan we often see a written lesson plan with a very detailed description of the process, including the teacher's behavior and pupils' activities. But actually the lesson will not go so well as in the planning. I was often bored reading lesson plans and thought I would enjoy them if they were written more like a work of literature.

- A lesson plan may be like the playbook or the scenario of a drama which permits the actor's timely digressions or ad libs in a large scale. In fact, a teacher may be an actor or actress, as Pólya (1963) said: The classroom may be the stage of a theatre, and a good lesson may be a good performance of a drama.

- But in many schools in Japan, a lesson may be seen as the time to cram knowledge into the brains of pupils to prepare for the entrance examination to the upper school. The lesson plan may necessarily turn to a recipe for cramming mathematics effectively.

Postlude

In Japan, we have traditional arts called *rakugo*, which is something like an entertainment held in a small theatre, telling a short comic story. Some years before, we invited to the annual conference of the Japan Society of Mathematics Education the famous rakugo teller named Katsura Beicho; he had a high reputation for his refined way of talking. The subject of the story was *tsubo-zan* (bottle math), with a very simple and very stupid plot.

A man went to the bottle shop and bought a bottle for 100 yen. But on the way home he changed his mind and wanted a larger one. He returned to the shop and changed to the larger one for 200 yen. When he was going out the shop, of course the master of the shop asked him to pay 100 more yen. But the man said to him, "I had already paid 100 yen when I bought a smaller one and just now I paid with another bottle worth 100 yen. In total, I paid to you 200 yen, and I can have a large bottle for 200 yen." The master was very confused and could say nothing.

That's the full story, and to tell the story takes only a few minutes, but this rakugo teller attracted the entire audience throughout one solid hour. It is the art not the technology that attracts the attention of the audiences.

Mathematics teachers should have such art in the classroom. For instance, the first-grade teacher has to teach $2 + 3 = 5$ to pupils taking at least one hour without boring them. Or, to tell the answer to the problem "how many remain in a box of 10 candies if 2 are eaten" needs only a few seconds. But it would be a marvelous thing for children to know eight candies remain in the box without opening the box and counting them. To make them understand this marvelous thing as such may take more time, and it is not only the technology of teaching but also the art of the teacher to do so.

Professional Development Through the Use of Records of Practice

The second day of the workshop focused on two examples from the United States of the use of teaching practice as a medium for professional development. Both sessions dealt with the use of records of practice—records of what teachers do as they teach—as a way to discuss mathematics teaching. Deborah Ball and Hyman Bass discussed the use of classroom video and addressed the questions

- How do observations of what teachers do in the act of teaching enable teachers to learn mathematics?
- How do such observations enable teachers to learn how to teach the mathematics they need to teach?

Margaret Smith presented two written cases of classroom teaching and addressed the questions

- How can cases designed to investigate teaching and learning be a site for learning about teaching?
- What does it mean for teachers to use the study of others' practice to learn mathematics and about teaching mathematics?

Professional Development Through Records of Instruction
Deborah Loewenberg Ball, Professor, University of Michigan
Hyman Bass, Professor, University of Michigan

Professional Development Through Written Cases
Margaret S. Smith, Assistant Professor, University of Pittsburgh

Professional Development Through Records of Instruction

Deborah Loewenberg Ball, University of Michigan
Hyman Bass, University of Michigan

Ball: Our focus today will be on professional development using what we call, "records of practice." Like "lesson study," this is a form of professional development that uses practice to learn about teaching. However, while lesson study engages teachers in examining their own practice and in the practice of colleagues, the work we will be discussing involves examining records of practice. What is a record of practice? It is a detailed documentation of teaching and learning. Examples might be videotapes, either segments from lessons or whole lessons; written cases of teaching and learning; students' written work from classrooms; transcripts of classroom discussions; teachers' notes and lesson plans. The point is that these are documents taken directly from teaching and learning of mathematics, without an analysis, which enable teachers to look at practice directly, together with other teachers.

WHY USE PROFESSIONAL DEVELOPMENT IN RECORDS OF PRACTICE?

Some of the reasons for using records of practice are intended to address a number of problems in our professional development and teacher education system. For example, records of practice provide a common context for teachers to work on teaching. Teachers in the United States do not usually have opportunities to work directly on teaching and learning with other teachers. When they do meet with other teachers, often all they do is tell each other about their work or work on something else like a new technique or a new curriculum or some mathematics. But rarely do they have the sorts of opportunities that we saw teachers in Japan have regularly. Records of practice provide a common opportunity to study teaching and learning.

A second advantage is that records of practice provide a way for professional development to be grounded in practice so that the problems and issues that teachers work on are directly connected to the work of teaching. Sometimes teachers learn from professional development experiences but are then unable to use that knowledge in their teaching. Records of practice provide an opportunity for teachers to learn knowledge as they would need to use it with students. Therefore, one compelling reason to use records of practice is to ensure that the knowledge that teachers generate as they work is both useful for practice and usable in practice.

Records of practice allow professional development leaders and teacher educators to select particular problems of mathematics or of the teaching and learning of mathematics. A teacher educator could select a specific challenge of teaching mathematics and then select records that provide an occasion for teachers to consider that challenge. This is different from discussing one another's teaching where the problems that arise are dependent on what teachers happen to bring up. Using records of practice allows a teacher educator to design work around a particular problem of practice.

Another benefit of using records of practice is that teacher educators can provide opportunities for teachers to see practices, problems, or issues that they have not seen yet in their own practice. They might see, for example, children discussing mathematics in a way that their own students do not yet know how to do. So it allows teacher educators to expose teachers to issues beyond teachers' own individual classrooms.

Working with records of practice can also develop teachers' abilities to learn from their own practice, to learn to look more carefully at student work, to learn to listen more attentively to students' talk, to analyze mathematical tasks in ways they have not done before. One thing that struck several of us while watching lesson study was how skilled many Japanese teachers are in the discussion, analysis, and study of practice. Records of practice provide opportunities for teacher educators and teachers to develop some of those skills and capabilities, not just of teaching, but of the study of teaching.

And finally, records of practice can enable teachers to talk safely about problems of teaching and learning, because the teaching and learning that they are looking at is not their own and not their colleagues. There can be more freedom to raise hard questions or to consider problems without the worry of being polite or not hurting someone else's professional pride.

Many of these advantages apply also to lesson study. One thing we might discuss together later is how using records of practice is similar to and different from lesson study.

POSSIBLE PROBLEMS IN USING RECORDS OF PRACTICE FOR PROFESSIONAL DEVELOPMENT

There are also problems in using records of practice. Because the material is not from a teacher's own classroom, it might not be relevant. Teachers might say, "I don't have this problem; these students are not like my students; this classroom is not like my classroom." So teacher educators may face problems of making sure that the work seems relevant to teachers. Similarly, it may not seem interesting to teachers when the problems they witness or study are not their own.

There are problems in developing good records of practice. Not every videotape is suitable for study. Not every lesson is provocative for teachers' learning. Not all examples of children's work are equally useful in professional development. Gathering, cataloging, examining, and becoming familiar with high-quality records of practice is a problem.

We have learned that for this work to be profitable for teachers, the tasks that teachers work on with these materials makes a difference. This is no different from the knowledge that the mathematical tasks that children work on make a difference for their opportunities to learn mathematics. The same is true for teachers' learning; not all tasks are equally useful in professional development. Quite often in our early work we neglected to frame tasks at all and thought that simply by looking at videotapes, teachers would learn. It matters what the task is.

In the United States we do not have, in general, highly developed norms for the study of teaching. Teachers are not used to discussing, analyzing, or closely probing teaching. Working with records of practice means that we also have to work on developing a culture and a set of norms for work of that kind. One challenge that we face is to move from a habit of evaluating and judging teaching to analyzing it. Yesterday we saw many examples of Japanese teachers—and of ourselves as workshop participants—closely analyzing the teachers' decisions, the nature of a task, a child's contribution. That sort of work, that kind of analysis is different from saying this was a good lesson, this was a smart child. Learning to do this kind of analysis is part of what we have to develop in the U.S. culture of teaching.

At the same time, too much analysis can move very far away from teaching. Teachers are not just researchers. They must act with students. In work that analyzes records of practice, it is important to maintain a balance between analytic work and practice and to strive for the development of knowledge usable for teachers' work. There is the challenge, like the challenge of working with children, of bringing sessions to closure so that teachers go away with knowledge and ideas that make them feel the work has been useful and they have something to take with them to their own classrooms.

DEVELOPING OPPORTUNITIES FOR TEACHERS' LEARNING USING RECORDS OF PRACTICE

Interestingly, the work using records of practice has much the same structure as the structure for lesson study: preparation, enactment, and analysis.

Preparation Phase: Design.

In developing opportunities for teachers' learning, there is a phase of design for the teacher educator that includes asking such questions as, What is the goal or purpose for teachers' learning? The preparation phase includes designing a task that teachers would work on together using records of practice and designing the enactment of that task in a session with teachers. It includes selecting resources to support that learning. For example, what sorts of records of practice would help? What other materials might be needed? Might teachers need the curriculum materials on which children were working in order to interpret a videotape? This process looks very much like the design work for teaching mathematics to children.

Enactment Phase: Facilitation.

There is the complicated process of enacting the work with teachers. What does it take to enact useful, constructive, productive sessions with teachers where analysis of teaching and learning are the subject? These are some of the tasks involved in this phase of the work: setting purposes; posing the task or problem to be worked on; organizing how time gets spent; attending to teachers' engagement and learning, to teachers' ideas and difficulties.

And there is the work of processing the discussions, sharing the work from the sessions, and developing ideas that everyone takes from the work. This involves keeping the work grounded in mathematics, so that teachers have opportunities to develop content knowledge. Keeping the work connected deeply to concrete materials of practice means learning to use evidence for statements that are made about teaching and learning. It includes learning how to generalize from studying particular examples and forming more general ideas that can be useful in classrooms other than the one being studied.

Analysis Phase: Reflection and Design of Next Steps.

And of course there is the phase of analyzing and reflecting on how the sessions with teachers work.

EXAMPLES OF USING RECORDS OF PRACTICE IN PROFESSIONAL DEVELOPMENT

We will take brief tours of two different examples of this work. There are many such examples in the United States, and although this is not the main form of professional development at this point, it is also not rare. Deborah Schifter (Schifter et al., 1998), Ed Silver (Stein et al., 1999), and Alice Gill (American Federation of Teachers, 2000), among many others, have all engaged in this kind of work.

So together, we will discuss some of the work we have been doing to develop approaches to the study of practice. These have some resemblance to lesson study but are also different from it. We have to examine how these are different, how these are similar, and to learn together ways that we might join some of the special features of each.

The example we would like to share draws on work that we have been designing over the past ten years with several of our colleagues at the University of Michi-

gan. We have been working with a very large collection of records from two classrooms—one grade three (8 year olds), and one grade five (11 year olds)—across an entire school year. We collected videotapes every day in these classrooms for a whole school year. We also collected all of the children's work, all the tests they took, all the materials they used. This includes a detailed teacher's journal with indications of what the teacher expected over a range of lessons. We have been designing materials and experiences for teachers' learning that draw from this very rich collection of records. What follows is one short exposure to the sort of work we do with teachers using this material.

THE PROBLEM OF THE DAY

Imagine you are a group of teachers. The problem on which we are going to work is that of designing and enacting mathematical work at the beginning of a school year, actually the fourth day of class. In many schools in the United States, teachers get entirely new groups of students at the beginning of every school year. Those children have often been in many schools and have not worked together before. The school where I was teaching, for example, was very mobile: Children moved in and out all the time. My school had the additional challenge of serving an international community and many of my students did not speak English—language and cultural differences increased the complexities of bringing the students together. But, even without cross-cultural and multilingual considerations, classroom teachers throughout the United States must take into account the fact that many children come from different schools with different past experiences and may never have done the sort of work in which the teacher aims to engage them. Teachers must find out what their students know how to do, and they must begin to teach them the curriculum. They must also teach them the ways of working that the teacher aims to use during that school year.

Before watching the classroom video, there are two kinds of questions we want you to consider.

CONSIDERATIONS FOR THE DESIGN AND ENACTMENT OF MATHEMATICAL WORK AT THE BEGINNING OF THE SCHOOL YEAR

Bass: Place yourself in the position of having to do this work which faces the teacher at the beginning of the school year. What are some of the considerations in the design of such a lesson, the enactment of such a lesson? What are the things you want the students to be doing? With what things should the teacher be concerned? What would the teacher want to find out in these early lessons? What are the problems that should be on the teacher's mind at this stage?

U.S. Participant: At the beginning of the school year, my most important goal is creating a mathematical culture, to get the students asking questions, making conjectures. I don't worry so much about particular content, starting the textbook or anything like that. So I have sort of favorite activities that I know are very engaging, that bring up a lot of ideas, and that bring up a lot of questions. I start the year, to set the stage for how they are to act for the rest of the year.

U.S. Participant: I think with the student population that Deborah Ball described,

the language issue is one that is especially critical for the teacher to both be understood and to be sensitive to understanding what the children are saying. So sensitivity to language is important.

U.S. Participant: For me, it's developing a culture of people being respectful to each other in these conversations. The content is one thing, but the social dynamics of listening, appreciating each other's ideas is very important to develop in the beginning of the school year.

U.S. Participant: I think one of the things that I like to do at the beginning of the year is to give students an opportunity to let me understand some of what they know and how they are used to working. Are they used to responding to a question, or are they simply looking for something the teacher says to say back?

CONSIDERATIONS OF THE MATHEMATICAL TASK AND ITS USE

Bass: Let us move now to another aspect and consider the mathematical work itself. You were given a homework assignment (Appendix G) that includes the mathematical task you will see worked on in this lesson. There are questions about the capacity of this task to support the considerations you brought up about doing serious mathematical work, establishing norms for communication with each other, learning and showing respect for other students. What are the kinds of questions you would pose in the enactment of the three-coin problem (Box 1)?

How would you pose the questions for the work on this task? How and when would you do so? What kinds of student response might you anticipate? What kinds of responses would you want to

I have pennies (1¢) , nickels (5¢), and dimes (10¢) in my pocket.

If I pull three coins out, what amount of money could I have?

SOURCE: NCTM (1989).

elicit? And what elaboration of the task might you want to be prepared to do in case it turns out to be too difficult or too easy? How can you be ready to incorporate responses from the students in the development of the lesson?

This task does involve some serious mathematical work. How do you reconcile that with the fact that this is a very diverse class? There are large differences in background and in background knowledge, in the students' sense of how to work with each other. What is the suitability of this kind of a task, given that kind of diversity, and so many unknowns?

U.S. Participant: It's a good task in that it has many entry levels. For example, the task could be set up in such a way that you could find one answer or many answers. And the ultimate part of the task, I would imagine for third grade, is considering how do you know you have them all? You might start by asking students in the whole group to think of one way, one amount of money they could have, and start to collect the ways. And then allow the students to go off, perhaps in pairs or by themselves, giving them choices about how they want to work initially. This would allow you to observe who works individually, who works with a partner, who works with a small group,

who knows who, who doesn't—all of those social issues. And who has confidence as they begin to solve the problem? Who takes it further?

U.S. Participant: In a class where children have many languages, I might take this problem and indicate that the pennies are worth one; the nickels, five; and the dimes, ten. I would not be certain that a multilingual class would understand the value of those coins. But I think it's a good task to get them to begin to think about things.

U.S. Participant: I guess I'm thinking just a little differently about it. Actually, I approach this at the beginning of the course in methods of teaching elementary school mathematics. I use a problem that I have already tried out, perhaps many times, and have developed a detailed lesson plan. So I'm familiar with the kinds of responses that I would likely get from the students and also how I would deal with those responses.

U.S. Participant: I would also have jars of money with the coins, for those students who felt they wanted them.

U.S. Participant: I don't teach elementary school, so I'm not quite sure if my concern would be valid, but listening to what Deborah Ball said about the kinds of students that she worked with, one of the concerns that I would have with this particular problem is the fact that there are many answers. And many children might not be used to this idea of a math problem having several solutions. I think that's something we want children to understand, but is that too big of a problem to bring up on the very first three or four days of the school year? I might consider actually softening that fact by maybe putting this into a game context or something that they see players playing, and whoever gets the most wins. Something where there are many solutions but where that doesn't become an initial focus.

Japanese Participant: It's important to know what students have learned in the previous years. What is the level of knowledge of those children in your classroom? I think that kind of context is a major concern for Japanese teachers.

Japanese Participant: I think the three-coin problem is too difficult for the elementary school student. How do you position this problem in the context of classroom teaching?

U.S. Participant: I did teach third grade most of my career, and I do think it is suitable for third graders. The problem would give me as a teacher a sense of whether or not these students were able to approach a problem in an organized manner. This is important to me as a teacher because if they can't, then I need to do some things to help them organize their thinking.

Bass: Your questions indicate where you want to speculate a little bit. When you

watch the enactment in the class, think about how to reevaluate that concern. One thing that is often emphasized is the importance of the teacher doing the math of the lesson prior to the lesson. The math is typically elementary, but the insides of it often involve intricacies and complications that vitally affect the instruction. That was part of the intention, in fact, of having you do the homework: It would allow you to be inside the territory where the children are working.

EXAMINATION OF THE RECORDS OF PRACTICE

Ball: A lesson plan (Appendix G) starts with the problem and provides an explanation of what the purposes are for the class. There were three purposes that I had as the teacher. The first was to develop students' habits of searching out multiple solutions and establishing whether all solutions to a problem have been found. This included developing students' ability to produce a mathematical explanation. In this problem, an explanation for a solution must establish two things. First, that three coins were used from among these three types, and second, that the amount of money produced is correct in total.

The second purpose is to communicate to the students what doing mathematics will mean this year in this class. For example, students will learn that mathematical work will include producing explanations for one's work to the teacher and to other students; they will learn to listen, to critique, and to use other students' ideas; and they will learn to be accountable for their own mathematical ideas.

The third purpose was for the teacher to begin to learn about the student—to learn, for example, about the students' addition and multiplication skills, their openness to multiple answers and solutions, the strategies they use for finding solutions, how they keep track of their work and of the solutions, how skeptical they are that they are finished, and how they go about determining whether they are done with the problem. How do they work with concrete materials, in this case coins? What is their disposition to confer with other students and to consider others' ideas?

The rest of the lesson plan outlines the steps. On the second page is a list of strategies that I knew that students of this age were likely to use and different approaches to recording their work that I anticipated them using. This was a problem that I had used many times before with this age and also with both younger and older students.

The video includes a segment from the beginning of the class. The problem was posed, and there was some discussion about what the problem meant, including an example of a solution. Then the children worked alone. After about ten minutes of work they came back into large group discussion of solutions to the problem.

(Transcript and class description in Appendix G)
See the video clip: Records of Instruction: Reasoning About Three Coins at Third Grade

ANALYSIS OF THE LESSON

Ball: The next phase of our work is to return to the problem that we're considering in this session, which has to do with organizing mathematical work in the beginning of the year in light of a whole host of considerations that bear on how one begins a school year. In this lesson segment we saw how the teacher's considerations about the beginning of the year were handled. What came up? How did the segment correspond to the teacher's goals and anticipations? What seemed unexpected either to the teacher or to you? How did this problem work out so far? Obviously, we haven't seen the whole completion of the work. How did this problem work out so far, given the teacher's goals? What surprised you? Was this what you had expected?

Having had an opportunity to examine one example of a teacher's work in this problem domain of designing and enacting mathematical work at the beginning of the year, what comments would you like to make?

U.S. Participant: The first question the teacher asked after bringing the class back together was to predict how many different solutions there were. Then the students worked on the problems a little bit more on their own. But when the class reconvened as a whole class, the discussion was on what amounts can you get. I was wondering what purpose that initial question served?

U.S. Participant: I thought the lesson just came to something of an abrupt end. I was anticipating some request of the students to think in a more structured way about the different solutions they were generating.

U.S. Participant: The third stated purpose for the goal included a list of the many things the teacher wants to learn. Unless the teacher videotaped a lesson and sat down afterwards, I saw no evidence or any specific way the teacher recorded that information. In other words, it is nice to ask, "What strategies did the children use?," but unless there is a systematic way to record that, especially the first week of school, it's very difficult to keep track of that sort of information. So I'm not sure how the teacher assessed that objective.

Japanese Participant: Three coins are taken out, and students asked what amount could be made. That was the situation. However, what was the motivation in this class? In this situation, the Japanese teacher would take three coins out of his pocket and say, for example, "This would buy you an apple." Then the children would think about wanting to purchase something and would get more interested in working on the problem. In the video, the children did not think about why they needed to solve the problem. It was just because the teacher said so. This content would be in the sixth grade in Japan where they would consider how many cases, not how much the value could be. The students would solve it structurally, by drawing a diagram or counting each case. The mathematical content would have a focus on analyzing the number of distinct combinations.

Bass: One of the advantages of having the very complete record of what happened over the entire year is that when we see something from a small window of a lesson, we can ask questions about how the students became acclimated to the meaning of the coins or how the children worked with the coins, and we can trace what happened in the earlier lesson where the teacher worked on the two-coin problem. And very much what you were suggesting a Japanese teacher might do, happened in that lesson. There was time spent moving around the room, showing the students the coins, asking for their

understanding of what the coins were worth, and things of that kind. So that preparation in fact was in place before the enactment of this problem.

Japanese Participant: In Japan, the same problem is also handled in the first year of senior high school. The focus is how to solve this problem and how to find those strategies. There needs to be time for students to think about the problem.

Japanese Participant: If students understand the structure of the two-coin problem, then they can utilize it in problem one (see the Homework handout in Appendix G) and also in problem three. If they understand the structure of problem two, even if they do not write out everything, they can use the results of problem two for problem four. By drawing tables they can grasp the structure of the problem. If they learn that in elementary school, and if they go up to the high school, they can always think about the meaning of the problem that is given.

U.S. Participant: What we have here is what happens with many rich problems. This problem is a different problem at the third-grade level than it is at the sixth-grade level, than it would be at the first year of senior high school. You look for different reactions from the students. The only concern I had about this problem at the third-grade level was that the entire time was spent in understanding the problem. At the end of the 30 minutes, the students had no better way to solve the problem than they had at the beginning, which was trial and error. But maybe at the third-grade level, that's all we want. That is, perhaps it is enough to simply introduce a problem of this kind, to introduce the idea of trial and error, and to solve it. At later grades of course, we look for systematic ways. And at the higher grades, we look for the underlying mathematics of combinations and so on to solve it.

Ball: The nature of these materials is important to highlight. Because there is a record of every day, the comments that people are making right now in a professional development context would be converted by the teacher educator into questions for further inquiry by the teacher—e.g., Did students at the third-grade level develop a more general structure for understanding this class of problems—rather than simply discussing whether children can or cannot do that? When someone wonders about these kinds of things, they would be invited to turn back to the record, to look at the next day's work, to look at students' written work perhaps, or to read the teacher journal. And this enables the kind of developmental tracing of children's learning not possible by simply visiting a school or by reading one example. This is a special feature of this kind of year-long record of practice. After all, teaching and learning occur across a school year, across time. One kind of work that this kind of record permits is the opportunity to look across days to see what happened at the beginning of the next class, or what sort of structure third graders ended up developing? And how did the children differ within the third-grade class?

U.S. Participant: I got the feeling that after you looked past the mathematics, one of the major purposes of this class was creating a community of learners. Especially from the way the teacher at the end remarked about the way students were listening to one another, giving each other enough time, promoting the thinking of students without interfering others.

A teacher can get a lot of information from the students about whether they were using multiplicative methods or additive methods in finding out the amount of money from the coins.

U.S. Participant: The lesson needs to be seen in the context of an ongoing activity, and the record we see is only a fragment of a particular lesson. I think it did very well in establishing certain rules of behavior and operation. Listening to each other, giving explanations, taking turns, getting input from many students, all these features were being established very carefully. The full story is certainly not here. But notice that Mick did come up with nine solutions. In fact, he came up with ten, which is also quite interesting. So I thought as a record, it would be very interesting to see whether from the record of the practice, the teacher was able to observe what the students did.

Japanese Participant: As teachers make a lesson plan for the lesson, it's very important to think about the multiple solutions that might come up and about motivation as a very important factor. Using the setting to naturally urge the students to come up with the questions, then come up with the solutions is important. We do our best to urge the students to come up with the solutions, to interest them. Take the coins out of your pocket. Then say, "Now I have three coins in my hand. How much it could it be?" This is one way to check whether the children understand this problem. Some people would say three cents or fifteen cents, just haphazardly. But that's a good chance to motivate them. Here you have a right answer. I would probably repeat this two or three times to interest the children. Then maybe I would ask what is the possible minimum amount of money?

What is the possible maximum amount of money? And I would say, is it possible to come up with four cents? Impossible. What about six cents? What about thirteen? Maybe it's possible. Here we have three coins. Some amounts they can make; some amounts they cannot. Okay, now let us think about the cases, impossible cases and possible cases, and let us come up with all possible cases. The question of how many solutions are there is a mathematically interesting question. But for children, is it very interesting? Maybe they will wonder why is it important to have knowledge about how many solutions there could be? Maybe the more important thing is four cents is impossible, five cents is okay. What about six, about seven? And do they have all of the possible solutions? I think this kind of approach is more important. If they can make the complete table of those cases, with three coins, they will list those impossible cases. What about with four coins? I think that could be the next step

Japanese Participant: The important thing is to urge the children to think about all of those possibilities and set up the steps. Usually the Japanese teachers try to think about how they can best set up several stages of thinking for students. But I know that this lesson is at the beginning of the school year, so the mathematical approach and the community making are also the priorities. I know that my comments should not be always applied to that kind of situation, but I think the important thing is motivation.

Can we ask the proper questions so that the children can follow the steps in a mathematical way?

Bass: One important feature of the work on this task that was not explicitly mentioned was beginning to teach the children how to reason mathematically. So the mathematical task provided a context for that, but the very detailed, fastidious explanations of why certain amounts added up to certain amounts were not only elementary exercises in addition but they were the first steps in learning what it means to give a reasoned, careful explanation for a claim. And this, as one would see in the later records of this class, became a very important theme in developing children's capacity to reason mathematically.

CONCLUSION

Thank you very much for those very interesting comments. I think we have used up our time. I just want to make one very brief remark. Some of the themes or directions that you proposed could be investigated in the actual record to see what was either in the lessons before and after, and also in the teacher's journal. And others of these, that are not necessarily enacted in the lesson but simply mathematical elaborations of the task, can become potential material for learning mathematics in the context of practice and using these for professional development.

Professional Development Through Written Cases

Margaret S. Smith, University of Pittsburgh

Over the past few years, my colleagues and I at the University of Pittsburgh have been exploring the potential of cases—written accounts of teaching—as sites for investigating and analyzing mathematics teaching and learning. The cases that we have created are based on data that was collected from QUASAR, a national project aimed at improving mathematics instruction for students attending middle schools in economically disadvantaged communities. Each case is based on actual events that occurred as teachers enacted reform-oriented instruction in urban middle school classrooms. The cases are not meant to represent best practice. Rather, they are intended to represent actual practice—what really happened when teachers set about to teach mathematics in new ways. The cases provide sites for teachers to engage in critique, inquiry, and investigation into the practice of teaching.

Each case has been constructed around a cognitively challenging mathematical task. Prior to discussing a case, we engage teachers in an opening activity intended to give them an opportunity to explore the mathematical ideas that are central to the case. This provides teachers with a personal experience in working through the mathematics on which to draw as they interpret and analyze the work of the teacher and her students during the class portrayed in the case. The opening activity also provides an opportunity to explore the mathematics in the task in more depth.

The remainder of this discussion focuses on a specific case entitled "The Pattern Trains: The Case of Catherine Evans and David Young" (see Appendix I for a copy of the case). This is one of a set of cases that was developed under the auspices of COMET (Cases of Mathematics Instruction to Enhance Teaching), project funded by the National Science Foundation that is creating materials for teacher professional development in mathematics. This case is one of four that explores ideas related to algebra as the study of patterns and functions.

The opening activity in the case of Catherine and David, as shown in Figure 1, provides an opportunity for teachers to look for the underlying mathematical structure of a pattern, to use that structure to continue the pattern, and to develop a rule that can be used to describe and build larger figures. The task provides an interesting context for discussing what algebra is and how algebraic reasoning can be developed.

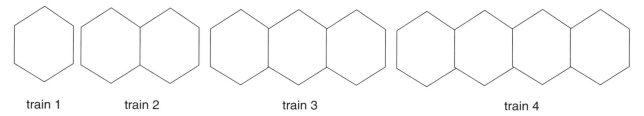

train 1   train 2   train 3   train 4

Solve

For the pattern shown, compute the perimeter for the first four trains, determine the perimeter for the tenth train without constructing it, and then write a description that could be used to compute the perimeter of any train in the pattern. (Use the edge length of any pattern block as your unit of measure.)

The first train in this pattern consists of one regular hexagon. For each subsequent train, one additional hexagon is added. The first four trains in the pattern are shown.

Consider

Find as many *different* ways as you can to compute (and justify) the perimeter.

The hexagon pattern task, featured in this opening activity, can be solved in several different ways. Consider, for example, the responses produced by five practicing middle school teachers who participated in a workshop during the summer of 1999. Linda's solution (Figure 2) involves a recursive approach. Linda recognized the general pattern of adding 4 to find the perimeter of each successive train, but her strategy required knowing the perimeter of one train in order to find the perimeter of the next train.

Barbara's solution (Figure 3) by contrast resulted in a generalization that can be applied to any train. She determined that each hexagon added four sides to the perimeter of a train and that the first and last hexagons also each contribute one additional side.

Kevin's solution (Figure 4) also involves adding four sides, but differs slightly from the one proposed by Barbara.

In this approach, Kevin explained that each hexagon added four sides to the perimeter of the train for each of the hexagons in the middle of the train and that each of the hexagons on the ends of the train contributed five sides to the perimeter.

Michael's approach (Figure 5) involved first counting all six sides of each hexagon. For each hexagon he then subtracted the vertical sides (two per hexagon), and then added on the two vertical sides on the ends of the train.

Chris's solution (Figure 6) is a bit more unusual. Chris thought about the hexagon train as having a bottom and a side and a top and a side (marked by bold lines). She noticed that the perimeter of the bottom and a side was the same as the perimeter of the top and a side. Chris noted that the bottom or the top was two times the train number so that 1 needed to be added to the bottom and to the top.

FIGURE 2   Linda's solution to the hexagon pattern task.

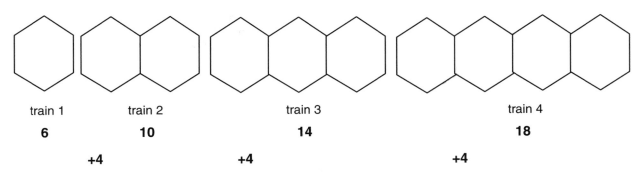

You just keep adding 4 each time. So the perimeter of the first train is 6, the perimeter of the second train is 10, the perimeter of the third train is 14, and the perimeter of the fourth train is 18.

FIGURE 3   Barbara's solution to the hexagon pattern task.

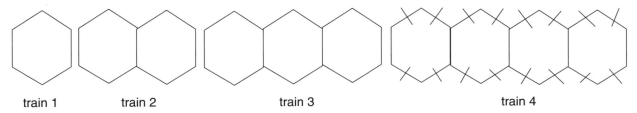

There are four sides for each hexagon plus two on the ends.

So for train 4: $4 \cdot 4 + 2 = 18$

$P = 4x + 2$

FIGURE 4 Kevin's solution to the hexagon pattern task.

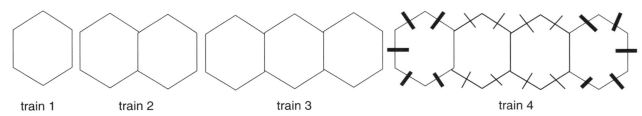

Each hexagon on the inside of the train adds four sides to the perimeter. The first and last hexagons in the train add five sides each to the perimeter.

So for train 4: $4 \cdot 2 + 10$

$P = 4(x - 2) + 10$

FIGURE 5 Michael's solution to the hexagon pattern task.

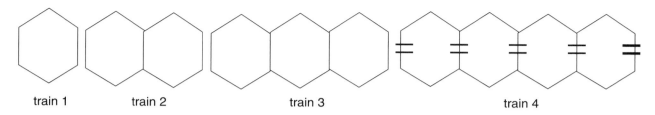

train 1　　　train 2　　　　　train 3　　　　　　　train 4

You find the total number of sides for all the hexagons and then subtract two sides for each hexagon for the insides. Then you need to add two back on for the ends.

So for train 4:　　　　　$6 \cdot 4 - 2 \cdot 4 + 2 = 18$

$P = 6x - 2x + 2$

FIGURE 6 Chris's solution to the hexagon pattern task.

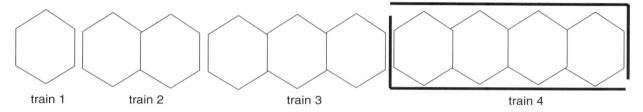

train 1　　　train 2　　　　　train 3　　　　　　　train 4

For each train, the perimeter of one side and the bottom is the same as the perimeter of one side and the top. So the perimeter of one side and top or bottom is 2x + 1, so you have 2 of these.

So for train 4:　　　　$2(2 \cdot 4 + 1)$ or $2(9) = 18$

$P = 2(2x + 1)$

As you can see from these sample solutions, teachers have many different yet interesting ways of connecting the diagram with a symbolic representation. After teachers have solved the task, we have found it helpful to explore the mathematics in more depth before moving on to a discussion of the case. One possibility would be to make a list of all the symbolic representations generated by the teachers, and ask them if the representations are equivalent and to explain the rationale for their decision. Alternatively, you may want to explore the mathematical content and processes embedded in the hexagon pattern task. This can lead to a discussion of mathematical ideas such as generalization, the order of operations, the distributive property, equivalence, and perimeter. There are many other questions that could be asked depending on your goals for teacher learning, the context within which you and the teachers are working, and the teachers' prior knowledge and experience.

Once teachers have had a mathematics experience related to the case, they are ready for the case discussion. Since the case is not self-enacting, you must create a professional learning task for teachers which serves to focus their investigation and analysis of the case. One task that my colleagues and I have found helpful in analyzing the case of Catherine and David is as follows: Indicate the ways in which you think Catherine's and David's classes are the same and the ways in which you think they are different. Be sure to cite line numbers from the case to support your claims. [At this point participants are given time to work in small groups to generate charts that made salient the similarities and differences between Catherine and David's classes.] This small group work was followed by a whole group discussion of similarities and differences. Table 1 contains a record of the responses produced by workshop participants during the group discussion.

This task of finding the similarities and differences between Catherine and David's classes requires comparing an event that occurred in one class with an event that occurred in the other class, analyzing the two events in order to determine whether they have anything in common, and noting what is the same or what is different about the events. This activity generally brings to light many key issues related to mathematics teaching and learning that can be further explored. Another example of a similarities/differences list generated by practicing middle school teachers is shown in Box 1 at the end of the document.

TABLE 1 Chart Generated by Practicing Middle School Teachers in Response to the Similarities and Differences Task

Similarities	Differences
<ul><li>Willingness to change</li><li>Same task</li><li>Positive attitudes</li><li>Encouraged student involvement</li><li>Commitment to new program</li><li>Same school and same grade level</li><li>Both teachers were part of a community</li></ul>	<ul><li>Catherine focused on doing procedures; David focused on understanding relationships (between number of blocks and perimeter).</li><li>Catherine was more concerned with success and directed student thinking so they would be more successful; David was more concerned with student understanding.</li><li>Types of questions: Catherine's had one right answer; David's required explanation.</li><li>Catherine made tasks easier; David helped students solve the original tasks.</li><li>David's students form generalizations "approaching symbolic"; Catherine's could apply rule to large numbers but not any number.</li></ul>

The COMET project shares Shulman's (1986) view that

> the strength of cases is that they can be used to straddle the space between generalizations and particularities, between the kinds of abstract, formal, codified knowledge that can be taught in the absence of context and the kinds of knowledge that are experientially derived, often informal, and perhaps lacking in precision.

Hence a case allows you the ability to go from the very particular things that happen within a specific classroom to seeing those instances as examples of some larger class of phenomena that we consider to be important in teaching and learning. For example, the case of Catherine and David was designed to provide specific instantiations of key mathematical ideas such as generalizations identifying patterns, perimeter, intuitive notions of variable, and connections among representations. Within the case, there are opportunities to look at particular examples of each of these ideas. In addition, if you look across the set of cases related to algebra as the study of pattern and functions, you would see the same set of ideas woven throughout the cases. This provides an opportunity to explore ideas in more than one context and from more than one perspective.

Each of the cases is also designed to make salient "pedagogical moves" that support or inhibit student learning. Moves that support student learning include teachers pressing for explanation and meaning, modeling high-level performance, allowing students sufficient time to explore and think, drawing conceptual connections, and building on prior knowledge. Pedagogical moves that inhibit student learning include shifting the focus to following rehearsed procedures; removing problematic aspects of the class, and allowing insufficient time for students

to explore and think. So again, in each case you can see specific events that connect to these more general ideas about mathematics teaching and learning. These ideas can be explored over a set of cases as well as in a teacher's own practice.

In facilitating the discussion of the case, we generally start by making a record of the similarities and differences that teachers identified, resulting in the creation of a chart similar to the one shown in Table 1. Our goal is to then move from the specific things that happen in the case (as represented in the chart) to more general ideas. So the chart becomes not an end in itself but rather a starting point for additional discussion. This discussion might begin by focusing on a specific difference that was noticed. For example, in further discussing the types of questions posed by Catherine and David (see Table 1, third bullet in the differences column), the facilitator might want to press teachers to analyze the learning opportunities that were or were not afforded by each teachers' questioning strategies, thereby explicitly connecting teaching and learning. The facilitator might also want teachers to look at the list of differences and to begin to look for commonalties across events in the list in order to see specific instances as a subset of a larger class of phenomena. For example, fostering students' thinking might serve as a bigger idea around which to organize a number of different classroom events such as helping students understand relationships and requiring students to provide explanations.

The ultimate goal of a case discussion is to create generalities that teachers will be able to draw upon in situations outside the case. The point is for teachers to take something away from the analysis of the case that can be used to think about their own teaching. For example, a discussion

BOX 1
The Similarities and Differences Between Catherine and David's Classes
Workshop Participants' Responses

Similarities Between Catherine and David
- Both teachers were struggling to change their practice.
- The classes were working on the same task. Each student in the classes just presents one idea. (In a Japanese class, each individual student is encouraged to present multiple ideas.)
- Both teachers asked students to share their thinking and asked for different solutions.
- Both tried to capitalize on student solutions. The problem about the 100th train is from the students (lines 490-495).
- Both do things that they hadn't planned on and so monitor and adjust their teaching as they are going. Both of them give homework directly from the class.
- Both seemed to realize it was important to work toward generalizations of what they were teaching. Both were going to get to big mathematical ideas in the end.
- There was no activity to create formulas for expressions in either of these classes.
- There is no evidence that the teachers were selecting students with a sequence of ideas in mind, or that the teachers knew what the students had done in small groups or individually. There was no evidence that they were calling on students in a particular order.

Differences Between Catherine and David
- One difference is that Catherine is in the first year of teaching this curriculum, and David is in his second year, which points out that teachers themselves need to learn how to deal with reform and what it might look like.
- Catherine had a set amount of time in mind for the lesson and when that time was over, she said, "We have to move on. It's time for another topic." Whereas, David felt more comfortable continuing his lesson into another day when the content was not covered to his satisfaction.
- Catherine used a square to measure perimeter versus David who used a segment to mark off and measure perimeter. This might have implications for students' understanding about what perimeter is.
- There was a difference in the level of support. Catherine was going through a change of practice with colleagues who were at the same place in learning how to do this. David was coming into an established community that had gone through this change and was trying to catch up. It wasn't clear whether he had the same opportunities to look at videos of his class and discuss it with colleagues. He did not seem to have the same opportunities to reflect as Catherine did.

- Catherine seems to get a little bit more impatient, and when a student doesn't seem to get an idea right away, she is there helping. For example, she seems to be literally moving the hands of the boy who was showing the perimeter on the overhead. David tends to be more willing to take time, ask more provoking questions, and wait for the students to make sense of things.

- David seems to push more for the multiple strategies, having one student explain, and then ask whether anybody else had done it a different way. He gave five different explanations for the formula, whereas Catherine got one from a student and presented another.

- They introduce the topic in a different way. Catherine starts the lesson by asking the students to make generalizations about the patterns and only brings up the word "perimeter" when a student mentions it. David's initial introduction to the lesson is to find the perimeter for the four trains.

- Catherine seemed to be narrow in how she asked questions, with answers that she wanted from the students, rather than being open to the answers that the students gave.

- David had questions for example, about noticing a relationship, giving a bit of direction to the student in terms of what are the kinds of things you might look for.

- Catherine asks questions such as, "How many on the end?" (line 164) How many will there be altogether? (line 166). They are very specific one-answer questions.

- David says "How are these two numbers related?" (line 569) in his effort to help students find a connection between the train number and the perimeter. He is giving questions with several possible answers.

- It seems as though Catherine was validating the students' answers, which would introduce something that the students would then seek, versus David who was encouraging open discussions and not necessarily commenting on correctness.

- The relationship between questions and evidence of student learning or understanding possibly came from the relationship between the questions Catherine was asking and what it was she thought she was getting (lines 205 and 245).

- Catherine seems to be focused on asking questions with a numerical answer. What's another perimeter? Whereas David seemed to be assessing student understanding based on their ability to explain how they got their answer and communicate an understanding that way.

regarding Catherine's concern about student success may provide teachers with a new lens for considering what it means for students to be successful and for considering whether "imitation" indicates understanding of mathematics. The hope is that this "lens" would sensitize teachers to similar decision points in their own practice.

What can be gained by using materials like this? My colleagues and I contend:

In order to grab hold of classroom events, to learn from examples, and to transfer what has been learned in one event to learning in similar events, teachers must learn to recognize events as instances of something larger and more generalizable. Only then can knowledge accumulate. Only then will lessons learned in one setting suggest appropriate avenues of action in another (Stein et al., 2000, p. 34).

Mathematical Knowledge of Teachers Panel

A panel addressed the following questions related to the mathematical knowledge of teachers:

- What are the mathematical resources that teachers need to teach well?
- How can teachers learn the mathematics they need to teach well?

The papers that follow are edited transcripts of their remarks.

Moderator: Deborah Loewenberg Ball, University of Michigan

Zalman P. Usiskin, Professor, University of Chicago
Deborah Schifter, Senior Scientist, Education Development Center
Haruo Ishigaki, Professor, Waseda University
Miho Ueno, Mathematics Teacher, Tokyo Gakugei University Senior High School

Mathematical Knowledge of Teachers Panel

WHAT MATHEMATICS DO TEACHERS NEED THAT THEY ARE LIKELY NOT TO ENCOUNTER IN THEIR MATHEMATICS COURSES?

Zalman P. Usiskin, University of Chicago

It is a truism. A teacher of mathematics should know a great deal of mathematics. The higher the level taught, the more the teacher needs to know. For a teacher of high school mathematics, this means knowing a good deal of number theory, algebra, geometry, analysis, statistics, computer science, mathematical modeling, and history of mathematics. This is what we might view as the traditional background of a teacher who is considered to be well prepared mathematically.

Even though it is good to take more and more mathematics, there is a problem that taking more mathematics creates. Often the more mathematics courses a prospective teacher takes the wider the gap between the courses taken and the courses the teacher will teach. The gap is both in the mathematical content and the ways that content is approached. An entire body of mathematical knowledge is ignored.

There is a substantial body of mathematics that arises from teaching situations in much the same way that statistics arises from data and applied mathematics arises from real situations, and that deserves to be viewed as a branch of mathematics in its own right. I call this "teachers' mathematics." A project currently underway entitled "High School Mathematics from an Advanced Standpoint" is developing a first course in teachers' mathematics for high school teachers, and second and third courses are being planned. I will attempt to describe the motivation and content of these courses.

THE PROBLEM

Every teacher of mathematics needs

1. to see alternate definitions and their consequences;
2. to know why concepts arose and how they have changed over time;
3. to know the wide range of applications of the mathematical ideas being taught;
4. to discuss alternate ways of approaching problems, including ways with and without calculator and computer technology;

5. to see how problems and proofs can be extended and generalized; and
6. to realize how ideas studied in school relate to ideas students may encounter in later mathematics study.

The result of the lack of teaching these ideas to prospective teachers is that teachers are often no better prepared in the content they will teach than when they were students taking that content. For instance, they may know no more about logarithms or factoring trinomials or congruent triangles or volumes of cones than is found in a good high school text.

THREE KINDS OF MATHEMATICS FOR TEACHERS

Three kinds of mathematics content are particularly needed by teachers. Each might be said to consitute a facet of looking at school mathematics content at a deeper level than is possible for high school students.

One focus is on mathematics particularly useful to high school teachers that might not normally be encountered in the standard courses taken by mathematics majors. Box 1 contains an example.

There is an analogous theorem for inequalities, which I do not have the time

---

BOX 1
Teachers' Mathematics Example 1
(mathematics that teachers do not usually encounter but would be useful to know)

You can add the same number to both sides of an equation, or multiply both sides of an equation by the same nonzero number, and the resulting equation is equivalent to the given one. But if you square both sides of an equation, you may gain solutions. And cubing both sides of an equation does not affect the solutions. What about taking the log of both sides? Or taking the sine of both sides? How can one tell, in general, whether an operation on both sides of an equation will change the solutions to the equation?

Here we are concerned with real-number solutions. Then an equation in one variable can be thought of being of the form $f(x) = g(x)$, where x is real.

Applying an operation to both sides is like applying a function h to both sides. This results in the equation

$$h(f(x)) = h(g(x)).$$

There is a very nice theorem: The two equations $f(x) = g(x)$ and $h(f(x)) = h(g(x))$ are equivalent if and only if h is a one-to-one function on the ranges of $f(x)$ and $g(x)$. Examining this theorem and its special cases unifies the solving of equations and gives the teacher new insight into the process of equation solving.

to mention here. But the more important point is that there is a lot of content of this type: theorems that integrate content that might be taught in different units or different years; theorems that shed light on formulas, figures, or functions; and so on.

The second focus is on the extended analysis of problems. Recall the four problem-solving steps of Pólya (1952): understanding the problem, devising a plan, carrying out the plan, and looking back. Most analyses of problem solving devote their time more to devising a plan than any other step. This is important, but it is also quite important to examine the last step: looking back. This means looking at a problem after it has been solved and examining what has been done. Will the method of solution work for other problems?

Here is an example from Dick Stanley of Berkeley (Box 2), who is one of the main authors of the materials we are devising.

The third type of mathematics is the explication and examination of concepts (Box 3).

BOX 2
Teachers' Mathematics Example 2
(extended analysis of problems)

Recall the well-known problem in which a rectangular sheet of cardboard is folded into a box by cutting out four congruent squares from each corner. What is the maximum volume of the box that can be created? If the cardboard is 12" by 18" and each square has side x, then the box has height x and length and width $12 - 2x$ and $18 - 2x$. So the problem is to maximize $x(12 - 2x)(18 - 2x)$ over the range of possible values of x.

The problem can be done these days by graphing the function $f(x) = x(12 - 2x)(18 - 2x)$, or it can be done with calculus, or in a numerical way by appropriate substitution. It happens that the volume is maximized when $x = 5 \pm \sqrt{7}$. But that tells us very little—it does not give us intuition into the problem. Why are there two solutions? Are they related in some way? If we leave the problem without examining such questions, then we have gone no farther than the typical class.

We can gain more intuition by letting the length of the rectangular sheet be 1 (say 1 foot) and the other dimension be w. If w is near zero, then the rectangle is long and thin. If w is near 1, then the rectangle is near a square. If w is large, then the rectangle again becomes long and thin. In our example, since 18 is 1.5 times 12, w is 1.5. How is the value that maximizes volume related to w? The relationship turns out to be interesting and gives insight into the problem that was not obvious.

Consider the idea of parallel lines. (1) Parallel lines are lines that are equidistant from one another. In this conception, parallel lines are an instance of parallel curves. This conception explains why train tracks are called parallel. (Tracks are parallel even when they curve.) (2) Parallel lines are lines that do not intersect. This conception places parallel lines as an example of disjoint sets. This is the usual definition of parallel lines. (3) Parallel lines are lines that go in the same direction. Algebraically, this means lines with the same slope and so under this conception—unless an exception is made—a line is parallel to itself. Sameness of direction intuitively underlies why, when parallel lines are cut by a transversal, corresponding angles have the same measure.

Virtually every mathematics concept—and all the important ones—can be examined in a variety of ways. When we give a definition for an idea, we almost immediately put blinders on the other ways of looking at the idea. By reexamining the variety of ways from a broader perspective, we can appreciate why students may have difficulty connecting various aspects of the same idea.

SUMMARY

"Teacher's mathematics" is a field of applied mathematics that deserves its own place in the curriculum. There is a huge amount of material that falls under this heading. However, this material is usually picked up by teachers only haphazardly through occasional articles in journals, or by attending conferences like this one, or by reading through teachers' notes found in their textbooks, or by examining research in history and conceptual foundations of school mathematics. This mathematics is often not known to professional mathematicians. It covers both pure and applied mathematics, algorithms and proof, concepts and representation.

Teachers' mathematics is not merely a bunch of mathematical topics that might be of interest to teachers but a coherent field of study, distinguished by its own important ideas: the phenomenology of mathematical concepts, the extended analyses of related problems, and the connections and generalizations within and among the diverse branches of mathematics. The importance of teachers' mathematics thus goes well beyond the needs of teachers to include all those who study the learning of mathematics and the mathematics curriculum.

Deborah Schifter, Education Development Center

When I spoke on Sunday, I mentioned that one problem with the implementation of the National Council of Teachers of Mathematics *Standards* is that many teachers and professional developers have emphasized new teaching strategies at the expense of what the reforms were actually about, i.e., mathematical understanding. If this is indicative of a deep-seated tendency in the United States—to adopt superficial strategies to get at deep problems—we must be aware of this in the context of lesson study too. I am concerned that people will get very enthusiastic about the *strategy* of lesson study and lose the essence of what it is about.

One question I have is whether there are shared ways of thinking about mathematics, learning, teaching, and classrooms implicit in the practice of lesson study in Japan, ways of thinking that would need to be cultivated among teachers in the United States to make lesson study profitable. For example, when we viewed the video of Mr. Nakano's fourth-grade lesson, we watched one student explain the reasoning behind his incorrect answer—reasoning that was quite easy for us to follow but which bypassed the mathematics of the problem. In our discussion of his lesson, Mr. Nakano commented that when students make an error or have difficulty with an idea, as this child did, this is when "the fun begins." My interpretation of his remark is that this is when his *work* begins—the teacher becoming aware of difficulties his students are having, figuring out what it is they do understand in relation to the learning objectives he has for his students, and then developing a path to reach these objectives.

My question is, is this understanding shared among Japanese teachers who engage in lesson study? And since it is not shared among teachers in the United States, is lesson study an appropriate context for developing it, or are there other, more propitious settings in which

teachers might better develop this disposition toward their work? Similarly, do Japanese teachers who engage in lesson study share an understanding of the mathematics of the curriculum they teach? Given the mathematical needs of many U.S. elementary teachers, is lesson study the appropriate context to address these?

There is evidence that many teachers, and Americans generally, lose touch with their capacity to think mathematically as early as in the primary grades. It's at this point that they start to learn that mathematics is memorization, in the process losing touch with their own powers of reasoning about mathematics. And so when we look at the work that teachers need to do, we must keep this in mind, understanding at the same time that this does not reflect on teachers' intelligence but is the result of their own schooling. As we discuss their serious needs in mathematics, it is very important to maintain a spirit of respect for the teachers who still have so much to learn.

In order to convey some of the issues raised by elementary teachers' mathematical deficits, I will describe three different reactions to one set of activities I frequently do.

In these activities, we look at some very common strategies children devise for solving multidigit calculations and then I ask the teachers to apply the children's methods to other pairs of numbers. When I begin a course this way, I consistently provoke several different reactions from teachers. Some actually get quite agitated and argue that all the children did the calculations the wrong way. Apparently, these teachers believe there is only one way to solve a given problem and that is to apply the algorithm they were taught in school. This points to a very important learning need for teachers: They must come to see that *understanding* the mathematics—knowing operations and calculations—involves more than being able to apply a single algorithm. This must be one of the goals for these teachers, and it is the work of their instructors to help teachers recognize that there is a larger world of mathematics they can enter. A second common response is one of relief: teachers recognizing that the children's procedures are ones they themselves have always employed. But under the impression that there was something wrong with their work, they had always kept it secret and felt some-what ashamed. So it comes as a relief to have their own strategies for calculating acknowledged as valid. However, having engaged in such "freelance" mathematical reasoning in secret, this capacity to think on their own remained underdeveloped. It is important now to encourage these teachers to move forward, to develop their powers of mathematical thought. In many cases, they learn, to their surprise, that they are strong mathematical thinkers. It is worth adding that many such teachers, once they discover that their ways of thinking were mathematically valid, go through a period of sadness or anger over lost opportunities, over the many years they could have been doing satisfying mathematics had they had the right encouragement.

A third common response is illustrated by what happened the first time I did an exercise like this with teachers. We had been working for some time, when one of the teachers blurted out, "I can follow the student's procedure. I can apply the method to a different set of numbers. But I don't understand why it works. This is another meaningless algorithm to me." And many of the other teachers in the class agreed with her. At that time, I was quite surprised, but since then I have

come to understand what was going on here. That is, again, the teachers have learned the mathematics by rote. But unlike those who react in the first way I described, these teachers do understand that reasoning must play some role in mathematics. However, they never developed models or representations, no sense of what the operations actually do, to call upon to make sense of mathematical procedures. To illustrate the kinds of models or representations, the kind of mathematical imagination, teachers need to develop, consider Mr. Kurosawa's students. They were working with a sequence of images of dots with an accompanying story—starting with one virus, the viruses grow by adding four each minute. Some students represented the number of viruses after three minutes as $4 \times 3 + 1$, others as $3 \times 4 + 1$. To explain these different arithmetic representations, students grouped the dots in different ways (Figure 1).

This is precisely the sort of mathematical imagination teachers need to develop. Given the mathematical needs of so many elementary teachers in the U.S., our first priority must be to help them reconnect with their own capacities for mathematical thought, to help them develop meanings for the symbols and objects of mathematical study. But how is this to be done? It certainly isn't happening in most mathematics courses offered at colleges and universities. One possibility is to work from records of practice, perhaps like those we have seen today, that highlight children's mathematical thinking. Such records, which reveal children's mathematical ideas in process, could provide access to those same ideas for teachers who did not have opportunities to develop these ways of thinking when they, themselves, were children.

FIGURE 1 Students show different ways to group the dots.

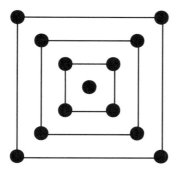 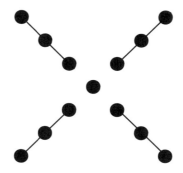

Haruo Ishigaki, Waseda University

What do teachers learn and how do they learn about mathematics? When it comes to that issue, then it is basically the same as how students learn and what students learn. Therefore, I would like to share with you the following four points.

First of all, the knowledge that any excellent teacher has is not a perfect one. Teachers need to be aware that their knowledge always has to be updated, and it has to be reconstructed. They should encourage students, but they should also encourage themselves. Good teaching is 80 percent confidence and 20 percent doubt. Teachers need to have both of these. When I just entered the university, I listened to the lecture of a Nobel laureate in quantum mechanics. And suddenly in the middle of the lecture, he stopped and started thinking. He had forgotten absolute zero. Was it minus 273 degrees or minus 237 degrees? He wasn't sure. If he was a Nobel laureate and forgot, it is okay to have doubt, I thought. That was a very big motivation for my work.

Second, students say extraordinary things and commit extraordinary mis-takes. And they give explanations which are not understandable to us. There are many situations, however, when there is some very valuable information in those little things that students or pupils say. I did not let a particular student take my graduate course, so he went to another university. After two years, he contacted me. He was going to talk at an academic meeting and wanted me to come and listen to his presentation. I realized that I had lost a very big treasure. I should have listened to his mathematics. This is true even when students are still children.

And third, in Japan the teachings of Confucius were common in education. One of his teachings is that you should always correct your mistakes. So at an appropriate place, you should recognize that you have already committed a mis-take and acknowledge it. Often if some-body asks a student questions, the student thinks he is being criticized. I listened to one of the lectures by a famous mathema-tician. He made a mistake, and the audience began to mumble and give him advice. But I was very much impressed by the professor's attitude. He asked the audience to wait for about ten minutes, as I remember. He went to the corner of the blackboard and worked through what he had explained. And then finally, he turned back to the audience and said, "you are right." And then he went on.

And finally, let me go back to the mathematics, the topic of today. A mathematical concept must be understood in context. While I was working as an editor of the academic society of mathematics, I happened to encounter a contribution about rounding off calculations. Take a very easy example, 3.1×3.9. Let's make it 3×4. And the answer should be 12. The students, however, repeatedly made a calculation of 3.1×3.9, and rounded the results to get 12.

The author wrote about how to correct the students' mistake. His intention was to teach the students that if you use substitutes which are very close to the exact numbers, the result will be very close to the real answer. In his explanation, however, he said that this is mathematically wrong, but in order to be efficient, using the substitutes is a good way to do the problem. Many students are good students and try to get to the right solution, not the wrong solution. I understood that this is why the teacher failed. I think, in this particular case, the teacher did not understand the real purpose of teaching this method to students. The approach should have been taught in a specific environment, where the teacher understood the real aim and the real purpose of the strategy.

Let me talk a little about concept building to conclude my presentation. The priority in concept building is to first define it as a collection of elements with something analogous and relate it to the external world. The contents, the common features inside, should follow the definition. That will come later. I think

we can learn something from this about knowing mathematics for teaching.

Miho Ueno, Tokyo Gakugei University

I'm from the Oizumi Campus of Tokyo Gakugei University Senior High School. The Tokyo Gakugei University has teacher preparation and an education faculty. I work for the senior high school and teach at the university. That means every year we receive the students from the Tokyo Gakugei University teacher training program and for lesson study. When students come to our school to have lesson study, I have a chance to see what level of knowledge they start out with in teaching mathematics. During the three weeks, I can also identify how they have developed their skills and their understanding of mathematics education.

Student teachers come to our school and try to remember what they did when they were high school students. This is their understanding of high school classroom activities. For example, one student said when he took mathematics classes in the past, students were always taking notes, and the teachers explained and let the students solve the problems. The next student said that when he was a high school student, he understood that mathematics was testing students' ability to memorize, and they learned mathematics in that way. The third student said that about 40 students were in the same class. Mathematics class was always quiet. Children used formulas and wrote them down in notebooks.

These students were typical. Every year when they conclude their three-week teacher training course, I ask them how their attitude about the classroom has changed. If students share the same impression about what they did when they were high school students, then they have a misunderstanding about mathematics teaching. They only know how to help students solve the problems as they are told to do in their textbook.

Prior to the training period, student teachers have certain anxieties about what they are supposed to do. But they are relatively confident about their abilities to teach mathematics. They believe that their ability is enough to attain the level required by the guidebook for their lessons. During the three-week period, student teachers have to compile a lesson plan prior to their classes. They have to describe the purpose of the class, what kind of teaching materials should be used, what they are supposed to say to the students, and what reactions they expect. The students understand that the definition of the formula is not the purpose. They recognize that they have to learn how they can help students solve problems and understand the mathematics. The student teachers realize that you cannot only rely on textbooks, but rather you have to convey the value and essence of the mathematics with your own wording and with your own understanding. You have to be very careful about how you lay out the mathematics on the blackboard.

The student teacher, at the beginning of the training, knows that his role as a teacher is to convey information to his students. But gradually they begin to realize that the class is the place where students have to learn. You have to devise teaching materials. You have to think carefully how you can use the pace of the class and how you can use the blackboard to help students learn. Their view of students changes while they teach during the training period. They begin to learn that you have to find out the value of the teaching materials, and you have to go into them deeper yourself so you can leverage what is written in the materials.

This is a capability teachers are required to have.

Teachers must understand the variable aspect of mathematical concepts and how deep the mathematical formulas are. When they are trying to find out and explain these deep aspects of the mathematics, they always discover that what they have as an analogy is not sufficient. This applies not only to the student teachers but also to experienced teachers. Teachers have to use their existing knowledge as a basis, but they also have to keep in mind that they have to improve their knowledge. As teachers try to acquire new knowledge of mathematics, they have to decide how to learn. They also have to know how formulas and algorithms came into existence. For example, you have to consider a particular mathematical task under certain conditions. But in other cases you have to change the conditions to the same task, or you may try to generalize the same task, and by doing so you will be able to see a pattern. Acquiring this kind of competence should be done not only by the student teachers but also experienced teachers as well as students in class. You have to encourage students to obtain and acquire this kind of thinking. Unless teachers have this competence, they won't be able to teach that concept to the students.

The basic attitude teachers should have toward studies is to be modest and try to learn as much as possible. Teachers are researchers at the same time as they are teachers, but they cannot stay only in a very narrow scope of their research. If teachers want to expand their scope of knowledge, they have to cooperate with their colleagues, and they have to enjoy discussions with other mathematics teachers. With this attitude they can deepen their knowledge of mathematics.

Small Group Discussion

Participants were divided into five small groups for discussion throughout the workshop. These groups were charged with responding to two of four questions using the experiences of the workshop to ground their thinking and discussion and to draw on the activities done together as a way to give meaning to their responses. Each group had assigned coordinators from the United States and Japan as well as a translator. Each U.S. coordinator was responsible for a summary of the discussion of their group. These small groups provided the opportunity for the participants from the countries to talk informally about teaching and professional development. This section contains summaries of the discussions, which varied depending on the focus of the groups, and an introduction to video clips of highlights of some of the small group work.

Questions addressed in small group discussion:

1. Teaching mathematics requires that teachers understand mathematics well themselves. In particular, what mathematics do teachers need to know beyond the content of the curriculum that they teach to their students?
2. How do teachers use mathematics together with other kinds of knowledge and skill in order to connect students with mathematics?
3. How do skilled teachers learn about and make use of their students' knowledge and capabilities to help them learn mathematics?
4. What are different approaches to helping teachers develop the mathematical understanding they need to teach? What are the advantages and potential problems of different approaches?

Group I
  Report Coordinator:
  Michelle Manes, Project Director, Education Development Center
Group II
  Report Coordinator:
  Denisse Thompson, Associate Professor, University of South Florida

Group III
    Report Coordinator:
    Susan Beal, Professor, St. Xavier University
Group IV
    Report Coordinator:
    Ramesh Gangolli, Professor, University of Washington
Group V
    Report Coordinator:
    Susan Wood, Professor, J. Sargeant Reynolds Community College
Video Small Group Discussion Highlights

Small Group Discussion Report: Group I

Group Members
Jack Burrill, Cindy Connell, Daniel Goroff, Toru Handa*, Keiko Hino**,
Jackie Hurd***, Shunji Kurosawa, Michelle Manes*, Toshio Sawada,
Deborah Schifter, Lee Stiff***, Mamoru Takezawa, Hajime Yamashita

*Report Coordinator; ** Translator; ***U.S. International Congress on Mathematics Education
(ICME) Travel Group

Teaching mathematics requires that teachers understand mathematics well themselves. In particular, what mathematics do teachers need to know beyond the content of the curriculum that they teach to their students?

RESPONSE

The question of what mathematics teachers need to know was a challenge for the group. One view is that perhaps that question is easier to answer for Japanese teachers than for teachers from the United States—the national curriculum in Japan defines the content teachers need to teach and therefore defines at least the minimal level of content they need to understand. One example of this from the workshop discussions: It was striking to participants from the United States that all of the Japanese teachers in the room were familiar with Deborah Ball's "coin problems," and that there was general agreement that these were "sixth grade problems." That degree of agreement about content at each grade level simply does not exist in the United States. It would be surprising if a group of teachers were all

familiar with the same problem, much less agreeing on the curricular purpose for the problem and at which grade level it belonged. Perhaps teachers in the United States get bogged down in particular pieces of content (both for themselves and their students) because they lack this consensus about what happens when in a child's mathematics education.

However, we agreed that there are some things teachers need to know, or be able to do, that transcend any particular curriculum. For example, it is important that teachers

- recognize the value of persistence
- understand mathematics as a science, something you explore
- recognize patterns
- understand mathematics as a system
- have the ability to follow a child's mathematical ideas and determine if there are problems with the logic
- have a positive attitude about mathematics and the expectation that it will make sense

There was also some discussion about the content teachers needed to know. One point of agreement was that elementary school teachers probably do not need to study calculus—and it seems, in both countries, it is unlikely that they do. There seemed to be consensus that teachers should know, at a minimum, the content of the courses that they teach in addition to the courses before and after theirs. As we dug into this idea, problems soon arose, however.

In a district where each school has a different curriculum, what does it mean to know the content of the courses before and after? If a teacher teaches different grade levels, how does the minimal requirement change? Some people felt that simply one year on either side was not enough, and it should be broadened. However, a teacher in the group reminded us that elementary school teachers are generalists, saying, "You can't make every elementary teacher into a math professor and a historian and a literature professor. Elementary teachers have to teach everything."

The closest we could come to consensus was to agree on the requirement of knowing the content of their own course and one course on either side, along with some particular pieces of mathematics— like the base 10 system in deep ways.

An interesting fact was that in both countries, there are concerns about what mathematics teachers need to know and about the weak backgrounds of elementary school teachers. In Japan, two recent books have been popular: *The University Student Who Can't Do Fractions* (Okabe et al., 1999) and *The University Student Who Can't Do Decimals* (Okabe et al., 2000). In Japan, the population decrease is making it easier to get into college, and there is concern that the elementary teachers are among the least prepared college students in terms of mathematical backgrounds. In the United States, the situation is similar, with schools of education having propor-

tionally more of the students with the lowest entrance test scores (U.S. Department of Education, 2000).

In both countries, there are claims about what elementary teachers do not know. In the United States, there is a strong research base that shows weakness of mathematical knowledge among prospective and practicing elementary teachers (Ball, 1990, 1991; Post et al., 1991; Ma, 1999). It is important, however, to talk about this research with respect for teachers, rather than disparage them.

How do teachers use mathematics together with other kinds of knowledge and skill in order to connect students with mathematics?

RESPONSE

The question of how mathematical knowledge comes together with pedagogical knowledge as teachers do their jobs was in a way easier to address.

- It is clear from the Japanese lessons that great care is given to planning things like blackboard use, order of problems presented, and thinking about what might happen during a lesson. All of the plans for "if students do this, I'll react this way..."—and even knowing what students are likely to say and do with particular problems—bring together both mathematical knowledge and the understanding of what students know and how they think about mathematics.
- Helping to connect students with content requires that teachers understand the content in deep ways and that they can think flexibly about it. Examples given include making topics like simultaneous linear equations more

interesting by setting the problems in a social science or physics context and connecting solving equations to a broader notion of "doing and undoing" which students understand. This goes beyond contextualizing problems to answer the question of "What is this good for? When will I use it?" to helping students better understand the content by showing the bigger picture and connections to things they already understand.

- In planning a lesson, teachers need to move beyond what *they* know as teachers and think about what the *students* know and understand. There is a difference between the way a teacher understands a piece of content and the appropriate level for students. Understanding a piece of content as a teacher means being able to talk about it appropriately for different levels of students.
- When an experienced teacher listens to a student's explanation, they are able to repeat back what the student said (an example of careful listening) and pick out the essential mathematics (bringing the careful listening together with the teacher's content knowledge). Inexperienced teachers are unable even to repeat what the students have said. Even if they know the mathematics, they are unable to really listen to their students. If they can not understand what their students are saying, they can not present the mathematics appropriately or address misunderstandings.
- In reading students' journal responses and problem solutions, experienced teachers are able to pick out the good ideas and provide guidance to students, whereas less experienced teachers may have difficulty making sense of what students write.
- Teachers need to know enough to make decisions about what is useful to pursue

and what they can skip. No course covers this.

CONCLUSIONS

One major concern, discussed during two of the three meetings, was the fact that lesson study is used primarily at the elementary level in Japan. According to the Japanese participants in the group, lesson study exists but is less common in middle school and not used at all in high school and college. The Japanese teachers explain this by saying that the high school teachers graduate from the mathematics department; they like math and have an easier time teaching it. Yet they also said that exploration of mathematics content by the teachers may be part of lesson study but is not always. Another explanation is the tracked high school system in Japan. In high school, the focus is preparation for university and entrance exams; this is much less of a worry at the elementary level. It seems that in Japan, elementary teachers take to lesson study because of an opportunity to learn content. It is not the only purpose, but it is a big attraction.

To the U.S. participants, it was clear that a lot of pedagogical learning went on in lesson study: how to plan a lesson, how to anticipate student responses, how to use the blackboard, and so on. The purpose of lesson study as described by one Japanese participant was to "look at the delta—the difference between what was planned and what actually happened in a class." That seems like a valuable experience for a teacher at any level, and in fact Daniel Goroff described a lesson study like program at Harvard University. The program is for mathematics professors, and the goal is to improve teaching, not content knowledge.

Another issue was around the evaluative nature of classroom observation in the United States. Teachers will still be observed as part of their evaluation, so how is this formal observation different from a lesson study experience, and how can it be made clearly different for the teachers? This brought up issues around evaluation of mathematics teachers: Some members of the group felt strongly that in evaluating teaching of mathematics, you have to have mathematics experts (and not just administrators) involved. The Education Development Center has a project called Lenses on Learning focused on designing materials and videos to help administrators look at teaching practice and understand what they should look for in a mathematics classroom.

In discussing the two main types of teacher professional development presented in the workshop, participants identified clear positives and negatives in both approaches.

One Japanese participant explained that one negative aspect of lesson study is that teachers try to create lessons that no one would criticize. That kind of pressure can keep a teacher from taking risks and from exercising creativity and originality. In addition, the point was made that when watching a real lesson with real kids, the issues that come up may not be about the lesson. Whatever happens happens, and you can not always predict or arrange to discuss particular ideas based on study lessons. Another point about lesson study, or at least its potential implementation in the United States, is that teachers see being observed as a "showcase." They do something they do not usually do with their students. The feedback received on a study lesson may not be useful if it does not apply to daily practice.

In thinking about records of practice, one participant compared that form of

professional development as training people to be opera critics rather than singers; he claimed that watching a video of teaching does not help teachers with their teaching practice. Defenders of the model, however, claim that it's not about being a critic, but rather to learn skills that are important in teaching. It is true that records of practice are removed from actual practice, but there are things you can learn: You can learn to examine students' talk, for example. What are they really saying? Do their mathematical ideas make sense? Also, records of practice are less threatening than having someone come in and examine your own practice. Using video and cases might be a way to cultivate the kind of atmosphere that would allow lesson study to happen. Deborah Schifter described a professional development exercise she uses: Teachers write a narrative of a classroom conversation. They read each others' narratives, and professional development staff read and comment on them. Some teachers say that the exercise makes them hear their students' mathematics differently. They need to attend differently to record it. This kind of activity can serve as a kind of bridge between examining videos and cases to examining one's own practice.

In comparing the two methods, there are some interesting points of contrast. In using records of practice for professional development, you can specifically select records for particular learning goals. In essence, you can build a curriculum around these records. However, it takes an outside expert to collect, examine, and catalog the records, and possibly to deliver the professional development. With lesson study, you cannot select for particular learning goals. Whatever happens is what there is to discuss. But lesson study can be done in a school without the participation of outside professional developers. Lesson study groups require leadership and organization but that can come from among the teachers in a school.

RESEARCH ISSUES

In looking at the issues raised in our discussion, some interesting areas for research emerged:

- What is the potential for implementing a lesson study or similar professional development structure at the high school level? Is there potential benefit for teachers at this level?

- Is there an impact of participation in lesson study on daily practice? One point made in the workshop is that Japanese teachers do not spend the same amount of time on a regular lesson as on a study lesson. So is it true that study lessons are "showcases" with little relation to a regular class, or does going through the process of carefully planning some lessons affect how a teacher presents all lessons? If there is an impact, what is it?

Group Members
Hyman Bass, Phyllis Caruth***, Frances Curcio***, Alice Gill, Ichiei Hirabayashi,
Tadayuki Ishida, Carole Lacampagne, Carol Malloy, Nobuhiko Nohda, Izumi Soga*,
Akihiko Takahashi, Denisse Thompson*, Hiroko Uchino, Tad Watanabe**

*Report Coordinator; ** Translator; ***U.S. ICME Travel Group

The group did not make any specific assumptions in order to answer the assigned questions. However, some misunderstandings among the American educators that were not clarified until Tuesday may have impacted the discussions. In particular, there was confusion about what was meant by lesson study. Not until Tuesday did it become clear that Japanese teachers might participate in several lesson study groups throughout the year on a regular basis to discuss a variety of instructional materials and content; participation in a long term lesson study occurred much less frequently.

From the discussions and from additional information provided by Tad Watanabe, it appears that lesson study is a practice that occurs typically at K-6 schools. Some of these may focus on developing a lesson over a period of time, and others may focus on providing mutual support for daily problems or for more broad-based issues, such as how to implement a new national course of study. At the lesson study sessions focusing on the development of particular lessons, different individuals may bring plans and have others critique these plans. Lesson study affords teachers the opportunity to talk about different aspects of lessons or to explain what happened when they tried a lesson in the classroom.

Formal lesson study with open-house study lessons occurs only a limited number of times during the school year and is for the explicit purpose of researching the lesson. These lessons often take place at elementary schools attached to universities; education researchers at the universities might serve as outside observers and reactors to the lesson study. The availability of lesson study at the elementary schools affiliated with universities seems to fulfill one of the missions of these schools, namely, to provide national leadership in improving teaching in all subjects including mathematics. It appears that not all Japanese teachers regularly participate in a formal lesson study as a teacher being observed teaching a lesson to children.

Additionally, lesson studies appear to be practices that occur primarily at the K-6 levels. Very little discussion occurred about professional development practices for teachers at grades 7-12.

In responding to the charge to discuss the two questions listed below, the group focused on both questions simultaneously.

Although responses do not fit neatly with only one of the two questions, this summary attempts to sort responses to provide some coherent comments to each question.

How do teachers use mathematics together with other kinds of knowledge and skill in order to connect students with mathematics?

RESPONSE

In the course of discussing this question, it became clear that the mathematics knowledge of the teacher is crucial at all points in the instructional process. Teachers design lessons, enact lessons, respond to students' ideas and make use of those ideas in furthering the lesson, analyze lessons, and study student work. All of these points require considerable mathematical knowledge. For instance, in the sixth-grade lesson the teacher explicitly wanted the children to construct the task of the lesson—the teacher's knowledge guided the lesson by guiding the children until the task for the day emerged. That is, students raised ideas related to area models; the teacher guided the children to consider other ideas until the linear growth model emerged. Clearly the teacher had to know what mathematical structure was inherent in his goal.

Other issues that arose in relation to the question are discussed below.

Teachers use their knowledge of mathematics as they develop appropriate tasks to use with their children. The teacher's mathematics knowledge is used in conjunction with his or her knowledge of children to develop tasks that will be of interest to the children and motivate them to learn. This intersection of the knowledge of children and mathematics was evident in the fourth-grade lesson in which the teacher used a quiz show format in an attempt to motivate children to deal with issues of large numbers.

Teachers use their knowledge of mathematics to consider real-life problems and examples that people need for everyday life. Japanese K-6 mathematics education seems to focus on "mathematical literacy," so that Japanese teachers attempt to begin a lesson with a context that children might encounter; this was evident in the fourth-grade lesson in which the teacher dealt with large numbers related to size and costs. It was also evident in the Japanese teachers' concerns about the U.S. third-grade lesson dealing with the number of pennies, nickels, and dimes to equal a given amount of money. Japanese teachers thought the problem would be more compelling if the teacher had the coins in her pocket to show to students or to have students consider what the coins might purchase.

Teachers use their knowledge of mathematics to understand the different aspects of the mathematics in a problem that may impede the work of the students on the given task. Teachers need to be aware of the cultural dimensions that provide gates that may have an effect on learning, either positively or negatively. For instance, in the fourth-grade lesson on large numbers, the numeration system involves grouping by ten thousands in Japanese, rather than by thousands as in English. The different mental structure required to comprehend the numbers in this system was a source of difficulty for some of the American educators watching the lesson; focusing so hard on comprehending the numbers represented in an unfamiliar way made it more difficult to focus on the mathematics embedded in the lesson. Although this difference in grouping was not a problem for the

Japanese children, the cultural differences caused a problem for the American educators. Given the cultural diversity of children in U.S. classrooms, it serves as a potent reminder of the need to be sensitive to children's perspectives. When cultural backgrounds cause children to think differently, it is often easy to dismiss their thinking as incorrect; however, student explanations and good questioning on the part of the teacher can help both students and teachers to bridge the cultural divide and enhance learning.

Teachers use their knowledge of mathematics when they take a simple problem from their textbooks and consider how the problem might be adapted or extended to explore the mathematics more deeply. This was evident in the sixth-grade lesson as the teacher took a basic problem dealing with growth by four per minute and had children look for patterns and attempt to express those patterns by means of functions and variables. As part of this work with functions, the teacher had children considering the different interpretations of $4 \times 48 + 1$ and $48 \times 4 + 1$ in the context of the situation. This functional work foreshadowed and laid the foundation for more advanced work in later grades.

Teachers use their knowledge of mathematics to anticipate various student solutions that may arise during classroom discussions about a task. Anticipating student solutions helps teachers determine where the discussion may go and enables them to make appropriate decisions on how to proceed with the lesson. For instance, in the sixth-grade lesson, children's ideas about area were leading to a quadratic relationship. By anticipating students' solutions, the teacher was able to steer the discussions until the linear relationship that he wanted the children to investigate was generated.

Teachers use their knowledge of mathematics as they make connections between mathematics and other disciplines.

What are different approaches to helping teachers develop the mathematical understanding they need to teach? What are the advantages and potential problems of different approaches?

RESPONSE

A number of issues arose regarding the various professional development approaches presented at the seminar—research study lesson, video case record, written cases, and professional development in general.

The discussions before and after the study lesson help teachers know and understand the mathematics embedded in the lesson. The discussions are important because they help teachers reflect on how to fix structural errors in the lesson. For instance, in the fourth-grade lesson, the fact that each successive question in the task increased by a factor of ten caused some students to focus on the pattern being generated rather than the underlying mathematical relationships, thereby obtaining an incorrect result for the comic book problem. Through discussions about the lesson after its presentation, teachers are able to think about this structural problem and how it might be resolved prior to teaching the lesson again.

One approach that is particularly helpful for teachers is to use vertical articulation of topics. That is, teachers should study topics and consider how they change and grow across the various grades and levels. If elementary and lower secondary teachers understand where topics eventually lead in high school, then they might teach those topics differently. For instance, the sixth-grade teacher taught his lesson to lay foundations for more formal work with functions in a later grade. It appears that in Japan, teachers are encouraged to participate in lesson study at various levels so that they have a good sense of the mathematics that is taught prior to and following the level at which they teach. The same is not necessarily true in the United States. Although the recently released *Principles and Standards for School Mathematics* (National Council of Teachers of Mathematics, 2000) encourages this vertical articulation through the content standards, it is not clear that such articulation typically occurs in practice. U.S. teachers have little opportunity to interact with teachers at levels other than their own to gain a better understanding of the mathematics taught at the different levels.

The national course of study in Japan helps teachers make assumptions related to the issue. This course of study helps teachers make assumptions about the mathematics that children should know, both in terms of instruction at their grade level and in terms of prerequisite knowledge. U.S. teachers are not able to make such assumptions quite so readily.

Materials need to be available in teachers' editions that show how ideas are related across levels. The materials in the Japanese teachers' editions are not the same as in the pupils' editions. The teachers' editions contain supplementary problems and discuss how a topic relates to previously taught ideas and to ideas that will appear in later grade levels. The Japanese teacher materials provide support to teachers, pointing out the important ideas of the lesson and where students might have problems; in addition, the teachers' edition may provide

different solutions or ways that children think about a problem. Some of these same instructional approaches are present in the teachers' editions of newer U.S. textbooks that provide additional problems, ideas for review, reteaching ideas if students have difficulties, or extensions for more advanced work. A big difference may be that the course of study in Japanese education helps focus on connections to earlier and later courses that are not possible in U.S. textbooks; hence, Japanese materials often seem more focused than corresponding U.S. teacher materials.

Research is needed to evaluate the relation between school mathematics that teachers are expected to teach and college mathematics that students are expected to learn. University mathematics does not necessarily help in teaching school mathematics. The mathematics teachers study should begin with the mathematics in the textbooks of the curriculum. This perspective closely relates to the workshop paper delivered by Zalman Usiskin in which he raised the issue that school mathematics is a rich source of study in its own right. Japanese and U.S. educators agreed that there was a need to study mathematics for teaching and not just mathematics for mathematicians.

The three different professional development approaches seen at this workshop facilitate the integration of content with methods. This integration is important because teachers' pedagogical content knowledge comes into play in understanding how students develop their mathematical knowledge.

The purpose of the formal study lesson is to provide research on the lesson and its effectiveness. However, written cases and videos could be used in lesson study groups and could help in the development of a research lesson. Published study lessons could also be used in study groups. In the study groups, experienced teachers mentor novice teachers. A question that arises with all of these approaches is how much mathematics knowledge a procedurally oriented teacher gains from studying such cases.

CONCLUSIONS

The group considered similarities in the ways that teachers in the two cultures look at the different models of professional development: lesson study, written case study, and video case analysis. In discussing the various approaches, Japanese teachers focused on the mathematics in the model, whether a written or video case, to determine whether or not the mathematics was appropriate for the level of the student. What was the mathematics that the teacher was trying to help students understand? With the lesson study approach, teachers have thought about why they are doing something, what mathematics has come before, and what mathematics they may want to foreshadow. That is, the Japanese teachers are interested in how the mathematics of a particular lesson relates to the curriculum for the whole year; the course of study provides a useful perspective on the content that should be taught in the classroom. In contrast, U.S. teachers often consider pedagogical issues first. Paying serious attention to the mathematics in the lesson development would likely be beneficial to U.S. teachers.

One issue that arose is that all the various approaches to professional development depend on the teachers' knowledge of mathematics and how this knowledge can be used to help students. If teachers do not know enough mathematics, they cannot take the ideas very far. A valuable aspect of lesson study is to

help the teacher understand the intricacies and details of a lesson—choice of numbers for problems, selection of manipulative materials to enhance learning, and so on. The detail in such discussion would be exceedingly valuable in the first few years of teaching.

Video and written cases provide an opportunity for teachers to learn the mathematics that is situated in their daily practice. Teachers analyze mathematical tasks, think about how the tasks might be selected, reflect on the mathematics the tasks elicit, and consider how the given task is embedded in a family of problems that can be scaled up or down as needed. Discussions begin with how the ideas play out in the given class being studied, and then teachers begin to think about extensions. The task is the seed for a lesson that ultimately can be generalized mathematically. If teachers are able to see how ideas grow from practice, they are not as likely to question the generalization of problems.

It seems important for teachers to develop the mathematics that is related to the school mathematics they must teach. Industrial mathematics, commercial mathematics, and economic mathematics all have different perspectives and emphases. At present, much of the mathematics taught in K-12 schools is based on the mathematics of mathematicians. When students understand all the mathematics in the K-12 schools, they are able to enter a collegiate mathematics program designed for future mathematicians, scientists, or others needing to use higher-level mathematics. The emphasis on the mathematics of mathematicians does not always seem relevant to prospective teachers. If the mathematics teachers learned was situated more in practice, such as in the video cases discussed by Hyman Bass and Deborah Ball, then perhaps teachers would focus more on the content of the mathematics and be more comfortable doing so.

The professional development discussed in the workshop requires a longitudinal commitment. Intensive work with cases or videos is the type of professional development we need to consider more often rather than the short variety that is common in the United States. At present, there is often no framework to put the different professional development experiences into a curriculum or into the larger mathematical picture. In the hands of a skilled facilitator, the approaches discussed in the workshop can provide a framework for professional development because of their focus on how children learn mathematics. The facilitator needs to be explicit in helping teachers make connections to the larger K-12 curriculum in order to understand how the math-ematical ideas fit together and to provide the forward and backward look into curriculum that appears to be a hallmark of the Japanese materials.

RESEARCH ISSUES

Several questions arose:

- Why is the study lesson conducted only at elementary school and not also at high school if it is such an important part of teachers' professional development?
- Teachers in the Japanese research study lessons are both instructors and researchers. Do American teachers have this dual perspective? If not, how could we begin to foster this dual perspective?

Small Group Discussion Report: Group III

Group Members
Susan Beal*, Jacqueline Goodloe***, Haruo Ishigaki, Yoshihiro Kubo,
Kouichi Kumagai, Carol Midgett***, Tatsuo Morozumi*(second day),
Keiichi Nishimura*(first day), Takaski Nakamura, Nanette Seago,
Yoshishige Sugiyama, Zalman Usiskin, Makoto Yoshida**

*Report Coordinator; ** Translator; ***U.S. ICME Travel Group

The group spent time understanding the three methods or approaches to professional development in Japan and the United States that were presented and discussed in the workshop: lesson study, video records, and written cases studies.

Teaching mathematics requires that teachers understand mathematics well themselves. In particular, what mathematics do teachers need to know beyond the content of the curriculum that they teach to their students?

RESPONSE

In summarizing the response to the first question, the group felt that the teachers needed to understand the mathematics they were teaching but did not discuss what teachers needed to know beyond the content of the curriculum. In two of the examples used during the workshop (sixth-grade lesson, $4n + 1$, and the hexagon example, $4n + 2$, in the case study), students could use a recursive formula to describe a pattern: add four each time. How do we know? What constitutes proof at these levels? The teacher is looking for an explicit definition of sequence, i.e., a closed formula for the nth term. In the United States studying the relation between recursion and a closed formula is not in the curriculum, and it was believed by the U.S. participants that U.S. teachers do not have much experience in working with this relationship. Adding four is related to the slope of the line. Do teachers know this?

Development of variables as a concept, although it is a major part of Japanese curriculum, is not explicit in Japan. Boxes represent x. The letter x is used in the seventh grade, and from there polynomials are introduced. The use of symbols in the linear equation, $y = mx + b$, where m is constant and x is a variable, is currently being researched in Japan; what should m and x be called? Moving from particulars to a more general mathematical idea is what teachers need to learn.

How do skilled teachers (master teachers, experienced teachers) learn about and make use of students' knowledge and capabilities to help them (the students) learn mathematics?

RESPONSE

Three aspects emerged as important elements in response to the second question: self-reflection, attention to details, and summary of the lesson. Points of cultural differences between the United States and Japan were also discussed: how teachers are known to be good teachers, direct comparison of teachers, working hard in mathematics verus "math people," and what it means to be a teacher.

Self-Reflection

The most important commonality among the methods and approaches expressed by the participants in our discussion group was the role of self-reflection. Each approach or method built on self-reflection is a vehicle to help teachers grow, mature, and learn more about pedagogy and mathematics. Participants commented that it was difficult to reflect on thinking and teaching in the context of actually teaching. One of the roles discussion plays in lesson study is to help teachers reflect on their lesson, on students' learning, and on the questions asked by the teacher to develop the concept being taught in the lesson. One participant mentioned that "they help you see what you can't about yourself." Another commented that "self-reflection is most important, but you have to actually test (your ideas in the) classrooms."

In the video records example presented by Deborah Ball, the teacher kept a journal each day, reflecting on the lesson, how the students were learning, and what they were doing during the lesson. The journal can be used by others to understand what the teacher was trying to accomplish in her lesson. The three phases of video records for professional development are design, enactment or

facilitation, and analyzing or reflecting. Thus, in the construction and use of records, self-reflection plays an important role.

In case study, self-reflection was indeed what Catherine and David related with respect to their lessons and with the process of change in which they were involved. For example, from page 10 of the case study: A "few weeks later when he met with his colleagues and shared a ten-minute segment of a videotaped lesson, their reaction to the tape led David into reflecting on how leading he was with the students." Our discussion group felt that you have to look at your teaching and, in doing so, share with colleagues.

Attention to Details

Attention to details was particularly important in lesson study. Sensitivity to detail was called the essence of lesson study, and a teacher's expertise in this area provides evidence of a skilled teacher. For example, if a teacher can explain clearly what a student said, the teacher has a "good eye" for teaching. Attention to detail includes such things as the importance placed on the example selected to introduce the lesson, and the order of examples used in the lesson, the language of questions and what it tells about the concept under investigation. Lesson study also tries to anticipate responses students would or could make and formulates plans to include accommodations for the different nature of the responses. Furthermore, the benefits derived from lesson study include paying attention to student detail.

Lesson study focuses on learning what the students are doing. Another teacher could use the concept of lesson study and teach a lesson to find how his or her students use or benefit from the materials (action research). Attention to detail for daily lessons is important as is the need to plan for every lesson.

Video records as an approach to professional development can focus on the details associated with the lesson. Materials available to be studied consist of detailed documentation of teaching and learning, although all of these are not necessarily analyzed. The materials are used to encourage teachers to learn how to observe, discuss, and make records— all important in learning a practice such as teaching as described by Deborah Ball in her opening remarks. Her study took place over an entire academic year in two classes. The richness of the detail allows explorations of what took place in the teaching-learning process over a period of time.

Lesson Summary

All three approaches for professional development have strengths and weaknesses. Many study lessons are transcribed, which is very time-consuming. One participant noted that he has one of his students copy what is on the blackboard and write about his or her thoughts on the lesson, rotating the task so that all students have the opportunity. In lesson study, the blackboard can be used as a record for research. Participants observed that it takes a long time in constrained circumstances to watch a video, while opportunities to read a case study were more flexible. All agreed that it is nice to have a summary of the lesson. However, whether it is video or written, a point of view is always present, depending on the person who videotaped the lesson or the one who summarized it. Since lesson study has many observers, there is not one point of view. Because each approach for summarizing or recording a lesson has strengths and weaknesses, the group thought that it would work well to combine the methods.

One characteristic of lesson study is that the physical records of the lesson are on the blackboard, which can help as teachers analyze the lesson. In fact, when discussing the sixth-grade lesson, we had the physical "blackboard" to help us in our analysis and recollection. The blackboard is organized to help students keep notes. Furthermore, we can categorize what the teacher said by using the notes from the blackboard.

CONCLUSIONS

Cultural Differences and Their Impact on Professional Development

How Teachers Are Known to Be Good Teachers

In Japan some teachers are known for their teaching and become known because they have been observed in the classroom, perhaps through lesson study. Many also write about their ideas in one of the many magazines for teachers. If the idea appears in a mathematics-specific issue, comments are made by mathematics educators. Also, Japanese bookstores have many books written by teachers to share ideas.

The U.S. participants felt that U.S. teachers become known by their professional affiliations and accomplishments and not necessarily by their teaching. The professional journals, for example those published by the National Council of Teachers of Mathematics, include articles by teachers that describe their ideas or classroom activities, but it is very difficult to know from this how a teacher actually teaches. And although there are magazines such as *Teacher*, which might mirror those in Japan, these magazines do not necessarily support the mathematics education community.

Direct Comparison of Teachers

Direct comparison of one teacher with another does not happen in Japan, as in the case study example with the comparison of Catherine's and David's classes. In Japan, the lesson study consists of a set of hypotheses on how to conduct the lesson, which are then tested. It is these hypotheses that are critiqued during the discussion following the observation of the lesson. Furthermore, to prevent overwhelming the teacher with too many suggestions during the discussion of the lesson study, focal points are established and the participant observers categorize what the teacher said, using the blackboard as a point of reference. Usually, the lesson has been planned with others, so the emphasis is on the work done by the group. The notion of "we will help you improve" in Japan starts as early as when you are a student and so naturally comes to the teaching process, but this is not so in the United States.

Working Hard in Mathematics Versus "Math People"

The attitude that all students can learn mathematics seems to be more prevalent in practice in Japan than in the United States, even though NCTM (and the Mathematical Association of America) specifically include this in the literature.

Being a Teacher

In the United States, teachers go back to college to get advanced degrees but not in Japan. Becoming a teacher is very difficult in Japan. Many teacher applicants fail the screening to become a teacher. The test to become a teacher is to teach in front of a set of examiners. As in the U.S., supply and demand has a lot to do with how rigorous the requirements are to become a teacher.

In Japan there is also a first-year teacher training program in lieu of student teaching. The year includes 30 days in school with a mentor to help. Every five years teachers go back to the education center for continued professional development. In the United States, 33 states require a small amount (minimal) of professional development (Dossey and Usiskin, 2000). In most states teachers have to do some form of professional development to retain certification.

Small Group Discussion Report: Group IV

Group Members
Jerry Becker, Shelley Ferguson***, Ramesh Gangolli*, Beth Lazerick***,
Shinichiro Matsumoto, Judith Mumme, Hiroshi Nakano, Yasuhiro Sekiguchi*,
Kiyoaki Shoda, Margaret Smith, Shinichi Suzuki, Daniel Teague***, Miho Ueno

*Report Coordinator; ** Translator; ***U.S. ICME Travel Group

Although an attempt had been made to focus the group's discussion on the questions suggested at the workshop, given the central position occupied by lesson study in the plenary sessions, it was perhaps inevitable that much of the small group discussion was related to assessing the role and effectiveness of lesson study as a tool of professional development. What follows is a summary of responses to the questions as they relate to Japanese teachers taken from the interaction at the workshop. It is based partly on what transpired in the small group sessions but also on information obtained through other opportunities (formal as well as informal) as they arose during the workshop. The remarks are directed toward mathematics (and not toward any other subject), and those that might seem to apply more generally to other subjects should be viewed as limited by this restriction.

BACKGROUND

Elsewhere in these proceedings one can find a full description of lesson study: what it is, how it is implemented, the contexts in which teachers encounter it, and the role it plays in their professional development. In this summary, it is not necessary to repeat that information. It will nevertheless be useful to mention here a few aspects of the process of lesson study that might run contrary to the conception of lesson study that some may have formed. These aspects will serve as a backdrop against which some of the remarks that follow may make more sense.

- Lesson study sessions are not as pervasive a part of the daily life of teachers in Japan as one might suppose. The extent to which individual teachers engage in formal lesson study sessions is quite limited. Thus, many elementary teachers might do so only a few times a year at their school. They might also observe such sessions as a part of professional development activities at professional meetings, etc. Secondary school teachers engage in it to an even lesser extent. Schools attached to university departments that do research in mathematics education are exceptions. There, lesson study is a far more recurrent feature of life.
- Moreover, the lesson study sessions in which teachers participate might deal

with any subject (not necessarily mathematics).

- There is a tremendous range in the type of experience afforded by such lesson study sessions, depending on grade level, context, and purpose. Sessions might range from very informal ones in which a couple of colleagues might casually observe a small change of presentation and comment on it, to very formal heavily attended "study lessons" in which new investigations or major changes in existing lessons might be launched or dissected. The latter type of session is typically held in a university context. The end product of such sessions (after many iterations) might well end up as a published lesson made available to teachers.

- Great care is clearly taken in the preparation and implementation phases of a lesson study session. Thus, there is continual stress on the importance of (a) clearly identifying the conceptual and cognitive goals of a lesson, (b) designing interesting questions that will promote those goals, (c) weighing and selecting from different pedagogical devices that might be useful in pursuing the problem, and (d) anticipating a variety of student approaches and/or misconceptions. Notwithstanding the scrupulous attention paid to these elements, the postdiscussion that follows a study lesson sometimes concentrates on conceptual content and at other times on individual pedagogical style. Discussions may range from polite noncommittal ones to long substantial debates.

- In spite of these variations in form and substance, there is a universal acceptance of the proposition that the process of reflection exemplified by the lesson study experiences is a powerful tool for professional improvement. The only qualifying proviso is that in order to be useful, this process must be undertaken on a continuing basis over a sufficiently long period.

Bearing in mind these aspects, a summary of responses to four questions follows.

What do teachers do?

RESPONSE

The simple answer is that they continually engage in the process of trying to become more effective teachers, thinking about what they teach and how they teach it. But this is a glib summary that does scant justice to a number of institutional and cultural forces that promote and indeed ensure this behavior on a continuing basis. Notable among them are the following.

Preservice Acculturation

Although classroom-based preservice training (e.g., as a student teacher) is short—typically just three or four weeks—we were told by our Japanese colleagues that throughout the preparatory years certain expectations of what is regarded as professional behavior are built in as an integral part of preservice education. Among these are (a) the notion that as a teacher, one is expected to strive for "continuous improvement" throughout one's career and (b) that lesson study or other activities like it (involving reflection and analysis of one's teaching) will form the most important tool for achieving continuous improvement.

Initial Mentoring

It seems to be a widespread practice that some structured mentoring is provided for the beginning teacher. (This is especially the case for elementary teachers, who are usually not specialists in mathematics.) It was not clear whether this mentoring is subject oriented (e.g., toward mathematics). The precise manner in which this is done was not clarified in our discussions, but it seems that it is usual to assign a fledgling teacher to a senior colleague who becomes responsible for mentoring that teacher for one or two years. A policy adopted in 1998 requires that such mentoring shall be provided as a rule to all beginning teachers. It is not clear whether this policy is fully implemented as of today, but it surely sends a strong message to the beginning teacher that her or his teaching effectiveness is of immediate concern to the school system. The system of mentoring seems to be an effective vehicle for transmission of the professional culture of the school and its cadre of teachers.

Inservice Integration

The mentor who is a part of the school's professional culture reiterates the expectations clearly conveyed during the preservice phase during the initiation phase. Simultaneously, the beginning teacher is also integrated as a part of a team of teachers in the school. Most of our Japanese colleagues seemed to indicate that this is the prevalent model. The integration is facilitated by the existence of a number of support structures that promote the implementation of the model. Among these are

a. Availability of time for teachers to prepare and discuss lessons among themselves.
b. Opportunities for getting expert advice; this may come via an ongoing or occasional liaison with a faculty at a university or by means of other specific

opportunities (e.g., at lesson study sessions at the ward, prefectural, or national level).

c. Stability of employment; after an initial probationary period, a teacher acquires tenure de facto. Implicitly, the other part of this social contract is the assumption that the teacher will fulfill the expectations of professional behavior described above. Fluctuations in the total number of teachers needed are handled by attenuating and adjusting replacements needed due to retirements or resignations, rather than by lay-offs. This encourages individual teachers to view themselves as a part of a permanent valued structure, contributing significantly to a national need, rather than as functionaries who are hired and fired based on random demographic exigencies.

d. Standardized, unambiguous curricular materials, supplemented by explicit implementation schedules and supported by detailed teachers' guides; the implementation schedules are expected to be observed scrupulously, so much so that we were told that in any given week, essentially all students at a particular grade level will be studying the same mathematical topic throughout the country. On the other hand, the extent to which an individual teacher would follow exactly the detailed lesson plan for teaching that topic as laid out in the teachers' guide varies. The variation seems to depend on the experience and initiative of the teacher, as well as the grade level. The adherence to a standard curriculum, both as to the sequencing of topics and the time spent on them applies without exception, so far we can tell, to elementary and middle school grades. There seems to be much more variation at the high school level, both in regards to the lessons used as well as the pacing. However, the order of development of the topics and the interconnections that are to be stressed seem to be governed by the collective wisdom of the national curriculum and is fairly uniformly observed.

What do teachers work on?

RESPONSE

The honing of specific lessons in order to make them more effective is the motif that seemed to run through the efforts of the individual teachers. Observations of lesson study sessions indicate that teachers devote considerable attention to (a) clearly articulating the specific intellectual goal of the lesson (it is noteworthy that the goal is often phrased as an abstract goal of achieving understanding of a concept rather than the mastery of a skill or technique); (b) selecting a problem or an investigation that will help students to arrive at an understanding of that goal; (c) seeking the most effective way of posing the problem to the class; (d) anticipating student responses, including alternative approaches as well as misconceptions; and (e) encouraging or eliciting generalizations.

Although these features are at the forefront in the lesson study sessions, one question that arose was to what extent does this type of thinking and reflection pervade the day-to-day activity of teachers? Necessarily, the role most often played would be that of an observer rather than a presenter, especially when the teacher is a novice, gaining experience. Presenters may be more experienced or reputed teachers. Thus, an important function

served by lesson study sessions seems to be to provide each teacher with an opportunity to experience and absorb the ingredients of a successful model as an observer but with the privilege of being an active participant as a friendly critic. Of course, soon a time comes for every teacher when that teacher needs to play the role of a presenter. By this time, however, the tension of being on the spot is dissipated by the previous experiences, in which they have observed that there is an impersonal protocol of criticism directed more at the content of the lesson (what works and what does not) or suggestions about how one might more effectively introduce a specific detail of the lesson, rather than at the inadequacies of the teacher.

Thus, lesson study sessions seem to provide a model for emulation rather than an active day-to-day operating procedure. Nevertheless, because the model is highly valued and the lessons produced and perfected by the model can be used on a national basis, it exerts a powerful exemplary force. The idea of continuous improvement through reflection and analysis of specific pedagogic decisions is implicit in the model, and the general agreement seems to be that it is a tried-and-tested operational model worthy of adoption on a routine basis.

What do teachers use?

RESPONSE

At the elementary level, the standard curricular materials, containing specific lessons, together with the detailed teachers' guides seem to provide the foundation on which classroom lessons rest. For the novice teacher they provide a safe, secure, and acceptably effective map that can be followed while that teacher is acquiring and honing professional skills. For the more experienced or enterprising teacher, they provide a template from which that teacher may depart by providing innovative variations of approach and treatment, while maintaining the conceptual goals of the lessons.

A striking feature of the lesson study sessions that we observed was the use of the blackboard as a vehicle for recording the ideas generated by students, thereby acting as an archive of the ideas under discussion in class, rather than as a written repository of the ideas sought to be conveyed by the teacher.

It was not clear what role manipulatives played in lessons at the elementary level. There was a short, oblique discussion of this at one point. The impression one gets is that they play a peripheral role, subject to the mathematical goal of the lesson.

Who works with teachers?

RESPONSE

Our Japanese colleagues said that during the preservice years interactions between faculty and students are formal for the most part. However, there seems to be some mechanism by which the student becomes aware quite early in the pre-service years that continuous improvement is the professional ideal, and that lesson study (or other similar reflective activity) is a powerful and effective tool for continuous improvement. The importance of the central role played by this cultural agreement about professional norms cannot be overestimated. Japanese colleagues made statements such as, "The importance of continuous improvement though lesson study is taken for granted in Japan," "One can always improve by studying one's own lessons with the help of colleagues", "How can you be a functioning teacher if you do not care to improve?," and "Even excellent teachers can always improve. One must continually seek to improve. Teaching is 80 percent confidence and 20 percent doubt."

During the initiation/mentoring phase, we were told that experienced teachers work with new entrants to the profession. This seems to have been a common practice of the profession, now adopted as official policy by the Ministry of Education since 1998.

During this novitiate phase as well as later in the teacher's career, teachers seem to have some opportunities to get advice directly or indirectly from disciplinary experts such as mathematicians or mathematics educators in higher educational institutions. In schools attached to university departments charged with the preparation of teachers, this happens quite regularly as a part of the ongoing implementation of lesson study in the research program of the university. In other schools it seems to happen less systematically. When it does happen, it would probably be in the context of lesson study events at the ward or prefectural level. On the whole, the development of deep conceptual understanding of the concepts that teachers teach seems to come from this continuing process of careful lesson planning and implementation, followed by reflection about its effectiveness, informed by constant analysis of student ideas. Few research mathematicians seem to be involved in school mathematics education.

CONCLUSIONS

The process of lesson study seems to be a key ingredient in the professional development of Japanese teachers, especially at the elementary and middle school levels. However, the precise manner in which this process facilitates the acquisition of disciplinary as well as pedagogical content knowledge by teachers is subtler than one might assume at first sight. Lesson study sessions are not numerous enough to act as vehicles through which teachers can acquire deep content knowledge of the great many mathematical topics they need to teach—teachers must necessarily seek other ways in which this knowledge may be acquired. Likewise, lesson study sessions are not frequent enough to ensure that teachers will absorb their methodology through force of habit. However, lesson study sessions serve as exemplary models for several aspects of practice. The thoroughness of preparation and presentation, the stress laid on analysis and reflection, and above all the single-minded focus on the effectiveness of the lesson (rather than the effectiveness of the teacher) are ideals that the teacher is encouraged to emulate in daily classroom practice. By the avowed acceptance of lesson study as a long-term professional development tool, the individual teacher affirms a belief in the value of these practices and a commitment to put them into practice. The opportunity to engage in lesson study sessions on a regular basis has a practical as well as symbolic value. A lesson study session forces the participating teacher to hone her or his skills to an edge sharp enough to withstand critical evaluation by colleagues and to continue to employ those skills in daily practice. On the other hand, due to the high status collectively accorded by the profession to the process of lesson study, the individual teacher can justly regard his or her successful participation in it as evidence of professional growth and competence. This periodic affirmation of exemplary professional values and practices greatly reinforces the teacher's image of himself or herself as a professional engaged in a process of continual improvement. Thus, in a roundabout way, the process of lesson study seems to have the effect of enabling the majority of teachers to arrive at and sustain a view of themselves as members of a professional community engaged in continual improvement. On-the-job acquisition of deep understanding of content and pedagogy depends on this attitude more than any other single factor. In the final analysis, this effect may be as valuable as any other effect of the process of lesson study.

RESEARCH ISSUES

In the short time span of the workshop, it was difficult to get an idea of the extent to which individual teachers implement on a day-to-day basis the practices exemplified in the lesson study sessions. A study of how lesson study effects day to day practice would be useful.

Also in discussions the Japanese indicated that teachers were generally expected to have a "good understanding" of the mathematics they are expected to teach. An examination of various certification requirements could give us an idea of the formal demands that are made on teachers in the way of technical content knowledge. How do teachers acquire the deeper conceptual understanding (involving major ideas and their interconnections) as well as the pedagogical content knowledge (such as effective strategies for communicating those ideas, awareness of common misconceptions and strategies of dealing with them, etc.)? Is it on the job, through a commitment to the ideal of continuous improvement through reflection and analysis, as described above?

Small Group Discussion Report: Group V

Group Members
Angela Andrews***, Deborah Ball, Toshiakira Fujii, Henry Kepner, Jr., Jean Krusi,
Marilyn Mays***, Keiichi Nishimura, Yutaka Sakai, Kayo Satou*, Mark Saul***,
Keiichi Shigematsu, Yoshinori Shimizu, Lucy West, Susan Wood*

*Report Coordinator; ** Translator; ***U.S. ICME Travel Group

The group asked and answered the questions listed below. Much of the discussion centered around the details of Japanese lesson study.

The group discussed the three models of records of practice presented in the workshop: video (Ball), written cases (Smith), and Japanese lesson study as seen through the video of a fourth-grade lesson and study group discussion and observation of a sixth-grade lesson and study group discussion.

How do teachers use mathematics together with other kinds of knowledge and skill in order to connect students with mathematics?

How do skilled teachers learn about and make use of their students' knowledge and capabilities to help them learn mathematics?

RESPONSES

Both questions were addressed through the discussion of the record of practice featured during the workshop.

Both video and written cases provide records of practice for long-term use. Video records of practice can record the learning of the same student over time. In one viewing, a spectator can see lessons from different parts of the year. The author of a written case study may affect how useful it is. Japanese colleagues found video an easier medium to work with than the case study. To them video is a familiar medium and easily allows forming of images. If a teacher poses a question and does not get any of the expected answers, live observation might provide insight into why the expected answers did not occur. In Japan, the lesson plan, student responses, and teacher's reflections form a sort of "case study," although not in written form.

Overview of Japanese Lessons

In the lesson write-up, like a script for a play, the left column gives student activities, the right side gives "cautious points" and "evaluation points." Usually, a middle column in the plan contains expected student responses.

The evaluation of the lesson must be consistent with the lesson's aim. Standards for evaluation are in terms of students'

- willingness, intent, and attitude toward learning;
- mathematical thinking displayed;
- representing and processing—originally called skills—of content; and
- understanding.

Each lesson is like a mountain, with a slow climb to the peak. Each lesson has a rhythm. Teacher personal satisfaction is not enough. To help students gain mathematical satisfaction, the teacher must sum up the mathematical objective of the lesson in which the teacher moves from naïve student solutions to those that are more sophisticated. Japanese teachers like whole group discussion, not the one-to-one discussion between student and teacher. Students often explain other students' ideas.

The parts of the lesson are introduction, development, and summary. Lessons must be set in a clear context. The use of the board is carefully planned and makes a summary of the whole lesson. Students can see what was learned, even if they do not completely understand.

Students' Notes

Students' notes and errors are valued by teachers. Japanese students are taught to take notes in first grade. They copy the task and conclusion and record their own work in the middle. They are encouraged to write their own ideas. The levels of student note taking are

- an impression —"it was fun";
- why I am interested in the lesson—the math content —"it was about x";
- classmates' ideas; compare my ideas and friends' ideas —see myself objectively; the student is the owner of an idea; and

- self-reflection —generalize the problem beyond the content of the lesson.

Lesson Study and Teachers' Mathematical Knowledge

In Japan, teachers' mathematical knowledge is important in enabling teachers to anticipate student responses which in turn strengthen that knowledge. Teachers also need mathematical knowledge to build on unanticipated responses and be ready to adapt to the students' responses and misunderstandings. Teachers select student examples that are close to their goal, then build on them to help accomplish the purpose of the lesson. Teachers must be alert to students' ideas that extend the lesson or for opportunities to probe for deeper understanding of the content. Working on and revising the teaching plan is one way to build mathematical knowledge. The teacher must think mathematically while creating the plan. Much attention is given in lesson design to the specifics of the lesson, even to details such as using the number 12 instead of 11. Emphasis is placed on finding a suitable task, with the structure of the task being very important. Teachers must stay focused on the goal of the lesson.

What is the nature of the postlesson discussion?

RESPONSE

The postlesson discussion focuses on

- the gap between the plan and the implemented lesson; and
- the gap between lesson study and the general sense of mathematics education.

There can be confusion between these two aspects.

Teachers of the same grade cooperate—they are given the opportunity to look at existing lesson study plans and read related books. Japanese teachers have very different backgrounds, much the same as U.S. teachers.

Lesson study focuses on the "whys" of lesson design. In lesson study, the conversation immediately following the lesson is crucial to understanding and improving the lesson. The Japanese believe that observing the class (seeing with your own eyes) is best for staff development.

What is the role of the advisor in lesson study?

RESPONSE

The advisor's role in lesson study is to identify key points to improve the lesson and teaching, to identify the most valuable things mathematically and pedagogically even in a disastrous lesson. In lesson study, the quick feedback from and to the teacher is very powerful. Advisors can ask "Why did you write in that place on the blackboard?" A brief record of the entire lesson should be on the black-board. The teacher evaluates the advisor and does not invite an advisor back if the comments are not deep.

How are teachers taught to be good observers during lesson study?

RESPONSE

Observation skills for live observation are very important. Teachers need to know how to observe well. When the teachers are students and first visit classes, they cannot even take notes—they do not know what to look at. They are taught to look at the relationship between the class purpose for that day and what happens in the class. They study one student, sometimes standing beside them to observe all they do, to determine whether the student's actions reflect the purpose of the lesson. Observation is from the teacher's side of the classroom, not the back of the classroom, in order to view the students' faces. Observers consider what the teacher asks, discriminating one question from another, and discerning the teacher's moves. It is difficult to teach teachers to observe well. A good advisor is needed.

Appendixes

Appendix A: Workshop Agenda

Appendix B: Participant List

Appendix C: Steering Committee Biographical Information

Appendix D: A Plan for the Lesson on Division by a Two-Digit Number

Appendix E: A Demonstration Lesson: Function Thinking at Sixth Grade

Appendix F: A Study Lesson: Large Numbers at Fourth Grade

Appendix G: Records of Instruction: Reasoning About Three Coins at Third Grade

Appendix H: Transcript of Excerpts from Small Group Discussions

Appendix I: A Written Case: Pattern Trains at Sixth Grade

Appendix J: To Become a Mathematics Teacher

Appendix K: Glossary

Appendix L: Workshop Reading List

Appendix M: References

Appendix A:
Workshop Agenda

The Study of Teaching Practice as a Medium for Professional Development
U.S. - Japan Teacher Preparation Workshop
Makuhari, Japan
August 6-8, 2000

Sunday, August 6

4:00-5:00 p.m.   **Registration and Informal Reception**

5:00-5:15 p.m.   **Welcome and Overview**
    Hiroshi Fujita, Tokai University
    Hyman Bass, University of Michigan
    Haruo Ishigaki, Waseda University

5:15-7:15 p.m.   **Background Context for Teacher Preparation in the United States and in Japan**
    Moderator: *Daniel Goroff, Harvard University*

    Elementary Mathematics Education in the United States
    Deborah Schifter, Education Development Center

    Secondary Mathematics Education in the United States
    Zalman P. Usiskin, University of Chicago

    A Study of Teacher Change Through Inservice Mathematics Education Programs in Graduate School
    Keiichi Shigematsu, Nara University of Education
    Keiko Hino, Nara University of Education

Recurrent Education in Japan
Mamoru Takezawa, Kanagawa Prefectural Education Center
Toru Handa, Waseda University Honjo Senior High School

7:15-8:30 p.m. **Reception**
Presider: *Hyman Bass, University of Michigan*
Remarks: *Lee V. Stiff, North Carolina State University*
Yoshishige Sugiyama, Waseda University

Monday, August 7
Lesson Study as Professional Development

9:00-10:00 a.m. **Introduction to the Focus of the workshop**
Presider: *Toshiakira Fujii, Tokyo Gakugei University*

Setting the Stage
- What can be learned from using practice as a means of developing teachers' knowledge of mathematical content and how to teach that mathematics?
- What questions should frame our thinking?

Deborah Loewenberg Ball, University of Michigan

What Is Lesson Study?
- How does lesson study work and what is its role in developing teachers' content knowledge and understanding of how to teach?

Yoshinori Shimizu, Tokyo Gakugei University

10:00-11:00 a.m. **Consideration of Lesson Study**
Framing Lesson Study for U.S. Participants
Makoto Yoshida, Columbia University-Teachers College

Japanese Study Group Fourth-Grade Lesson and Rationale
Hiroshi Nakano, Tokyo Gakugei University Elementary School

11:00-11:15 a.m. **Break**

11:15 a.m.- **Fourth-Grade Lesson Observation**
12:30 p.m. **Video of Fourth-Grade Lesson on Large Numbers**

12:30-1:30 p.m. **Lunch**

| 1:30-2:30 p.m. | **Group Discussion of Fourth-Grade Lesson** |
| | Facilitator: *Akihiko Takahashi, University of Illinois at Urbana Champaign* |

- What was the role of lesson study in enabling the teachers to learn how to teach the lesson?
- What observations about the lesson seem important?
- What potential adjustments might be made in the design of the lesson?

| 2:30-3:15 p.m. | **Video of Study Group Discussion of Sixth-Grade Lesson** |

| 3:15-3:30 p.m. | **Break** |

| 3:30-4:30 p.m. | **Small Group Discussion: Objectives and Effectiveness of Lesson Study Groups as a Resource for Professional Development** |

- What are the advantages of using lesson study and lesson study groups as a resource for professional development for teachers?
- What are the limitations?
- Does this approach raise any research issues that should be considered?
- How does this approach address issues of teacher content knowledge?
- How does this process create effective teachers in relation to content knowledge, pedagogy, and the role for research in continuing the discussion?

| 4:30-5:30 p.m. | **Reflections on the Two Lessons: Fourth and Sixth Grade** |

- How do the two lessons compare?
- What are the differences and the similarities?
- What was the mathematical content and how did the lessons develop student understanding?

Moderator: *Keiichi Shigematsu, Nara University of Education*
Panelists: *Jacqueline Goodloe, Burrville Elementary School*
Jerry Becker, Southern Illinois University
Ichiei Hirabayashi, Horoshima University
Keiichi Shigematsu, Nara University of Education

| 5:30 p.m. | **Homework** |

Tuesday, August 8
Professional Development Through the Use of Records of Practice

9:00-10:30 a.m.   **Professional Development Through Records of Instruction**
- How do observations of what teachers do in the act of teaching enable teachers to learn mathematics?
- How do such observations enable teachers to learn how to teach the mathematics they need to teach?

Presider: *Zalman P. Usiskin, University of Chicago*
Deborah Loewenberg Ball, University of Michigan
Hyman Bass, University of Michigan

10:30-10:45 a.m.   **Break**

10:45 a.m.-
12:00 p.m.   **Professional Development Through Written Cases**
- How can cases designed to investigate teaching and learning be a site for learning about teaching?
- What does it mean for teachers to use the study of others' practice to learn mathematics and about teaching mathematics?

Presider: *Judith Mumme, Program Director, Mathematics Renaissance*
Margaret Smith, University of Pittsburgh

12:00-1:00 p.m.   **Lunch**

1:00-2:00 p.m.   **Small Group Discussion: Professional Development Through Records of Practice**
- What are the advantages and disadvantages of each approach to delivering professional development?

2:00-3:00 p.m.   **Panel: Mathematical Knowledge of Teachers**
- What are the mathematical resources that teachers need to teach well?
- How can teachers learn the mathematics they need to teach well?
Moderator: *Deborah Loewenberg Ball, University of Michigan*
Panelists: *Deborah Schifter, Education Development Center*
Haruo Ishigaki, Waseda University
Miho Ueno, Tokyo Gakugei University Senior High School Oizumi Campus
Zalman P. Usiskin, University of Chicago

3:00-4:00 p.m.   **Reflections on Relation to Professional Development Small Group Discussion**
- Based on the workshop and on the nature of professional development, what offers promise and why?
- What does not offer promise and why not?
- What areas call for further research and what are possible strategies to use in framing that research?

4:00- 4:30 p.m.   **Conclusions**
Deborah Loewenberg Ball, University of Michigan
Toshiakira Fujii, Tokyo Gakugei University

Closing Remarks
Hyman Bass, University of Michigan
Haruo Ishigaki, Waseda University

The U.S.- Japan Teacher Preparation Workshop is sponsored by the National Science Foundation, The Spencer Foundation, and the MCI WorldCom Foundation.

Appendix B: Participant List

Deborah Loewenberg Ball
Professor
University of Michigan
Ann Arbor, Michigan

Hyman Bass
Professor
University of Michigan
Ann Arbor, Michigan

Susan Beal
Professor
St. Xavier University
Chicago, Illinois

Jerry Becker
Professor
Southern Illinois Universtiy
Carbondale, Illinois

Gail Burrill
Director
Mathematical Sciences Education Board
Washington, DC

Jack Burrill
Outreach Specialist
University of Wisconsin at Madison
Madison, Wisconsin

Cindy Connell
First-Grade Teacher
Ben Franklin Elementary
Spartanburg, South Carolina

Toshiakira Fujii
Professor
Tokyo Gakugei University
Tokyo, Japan

Hiroshi Fujita
Professor
Tokai University
Tokyo, Japan

Ramesh Gangolli
Professor
University of Washington
Seattle, Washington

Alice Gill
Associate Director
American Federation of Teachers
Washington, DC

Daniel Goroff
Professor
Harvard University
Cambridge, Massachusetts

Toru Handa
Mathematics Teacher
Waseda University
Honjo Senior High School
Honjo, Japan

Keiko Hino
Associate Professor
Nara University of Education
Nara, Japan

Ichiei Hirabayashi
Professor Emeritus
Hiroshima University
Hatsukaichi, Japan

Tadayuki Ishida
Mathematics Teacher
Keio University Secondary School
Hachioji, Japan

Haruo Ishigaki
Professor
Waseda University
Tokyo, Japan

Tsuyoshi Kamaike
Videographer
Chigasaki, Japan

Henry Kepner, Jr.
Professor
University of Wisconsin-Milwaukee
Milwaukee, Wisconsin

Jean Krusi
Mathematics Teacher
Ames Middle School
Ames, Iowa

Yoshihiro Kubo
Mathematics Teacher
Kyoritu Girls Junior High School
Kunitachi, Japan

Kouichi Kumagai
Associate Professor
Joetsu University of Education
Joetsu, Japan

Shunji Kurosawa
Elementary Teacher
Tokyo Gakugei University
Setagaya Elementary School
Tokyo, Japan

Carole Lacampagne
Mathematics Consultant
RAND
Arlington, Virginia

Carol Malloy
Professor
University of North Carolina-
    Chapel Hill
Chapel Hill, North Carolina

Michelle Manes
Project Director
Education Development Center
Newton, Massachusetts

Shinichiro Matsumoto
Mathematics Teacher
Tokyo Gakugei University
Oizumi Junior High School
Moriya, Japan

Tatsuo Morozumi
Lecturer
Shizuoka University
Shizuoka, Japan

Judith Mumme
Project Director
Videocases for Mathematics
    Professional Development
Math Renaissance
Camarillo, California

Takashi Nakamura
Associate Professor
University of Yamanashi
Yamanashi, Japan

Hiroshi Nakano
Elementary Teacher
Tokyo Gakugei University
Setagaya Elementary School
Tokyo, Japan

Keiichi Nishimura
Mathematics Teacher
Musasigaoka Senior High School
Asaka, Japan

Nobuhiko Nohda
Professor
University of Tsukuba
Institute of Education
Tsukuba City, Japan

Yutaka Sakai
Professor
Tokyo Gakugei University
Tokyo, Japan

Kayo Satou
Mathematics Teacher
Tokyo Gakugei University
Setagaya Elementary School
Tokyo, Japan

Toshio Sawada
Professor
Science University of Tokyo
Tokyo, Japan

Deborah Schifter
Mathematics Educator
Education Development Center
Newton, Massachusetts

Nanette Seago
Video Study Director
Math Renaissance
Camarillo, California

Yasuhiro Sekiguchi
Associate Professor
Yamaguchi University
Yamaguchi, Japan

Keiichi Shigematsu
Professor
Nara University of Education
Nara, Japan

Yoshinori Shimizu
Associate Professor
Tokyo Gakugei University
Koganei, Tokyo

Kiyoaki Shoda
Mathematics Educator
Tokyo Educational Institute
Tokyo, Japan

Margaret Smith
Assisstant Professor
University of Pittsburgh
Pittsburgh, Pennsylvania

Izumi Soga
Elementary Teacher
Nakamura Elementary School
Higashiyamato, Japan

Yoshishige Sugiyama
Professor
Waseda University
Tokyo, Japan

Kara Suzuka
Graduate Student
Michigan State University
East Lansing, Michigan

Shinichi Suzuki
Professor
Waseda University
Tokyo, Japan

Akihiko Takahashi
Mathematics Researcher
University of Illinois at Urbana-Champaign
Urbana, Illinois

Mamoru Takezawa
Mathematics Educator
Kanagawa Prefectural Education Center
Nakagun, Japan

Denisse Thompson
Associate Professor
University of South Florida
Tampa, Florida

Hiroko Uchino
Mathematics Educator
Turuda Junior High School
Satsuma, Japan

Miho Ueno
Mathematics Teacher
Tokyo Gakugei University
Senior High School Oizumi Campus
Tokyo, Japan

Zalman P. Usiskin
Professor
University of Chicago
Chicago, Illinois

Tad Watanabe
Associate Professor
Towson University
Towson, Maryland

Lucy West
Mathematics Teacher
School Community District 2
New York, New York

Tamae Wong
Senior Project Officer
U.S. National Commission on
 Mathematics Instruction
Washington, DC

Susan Wood
Professor
J. Sargeant Reynolds Community College
Richmond, Virginia

Hajime Yamashita
Professor
Waseda University
Graduate School of Education
 Honjo Senior High School
Tokyo, Japan

Makoto Yoshida
Senior Researcher
Columbia University Teachers College
New York, New York

POST-ICME-9 SEMINAR TRAVEL GRANT AWARDEES PARTICIPANT LIST

Angela Andrews
Mathematics Teacher
Scott School
Naperville, Illinois

Phyllis Caruth
Mathematics Teacher
Little Rock Central High School
Little Rock, Arizona

Frances Curcio
Professor
Queens College, CUNY
Staten Island, New York

Shelley Ferguson
Mathematics Specialist
San Diego City Schools
San Diego, California

Jacqueline Goodloe
Elementary School Teacher
Burrville Elementary School
Washington, DC

Jackie Hurd
Elementary School Teacher
Highlands Elementary School
Pacifica, California

Beth Lazerick
Mathematics Teacher
St. Andrews School
Boca Raton, Florida

Marilyn Mays
Professor
North Lake College
Irving, Texas

Carol Midgett
Elementary Teacher
University of North Carolina at
    Wilmington
Wilmington, North Carolina

Mark Saul
Mathematics Teacher
Bronxville Public Schools
Bronxville, New York

Lee V. Stiff
Professor
North Carolina State University
Raleigh, North Carolina

Daniel Teague
Mathematics Teacher
North Carolina School of
Science and Mathematics
Durham, North Carolina

Beverly Williams
Web Administrator
National Council of Teachers
    of Mathematics
Reston, Virginia

SUPPORT STAFF

Saitou Harumichi
Graduate Student
Tokyo Gakugei University
Tokyo, Japan

Yoshimichi Kanemoto
Graduate Student
Saitama University
Urawa, Japan

Eri Matsuda
Graduate Student
Tokyo Gakugei University
Tokyo, Japan

Tatsuhiko Seino
Graduate Student
Tokyo Gakugei University
Tokyo, Japan

Kaori Tabeta
Graduate Student
Tokyo Gakugei University
Tokyo, Japan

Yoshihisa Tanaka
Graduate Student
Tokyo Gakugei University
Tokyo, Japan

Appendix C:
Steering Committee
Biographical Information

Deborah Loewenberg Ball is a professor of educational studies at the University of Michigan and currently serves on the Mathematical Sciences Education Board (MSEB), was a member of the Commission on Behavioral and Social Sciences and Education, and also the Glenn Commission. Her work as a researcher and teacher educator draws directly and indirectly on her long experience as an elementary classroom teacher. With elementary school mathematics as the main context for the work, Ball studies the practice of teaching and the processes of learning to teach. Her work also examines efforts to improve teaching through policy, reform initiatives, and teacher education. Ball's publications include articles on teacher learning and teacher education, the role of subject matter knowledge in teaching and learning to teach, endemic challenges of teaching; and the relations of policy and practice in instructional reform. Ball was on the writing team for the National Council of Teachers of Mathematics (NCTM) *Professional Teaching Standards*.

Hyman Bass is the Roger Lyndon collegiate professor of mathematics and professor of mathematics education at the

University of Michigan. His mathematical research publications cover broad areas of algebra, with connections to geometry, topology and number theory. Bass is a member of the National Academy of Sciences and the American Academy of Arts and Sciences. Bass is president-elect of the American Mathematical Society, past chair of the MSEB at the National Research Council, and the Committee on Education of the American Mathematical Society, and he is President of the International Commission on Mathematics Instruction. During the past four years, he has been collaborating with Deborah Ball and her research group at the University of Michigan on the mathematical knowledge and resources entailed in the teaching of mathematics at the elementary level. In all of this work, a major challenge has been to build bridges between diverse professional communities and stakeholders involved in mathematics education, both here and abroad.

Jerry Becker is a professor of mathematics education at Southern Illinois University-Carbondale. He received his Bachelor's and Master's degrees in mathematics from the University of Minnesota (1959) and the University of

Notre Dame (1961), respectively, and his Ph.D. degree in mathematics education from Stanford University (1967) with Ed Begle, Director of the School Mathematics Study Group. He has taught mathematics at both the elementary and secondary levels. His interests include improving practices in teacher education, international mathematics education, cross-cultural research on problem solving, and the cognitive development of learners in mathematics. He has been president of the School Science and Mathematics Association and has served two terms on the U.S. National Commission on Mathematics Instruction. He is a member of the National Mathematics Advisory Committee for the Eisenhower National Clearinghouse and recently completed a term on the Board of Directors of the NCTM. He served a three-year term as a member of the Editorial Board of the *Journal for Research in Mathematics Education.* He is co-author of "Elementary School Practices" in the *International Handbook on Mathematics Education* (1997) published by Kluwer Academic Publishers and co-edited, with professor Shigeru Shimada, the translation to English of *The Open-Ended Approach - A New Approach to Teaching Mathematics* published by the NCTM (1997). He is co-author of "The Politics of California School Mathematics: The Anti-Reform of 1997-99" in the *Phi Delta Kappan* (March 2000) and is co-editor with professors Toshio Sawada and Yoshio Takeuchi of *From Problem to Problem - Developmental Treatment of Problems* that has been translated into English for publication.

Frances Curcio is a professor of mathematics education in the School of Education, Department of Teaching and Learning, at New York University (NYU). She works closely on campus and in the schools with preservice and in-service elementary and secondary mathematics teachers. Her research interests are in graph comprehension, language and communication in mathematics, and mathematical problem solving. She is a co-principal evaluator for a five-year National Science Foundation-funded professional development project in Community School District Two, New York City. She is the conference chair for the national conference, Diversity, Equity, and Standards: An Urban Agenda in Mathematics Education, to be co-sponsored by NYU and the NCTM, in March 2000. She is the project director for the ICME-9 Travel Grant Program and the general editor for the 1999-2001 Yearbooks of the NCTM. Professor Curcio served as a member of the Board of Directors of the NCTM from 1990 to 1993, and was a member of the United States National Commission on Mathematics Instruction from 1994 to 1997. Since 1985, professor Curcio has conducted study tours and led mathematics education delegations to China, Russia, Spain, and eight of the fifteen former Soviet republics. She led a delegation to South Africa in November 2000.

Toshiakira Fujii is currently professor of mathematics education at Tokyo Gakugei University. He received a Master of Arts Degree in Mathematical Education in 1985 from Tsukuba University, and one in 1981 from Tokyo Gakugei University and a Bachelor of Arts Degree in Mathematics in 1974 from Tokyo Gakugei University. Professor Fujii's career began with the position of elementary school teacher in Tokyo between April 1977 and March 1979. He then moved into the position of research associate in education at Tsukuba University between April 1986 and March 1988. From April 1988 to

October 1989, Professor Fujii was Lecturer of Mathematics Education at Yamanashi University, and from October 1989 to March 1997, he held the position of associate professor of mathematics education at Yamanashi University. This tenure began in April 1997 at Yamanashi University and concluded in March 1999, only to be resumed in April 1999 at Tokyo Gakugei University where he continues. Professor Fujii has written more than 70 articles on understanding, teaching and learning mathematics, and problem solving in different journals such as *Arithmetic Education* (Journal of Japan Society of Mathematical Education) and *Tsukuba Journal of Educational Study in Mathematics*.

Hiroshi Fujita is currently professor emeritus at the University of Tokyo. Prior to his retirement from the University of Tokyo in March 1989, Dr. Fujita served as assistant in the Department of Physics on the Faculty of Science in 1956. Dr. Fujita then served as Lecturer in the Department of Applied Physics on the Faculty of Engineering between 1960 and 1964, and as an associate professor between 1964 and 1967. From April 1966 until his retirement in March 1989, Dr. Fujita served as a professor in the Department of Mathematics on the Faculty of Science at the University of Tokyo. Other positions held were professor in RIMS, Kyoto University, 1971 to 1988; University Senator, 1987; Dean of Faculty of Science, April 1988 to March 1989, and professor in the Department of Mathematics at Meiji University, March 1989 to March 1999. Since April 1999, Dr. Fujita served as professor at the Research Institute of Educational Developments at Tokai University, and he served as a professor at the University of Air from April 1989 to present. Dr. Fujita's public and academic

services include President of Mathematical Society of Japan, 1982 to 1984; President of Japan Society of Industrial and Applied Mathematics, 1994 to 1995; Advisor of the Japanese Society of Mathematics Education, 1987 to present; Advisor of the Japanese Society of Science Education, 1996 to present. With respect to his affiliation with the International Commission on Mathematical Instruction (ICMI), Dr. Fujita has been a member of the Executive Committee from 1986 to 1990 and was the National Representative of Japan to ICMI from 1984 to 1994. He has also served as Chairman of the International Program Committee of ICME-9 and as President of the National Organizing Committee of ICME-9 since 1996 to present. Professor Fujita's overseas visiting positions include Stanford University, Research Associate and Lecturer, September 1962 to March 1964; Stanford University Visiting Professor, June 1967 to August 1967; New York University, Courant Institute of Mathematical Sciences, Visiting Member, September 1967 to August 1968, and Wisconsin University, Visiting Professor, September 1968. Dr. Fujita is also associated with the following publications either as author or co-author: "School Mathematics in the 1990's, ICMI Study Series;" 1986: "The Present State and Current Problems of Mathematics Education at the Senior Secondary Level in Japan" (Plenary Lecture); "The Reform of Mathematics Education at the Upper Secondary School (USS) Level in Japan". "Highlights and Shadows of Current Japanese National Curriculum of Mathematics for Secondary Schools"; "An Interim Announcement of ICME-9".

Jacqueline Goodloe is the elementary mathematics resource teacher at Burrville Elementary School in Washington, D.C. She spent the 1998-1999 school year as the National Council of Teachers of Mathematics Teacher in Residence, where she served as a teacher resource to the headquarters staff. During that year she also assisted with the coordination of the first Mathematics Institute for elementary teachers at The Carnegie Institution of Washington, D.C. She has taught in the D.C. Public Schools for 26 years and received the 1991 Presidential Award for Excellence in Science and Mathematics Teaching. She is a member of the D.C. Council of Teachers of Mathematics, the Benjamin Banneker Association, and the NCTM Committee for the Comprehensive Mathematics Education of Every Child. She has served on advisory boards with the PBS MathLine series, "Teaching Children Mathematics" editorial panel, and most recently MathMastery.com, a mathematics tutorial website.

Daniel Goroff is professor of the practice of mathematics at Harvard University and Associate Director of the Derek Bok Center for Teaching and Learning. He earned his Master of Arts summa cum laude at Harvard, Master in Philosophy in Economics as a Churchill Scholar at Cambridge University, and a Ph.D. in Mathematics as a Danforth Fellow at Princeton University. Winner of a Phi Beta Kappa Teaching Prize in 1988, Goroff has served on the Board of the American Association for Higher Education and as Director of the Joint Policy Board for Mathematics. He worked for the National Research Council during 1996-1997 and for the President's Science Advisor at the White House during 1997-1998. In 1998, he was named one of the Decade's Young Leaders in Academia by "Change: The Magazine of Higher Education."

Keiko Hino is an associate professor of mathematics education at the Nara University of Education, in Takabatake-cho, Naro, Japan. In addition, Dr. Hino is a member of the Production Staff of the Japan Society of Mathematical Education, the Japan Society of Mathematical Education, the Japan Society for Science Education, the National Council of Teachers of Mathematics, and the American Educational Research Association

Haruo Ishigaki is a professor of education and director of the Institute for Advanced Studies in Education at Waseda University. He holds a Master of Science Degree. Professor Ishigaki has served as Chairman of the Editorial Committee of Mathematics Education and Arithmetic Education for the *Journal of Japan Society of Mathematical Education* between 1997 and 1999, and from 1997 until summer 1999, Professor Ishigaki has been a member of Natural Sciences, Science Council of Japan. He has been involved in a recurrent program of the institute for teachers, which holds summer courses for technology and its application to education since 1995. In addition, Professor Ishigaki has served as a member of the Committee for Cooperative Research of Natural Sciences, Science Council of Japan since 1997.

Zalman P. Usiskin is professor of education at the University of Chicago, where he has been a faculty member since 1969. He is interested in all aspects of mathematics education, with particular emphasis on matters related to curriculum, instruction, and testing; international mathematics education; the history of mathematics education; and educational policy. He is the author or co-author of

14 books and over 100 articles on mathematics and mathematics education. From 1964 to 1984 he taught mathematics in nine secondary schools in Illinois, Michigan, and Massachusetts. He has been directly involved with the work of the grades 7–12 component of the University of Chicago School Mathematics Project (UCSMP) since its inception in 1983, and since 1987 he has been overall director of UCSMP. He was a member of the advisory board to the Children's Television Workshop program Square One TV from 1984 to 1992, the Mathematical Sciences Education Board of the National Research Council from 1988 to 1991, and the Board of Directors of NCTM from 1995 to 1998. He is currently a member of the steering and test development committees for mathematics of the National Assessment of Educational Progress and chair of the United States National Commission on Mathematics Instruction. Among many awards, he received the Max Beberman Award for his work in curriculum from the Illinois Council of Teachers of Mathematics in 1981, the first Distinguished Service Award from the Metropolitan Mathematics Club of Chicago in 1984, the Glenn Gilbert National Leadership Award from the National Council of Supervisors of Mathematics in 1994, and a Lifetime Achievement Award from NCTM in 2001.

Hajime Yamashita is a professor of education at Waseda University and the Principal of Honjyo Senior High School at Waseda University. Professor Yamashita received a Bachelor of Science Degree in Mathematics (Complex Analysis) from Waseda University in 1962 and also holds a Master of Science Degree. He has been a teacher at the Senior High School of Waseda University since 1962. He was also a Lecturer in the School of Politics and Economics at Waseda University since 1972. In addition, Professor Yamashita has lectured in the School of Politics and Economics at Waseda since 1985 and in the Graduate School of Education since 1998. Finally, professor Yamashita has been the principal of Honjo Senior School, Waseda University since 1999.

Appendix D:
A Plan for the Lesson on
Division by a Two-Digit Number

1. Topic of the lesson: division by two-digit numbers.
   (The first lesson out of nine lessons in the unit "Division".)
2. A plan for the entire unit (nine lessons)
   (1) Regularities of divisions (two lessons)
      - Methods to find the answer to expressions like "128 ÷ 16" (this lesson).
      - Divisions by "tens" and by "hundreds."
   (2) Division by a two-digit number (six lessons).
      - Dividing by a two-digit number.
      - How to check the results of divisions.
      - Division by a two-digit number that needs an adjustment of a supposed quotient.
      - Standard algorithm for "(three-digit) ÷ (two-digit)."
   (3) Summing up the unit (assessment) (two lessons).
3. Objectives of the lesson
      - Finding the methods to get the answer to the division "128 ÷ 16" by students themselves.
      - Understanding the regularities of divisions such as, "The answer remains the same when we divide both the divisor and dividend by the same number" or "By making a divisor half, the answer becomes double."
4. Development of the lesson

	Main Learning Activities	Anticipated Students' Responses	Remarks on Teaching

Posing today's problem	• presenting a problem;
	
	"We are going to plant 128 bulbs of tulips into 16 planters. The same number of bulbs are to be planted in each planter. How many bulbs will be planted in each planter?"
		• drawing a figure of the problem situation
		
		• the expression for getting the answer is "128 ÷ 16"
		
		• using a number line
			• talk about the previous class activity of planting bulbs on the school ground
			• show a picture and model to the students
			• If needed, ask questions to those students who could not understand the problem well;
			  • what is the unknown?
			  • can you draw a figure?
			  • what if we change the numbers in the problem?

Students' problem solving on their own	• finding out the way to get the answer to the expression $128 \div 16$	(0) By guessing
		(1) By thinking how many "16s" are there in 128 ?
		   $128 - 16 - 16 - 16 -. ....= 0$
		   (a repeated subtraction)
		(2) By substituting numbers into the expression
		   $\triangle \times 16 = 128$ by turns, we can get the answer.
		   $1 \times 16 = 16, 2 \times 16 = 32,$
		   $3 \times 16 = 48,... 8 \times 16 = 128$
		(3) "Dividing by 16" means divided first by 8, and then by 2.
		   $128 \div 16 = 128 \div (8 \times 2) = (128 \div 8) \div 2 = 16 \div 2 = 8$
		(4) Dividing both dividend and divisor by the same number like 2 or 4.
		   $128 \div 16 = (128 \div 2) \div (16 \div 2) = 64 \div 8 = 8$
		(5) When the divisor is multiplied by 2, the quotient becomes half; $128 \div 2 = 64$,
		   $128 \div 4 = 32$.
		   So, we can get the answer of $128 \div 16$ as a half of $128 \div 8$
			• give hints to those students who can not find a solution
			
			• ask the students to explain how and why the methods do work
			
			• request another method for those students who got one method

	Main Learning Activities	Anticipated Students' Responses	Remarks on Teaching
Whole-class discussion	• presenting the ideas you came up with and listen to the other students' ideas • comparing the methods presented to find the connections among them • which method might be more effective?	Focus on the following ideas to integrate the students' methods. • by estimating the number, find the number that applies to the equation; using $\triangle \times 16 = 16 \times \triangle$ (repeated subtraction falls into this idea) • thinking by two steps • using multiplication table, applying the regularity (If we make the number of planters half, the number of bulbs also becomes half)	• pick a naive method like guessing first • focus on the regularities of division
Summing up	• reflecting on the regularities of division we found	• when we divide both the dividend and divisor by the same number, the answer remains the same • so, we can get the answer to division by a two-digit number, in certain cases, by reducing it into division by a one-digit number	
Applications	• try the other cases, divisions by 12 or 18, by applying the regularities	• $96 \div 12 = (96 \div 2) \div (12 \div 2) = 48 \div 6$ • $96 \div 12 = (96 \div 3) \div (12 \div 3) = 32 \div 4$ and so on	• give such expressions like $96 \div 12$ or $144 \div 18$ as examples

Appendix E:
A Demonstration Lesson:
Function Thinking at Sixth Grade

Lesson Plan   158

Lesson Transcript   161
   Shunji Kurosawa, Teacher, Tokyo Gakugei University, Setagaya Elementary School

Postlesson Discusssion Transcript   168
   Takashi Nakamura, Professor, University of Yamanahi

Postlesson Discussion: Questions and Responses   175

LESSON PLAN
A DEMONSTRATION LESSON: FUNCTION THINKING AT SIXTH GRADE

August 3, 1999
Setagaya Elementary School
Sixth Grade
Instructor: Shunji Kurosawa

BACKGROUND

The Name and the Situation

(1) Two changing variables

Starting at the third grade, the field of quantity-related mathematics is brought into the curriculum, dealing with equations, graphs, statistics, and functions. This particular lesson will be focusing on functions but not the functions defined in a math textbook. The lesson's idea is based on the "function-like thinking process" that deals with comparing two variables, one increasing and the other in relation to the first, finding the relationship, and expressing the realizations of the relationship to solve the problem.

In the fourth grade, a lesson called "examining change" is introduced, and students are asked to compare two variables to examine the relationship. The relationship is described in graph and equation forms at the fifth-grade level. Now in the sixth grade, the comparison of direct and inverse proportions is used to develop the "function-like thinking process."

(2) The situation

This lesson is at the stage a step before studying proportions. So the objective is to solve a problem by applying the method already learned, like the one in "examining change." That is, to solve a problem by finding a variable number within a given situation, compare it with another

variable number that is dependent on the first one, and to find the rules of the relationships between the two. This kind of thinking process will be used as the evaluation of the lesson.

The Purpose

The development of "function thinking" is the basic foundation for understanding functions and a goal that should be taught at an early stage. This is due to the fact that it develops a scientific mind by comparing the unknown to a known to construct an explanation. Yet it does create boredom just to experience each step of the basis of functions in order, no matter how important it may be. Function thinking begins to develop only when there is an unknown and a desire to want to know the unknown. The aim here is to create a situation for students to be curious enough to find their own question within the given subject and evaluate the thinking process while solving the problem. There is an unfortunate fact that this sort of thinking process is not commonly taught. Even if it was being taught, it often jumps to the stage of learning rules and practicing, with two variables already provided. The truth is that the first step is being skipped most of the time. In today's lesson, students will see where each variable comes from while observing the growth of an abstract image.

The Development

(1) Objectives

(a) Find a variable and raise a question about what is going to happen.
(b) Find another variable that is in relation to the first one, realize how they are related, and find an answer to develop the thinking process of functions.
(c) In addition, encourage students to find their own rules describing the changes to achieve developmental thinking.

The stages of learning and students' activities (●)	Cautious points (▲) and evaluation points (◆)
1. Observe the image shown below. 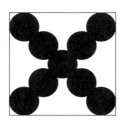 ● Each of the squares is moving away from the one in the center. ● The number of squares is increasing by four. ● It is like a virus.*	▲ Begin with students' responses to the image. Listen to comments such as, "Like fireworks," "An explosion," "There are nine squares," "They are expanding," etc. ◆ Make sure to value comments that describe the change in the image, such as, "The number is growing," and "away from the one in the center." after 1 min
2. Make it into a question. ● If the amount of squares increases by four from the one in the center every minute, how many squares will there be after ten minutes?	◆ Let them think of the variable (time) that is related to the image. (?? at the beginning, ?? a minute later) ▲ Develop the class according to their comments.
3. Each will come up with their own solutions and answers.	▲ Comment on each other's solutions and the reason behind the equations they built.
4. Argue the solutions. ● The answer is 41 squares. ● The reason is: $4 \times X + 1$ or $X \times 4 + 1$. ● Create own situations with changing variables.	◆ Were they able to explain the reasons well by using graphs and equations? ▲ Go over each problem, and plan to use them in the upcoming class.

*Editor's note: The teacher stated as an assumption that we may not know how all viruses grow and that it may be the case that some grow at a constant rate.

(3) Evaluation

Were students able to consider the two changing variables well enough to create a problem?

LESSON TRANSCRIPT

A Demonstration Lesson:
Function Thinking in the Sixth Grade
August 3, 2000
Tokyo Gakugei University, Setagaya Elementary School
Teacher: Shunji Kurosawa

Kurosawa-sensei[1] began the lesson by posting a yellow sheet of paper with a single black dot on the blackboard.

He then posted another sheet with five black dots.

This was followed by a sheet with nine black dots.

And finally, there was a sheet with thirteen black dots.

One student mentioned that it seemed to be "growing."

Kurosawa-sensei asked students, "What is the subject of 'growing'? *What* is growing?"

---

[1] Sensei means teacher

Students came up with a variety of responses. The line is getting longer.

The triangular area between the lines is getting larger.

The size of the cross is getting bigger.

The number of black dots is growing.

After approximately 10 minutes of discussion, Kurosawa-sensei posed the same question again...

Teacher:	I'll ask the question one more time.
	You have come up with some answers seeing only this one.
	(Do you see other things) by looking at this one?
	Is there something else that is changing?
	Is there anything else that is changing rapidly?
	Arita-san, you can keep it, I will get it later.
	Yes, Ota-kun.
Ota:	The number of the dots will increase four pieces at a time.
Teacher:	Okay. I'll note that point.
	...
(Writing)	(Ota) Increase 4 at a time.
Teacher:	Increasing by four pieces. Yes.
Student:	Ota-kun also said that, if the dots, which increased by four pieces, were connected by lines,
	Then it would make a square and the squares would be increasing.

Teacher:	Oh, you have said something interesting. You can see the square.
	Write it down please.
	Yoshida is sharp.
	The squares have increased.
(Writing)	(Yoshida) The square is increasing.
Teacher:	Okay, the squares are increasing rapidly.
	I see.. Yes? ...
	Do you know anything that increases rapidly like this in the world? (Is there anything) in your everyday life?
Student:	Debt.
Teacher:	What?
Student:	I said debt.
Teacher:	Debt! You —
	Debt. Is there anything that—"pohn!"—increases rapidly in your daily life?
Students:	There's nothing, Kurosawa-sensei!
Teacher:	Is there really nothing?
Students:	Increase? This is tough. What?
Teacher:	Nothing?
	What? Water? Water?
Student:	If the water falls. . .
Teacher:	I see, the water falls—" pohn"—then it will increase, I see. I see. Water. Water. Like water goes "pohn" if stone falls into the water—"pohn."
Teacher:	What else? Are there any other images?
Student:	A balloon.
Teacher:	What? A balloon?
Student:	I mean the air makes it bigger.
Teacher:	(Blowing) Like this? A balloon, as you blow—"bwah"—into it more and more—"bwah"—is that what you mean?
Teacher:	It will expand and in the end—BANG! I see.
	I see. I came up with a much better idea when I saw this.
	I came up with cell division.
Student:	No such form exists.
Teacher:	You think so? What is it then? The thing which will increase. Bacteria!
Umeki:	It can increase in a fixed pattern.
Teacher:	Wait a minute. Umeki said a great thing. Say it again.
Umeki:	The black dots will increase in a fixed pattern.
Teacher:	Since the dots will increase in a fixed pattern, then you want to say it looks like what?
Umeki:	A virus.
Teacher:	A virus?
Students:	... It is not constant.
Teacher:	Isn't a virus constant?
Students:	It's not constant.

Teacher:	Is that so? We never know.
	Natural science behaves by rules, the virus may increase constantly.
	Virus. I understand.
	"Pohn!" There's one (black dot). This is the beginning. This—I wonder how we should do this.
	This is after one second.
Students:	...
Teacher:	It's fast? After one minute.
	Then this diagram is after one minute.
	"After one minute." After one minute.
	So this is the diagram after the second minute. Therefore, after that—one minute later, one minute later—the virus...
	The black dots became a virus. It's like the movie, My Neighbor Totoro, (about) that ghost who had a virus.
	Kobayashi, how much will the virus be increased after 5 minutes, if it increases every one and two minutes?
	It is easy to answer for five minutes or six minutes.
	How many minutes would you like to try?
Students:	One hour. Forty-three minutes. Ten minutes. Thirty-five minutes.
Student:	An appropriate number is better.
Teacher:	Appropriate! What is the most appropriate number of minutes?
Student:	A number that is easy to calculate.
Teacher:	That is correct. That is right. Umeki.
Umeki:	There is no number that is hard to calculate...
Teacher:	There is no number that is hard to calculate.
	Umeki, speak. Umeki please make a problem. Please give us your virus problem. Please, go ahead.
Umeki:	Well, a virus will ... 48 minutes later.
(Writing)	(Umeki) A virus after 48 minutes, how many are there?
Teacher:	Then, from now. Okay? Is there anything about the problem that you don't understand?
	Is it hard for you to calculate 48 minutes? Is it all right?
	Yes, what is it?
Students:	...
Teacher:	Just a moment. Did you try to say the answer? Just a minute. Is this okay as a question? 48 minutes later.
	Then, I will give you 3 or 4 minutes from now, to calculate how much the virus will increase after 48 minutes.
	Start now.

The students worked independently on the problem for about eight minutes.

During this time, Kurosawa-sensei walked among the students. He watched them work and occasionally stopped to talk with individuals. When he felt enough students were ready, he called the class together to discuss the problem.

Kurosawa-sensei surveyed the students to find out their answers. Most students answered 193; a few had 189. Kurosawa-sensei began the class discussion, concentrating on the solutions that led to 189 as the answer.

	Then, let's start with someone who has the answer 189.
	Kawamura-san, please.
Kawamura:	It increases by 4 pieces 47 times, so that's 47 times 4.
	And there is the dot in the center, but that does not increase 4 pieces at a time, so you only need to add 1.
	So it is 47 times 4 plus 1.
Student:	...
Teacher:	You can speak after Kawamura-san is done.
(Writing)	(Kawamura) 47 times, it increases by 4. 47 times 4, plus 1 in the center.
	47 times 4 plus 1 is 189.
Kawamura:	The dots surrounding the four increase 4 at a time,
	But the first time is not included, and it increases by 4 pieces 47 times which is 188,
	And the dot in the middle is added to it.
	Does anyone have an objection to my answer?
Yoshida:	Kawamura says that four pieces increased 47 times,
	This means that since four pieces will increase 47 times after one minute,
	Then I think 5, instead of 1, should be added for the first minute.
(Writing)	(Yoshida) That is what happens one minute later therefore, must add five.
Yoshida:	Does anybody have any questions regarding my answer?
Teacher:	Kawamura-san...
Kawamura:	...
Teacher:	You should say your opinion.
	Yoshida ...you should name someone...
Yoshida:	Dobashi-kun.
Dobashi:	I agree with Yoshida's opinion.
Teacher:	Ikeda-kun, did you understand?
Student:	Yes.
Teacher:	Kawamura-san, are you okay also?
Kawamura:	Yes.
Teacher:	It does not become 193 after adding 5.
Student:	It will. 47 times 4 plus 5.
Teacher:	I see, I see. I understand. You mean that 47 times 4 plus 5. Is that what you mean?
Student:	4 times 48.
Teacher:	Please speak.
Student:	It is not 47 times 4 plus 5. Well, it's okay if it's 48 times 4, plus 1.
(Writing)	(Umeki) 48 times 4 plus 1 is correct
Teacher:	I see. Then, can anyone explain Nakahara's answer?
	Okay, not very many people.
	So, Nakai-kun please.

Nakai:	Since four pieces will increase every minute, so four pieces will increase in one minute, 48 times 4 plus 1.
(Writing)	(Nakai) Every minute it increases by 4. 4 times 48 plus 1.
Teacher:	...
Nakai:	Does anybody disagree with my opinion?
Teacher:	Nakai's answer is the same as this one.
	But, it is slightly different.
	Is that okay? 48 times 4 plus 1 and 4 times 48 plus 1.
	Can anybody explain the difference between the two?
Student:	...
Teacher:	Someone has a different method. Wait a minute. There are others.
	Then, please explain it.
Ogawa:	I did 1 plus 4 times 48 ...
(Writing)	(Ogawa) Another way to describe it is 1 plus 4 times 48.
Teacher:	Say it again.
Ogawa:	1 plus 4 times 48.
Teacher:	Oh, this way. What did you say?
	Okay, I will let you explain what the differences and similarities are regarding these three methods...
	It is easier to understand if it is marked as A here, and marked as B here.
	Tatsumi-kun, please explain Umeki-kun's way.
Tatsumi:	...
Teacher:	...
	A is—
	Please come up ...
Tatsumi:	You mean I should draw a picture?
Teacher:	I don't know, please ask.
Tatsumi:	A is, A is... on the number line... it assumes that 48 is 1, and seeks what is... over 4...
Teacher:	What you're saying is, 48 times 4?
Tatsumi:	4 times 48 means 4 multiplied by 48, but
	what it means is that every 1 minute it increases by 4,
	and it is not increasing by 48 every minute,
	So I think it is better to say 4 times 48.
Teacher:	So A is better? I mean, B is better?
Tatsumi:	Between A and B, I thought B was better.
	But between B and C, there is a 1 at the very beginning, and I thought that was even better.
Teacher:	Then C is better?
Tatsumi:	Yes
Teacher:	Okay, Tatsumi-kun says that this one says 48 multiplied 4 times,
	and that one says 4 multiplied 48 times.
	So if it is increasing by 4, then B is the better choice. That is his opinion.
	Ok? Anyone disagree?

	B is better?
Tatsumi:	48 is a little big, so...
Teacher:	OK, let's use this. Let's think of 3 minutes elapsed time. Yes, please.
Tatsumi:	... 48 is...so every minute, this part, not there, here... increases by 1, by 4. Here, next to the [center] dot, after the first minute there is one dot, and in 2 minutes there are 2, and after 3 minutes there are 3, but then, over here there's 3 more, and 3 more here, and 3 here. So if you multiply 3 times 4, and then add 1 for the one in the center, you will get the answer.
Teacher:	How's that? Now there are some of you who understand. Do you really understand? So after 48 minutes, there will be 48 more lined up here. Understand? After 1 minute, there's one, after 2 minutes there are 2, and after 3 minutes, 3 and so after 48 minutes there will be 48. Please, go ahead.
Student:	I think that's okay, but the virus increase takes place uniformly 4 at a time, not 4 here at once, then 4 more there, so...
Teacher:	Hmm. So we can think of the increase this way... or as 4 times 3. This is the difference, right? Do you see the difference? As long as you see the difference, that's fine. But judging from the manner of the increase, the opinion is that B is better...or I mean C, because it adds the 1. Now, we're starting to run out of time. Hmm. Lastly, is there anyone who can produce a formula that will allow for the calculation of the increase no matter how many minutes have elapsed?
(Writing)	In order to know the number of the viruses after an unspecified number of moments have elapsed....
Teacher:	What if you want to figure out the number of viruses after an unspecified number of elapsed minutes?

The class continued for only a few more minutes. Kurosawa-sensei ended class by asking students to consider "other scenarios that increase" for the next time they met.

The sixth-grade lesson was followed by a postlesson discussion with the classroom teacher and the Japanese mathematics educators who were in attendance. Participants from the Congress observed the discussion.

POSTLESSON DISCUSSION TRANSCRIPT:

Function Thinking at Sixth Grade
August 3, 2000
Tokyo Gakugei University, Setagaya Elementary School
Facilitator: Takashi Nakamura
Teacher: Shunji Kurosawa

Takashi Nakamura from the University of Yamanashi facilitated the postlesson discussion. Nakamura-sensei began the session by having Kurosawa-sensei give his goals for the lesson.

Facilitator:	Let's start our postlesson discussion now.
	As I have explained, the content of our postlesson discussion is the subject of this meeting.
	First I want to note that we do not have much time.
	For about five minutes I suggest the teacher who conducted the classroom lesson tell us the goals of the lesson.
	Then, we will ask him questions and target the issues to discuss.
	First of all, I would like Kurosawa-sensei to talk about the goals of the lesson and the classroom teaching today.
Teacher:	Today, I had three goals.
	The first goal was to run the class in such a way that students come up with the math questions by themselves.
	To meet that goal, I showed them this chart and used the students' words.
	I wanted to set up the lesson to allow the students to come up with the questions.
	I would like your comments.
	The second goal was to teach students the concept of a function, which is an important subject in math education.
	As you know, the concept of a function is important to understand measurable changes of a subject.
	We need to understand two variables and find out the "rule of the change" between them.
	And by using the "rule of change," we can solve math problems. This is how I think about teaching a function, step by step.
	And for the third goal, I wanted to teach students how to read and understand the equation that represents how things change.
	Now, I want to evaluate whether I accomplished these three goals in the class.
	Regarding the first goal—to let the students generate the questions—and whether or not we achieved it...
	I welcome your opinion. Please tell me about it later.
	Today's math question was, "How many black dots will you have after 48 minutes?"

I think students came up with the right questions on their own.

That is because they used words such as "rapidly" and "virus." Unfortunately, I introduced words like, "After certain minutes."

I believe my students did indeed come up with the math questions on their own. The second point was the concept of a function.

The concept of function involves finding how things change— then using examples associated with the change, and finding the "rule of change."

My students used the word "rapidly."

Regarding the use of the word "rapidly"—I would have preferred such terms as "spreading" or "increasing."

But they were able to find many words to indicate change.

For example, students knew the lines and area increased.

However, as I've explained, I didn't do enough to help students with changes involving independent and dependent variables.

Still, aspects such as shape and number of squares were used effectively to solve the fourth problem.

The third goal was to help students understand the equation; I tried to get them to appreciate the difference between 48 x 4 and 4 x 48. Although they had some problems, they understood the meaning of not only 4 x 48 but also 48 x 4.

For me, it is acceptable that one student understood, and the students around him understood by learning from him.

Therefore, I think they learned how to read the equation appropriately.

Additionally, I had hoped they would come up with an expression for dividing this into four parts.

It produces a formula like this: 3 minutes plus 1/4, parentheses. (laughter)

Teacher: I wondered if these kids could come up with this concept.

Whoops! That's wrong. It's actually multiplied by this, right? (laughter)

I thought there might be a chance that these kids could have come up with this idea, but it did not happen.

For them to do that, I should have taught them how to think about the concept of 1/4 or how to divide the element at the line.

I thought it would be fun to see if they could come up with it.

Anyway, I thought they more or less understood how to comprehend the equations.

The participants were given the opportunity to ask Kurosawa-sensei clarifying questions about his goals. Nakamura-sensei took seven questions from participants then asked Kurosawa-sensei to address each of them. A summary of the questions and responses can be found following this transcript.

The general discussion started with Kurosawa-sensei's first goal: To have students come up with the mathematical question.

Facilitator: If you do not have any more questions, I want to start the general discussion. When you ask your questions, please state your thoughts and critical views on today's class.

As Kurasawa-sensei stated before, there are three goals.

The first one was to let students come up with the math problem on their own.

Regarding (the second) goal—was this approach effective for teaching mathematical functions?

The last goal involved reading and interpreting the equations.

Another item has to do with pedagogy as it relates to how to teach students to express their mathematical ideas.

So, there are four major items.

The first item is how to present a math problem.

That means letting the students formulate the math problem. Do you have any opinions? Yes, please.

Facilitator: Regarding the lesson, there was perhaps a spectrum of opinions.

One view is that students be encouraged to come up with a variety of questions and explore different problems.

On the other hand, if the lesson focus was on the number of dots rather than area, he should have begun this sooner.

What the teacher wanted students to accomplish was to get a number. Therefore you should undertake the more direct approach.

Are there any teachers with this opinion? That part of the lesson took 25 minutes.

Do you really think what you did was correct?

Are there any teachers who question the approach or usage of time? Therefore, if you want to teach the concept of a function-

Why not show 48 from the beginning and ask students what would happen?

Is there anyone with such an opinion? Perhaps not... Yes, please.

Participant: My point is a little different. I feel that the lesson was incomplete.

If you want them to come up with their own math problem, you should consider more thoroughly how to set it up.

You showed them these sheets, and they explored different questions. But, as you said, you helped them get to the problem.

However, if you want to focus on the number of dots, you should wrap up the discussion more quickly to get to that point.

I think it's meaningful to allow time to explore different questions rather than focusing on the dot problem too soon.

Facilitator: Yes. What do you think? Yes, please.

Participant: I agree more with the method of teaching today...

From today's presentation of functions, I think it's possible to further expand students' understanding of functions.

In today's class, students saw how it's possible to generate different mathematical problems from a simple example.

	And, overall, by focusing on the problem of the number of dots...
	Then the students learned the relationship of variables and the concept of functions.
	They were taught different ways to view the problem and express it in an equation.
	For all these reasons, I agree with the way he conducted the class if we have to complete the lesson in 45 minutes.
Facilitator:	Let's consider other types of issues.
	By exploring the area of a triangle or length of the lines, at what point do students internalize the problem?
	Is there any guarantee that will happen in the class?
	Or is that the responsibility of the teacher to have them learn it at home?
Participant:	This is related to what was discussed before.
	It is not important to let students think about what the teacher is thinking about.
	The important thing is to understand what students are thinking about.
	The opinion expressed by the teacher at the beginning was—using his words—he was bringing out students' awareness.
	Through his remarks it was evident that the teacher was drawing the students closer to his way of thinking—
	and the students started wondering what the teacher was thinking and wanted.
Facilitator:	I agree with your opinion. Yes, please.
Participant:	I also agree. It took 25 minutes to produce the math problem.
	While many math problems were expressed– Kurosawa-sensei tried to lead his students towards one problem.
	I think the students clearly saw his intent. Then, they knew the important problem was to find the total number of dots.
Facilitator:	Finally we are getting a variety of views. (laugh)
	Yes, please.
Participant:	It took 25 minutes to develop the math problem.
	Nevertheless, the time it took is less important. The important thing is what you were able to accomplish within the time.
	If you listened carefully, they said the picture has plane symmetry or line symmetry.
	Students came up with a number of concepts that are associated with mathematics.
	Usually we see many nonessential things that are not related to mathematics.
	Still, depending on the content of the class, like today's, we should determine the right amount of time and work hard on it.
	Although I do not disagree—students used the word "spreading" repeatedly as Kurosawa-sensei told us before.
	They did not use the word "increases."

You said, "I finally used the words 'increasing rapidly' because I couldn't wait any more for them to come up with those words."

I have one more thing. After students mentioned the problem on the number of black dots, you said,

"Is there anything else changing rapidly?" I wondered if you said that by mistake.

How should the teacher conduct the class to draw out those words from the students?

I cannot offer a solution. (laugh)

Facilitator: Yes, please.

Participant: Regarding the concept of a function, I find the process of finding the variables of the problem to be important.

In this sense, the beginning of the class was very interesting.

However, it was the teacher who said, "This changes with time."

What should we do to let students come up with that point?

In your presentation you clearly state, "The first chart, the second chart, the third chart."

Students can point out what they see.

Time cannot be seen, but it is being shown—the first chart, the second chart, and so on.

Therefore, I think it should be possible to relate after one minute, the first chart, then the second, and so on.

However, its difficult because the children relate the first sheet (with the single black dot) to the first minute.

Therefore, I think you should start with the second sheet with five dots.

Facilitator: The second goal was how to develop the concept of a function in students' mind.

What do you think? Should we start from the sheet with a single dot or 5 dots?

Participant: That is not what I have in mind. A problem existed much earlier.

The teacher used the word "virus" and that focused the subject at the beginning.

I think students produced mental images of the virus increasing over time.

Nevertheless, were they all able to understand and visualize the problem? Would they have gotten it without being told -

"Today's subject is about the virus" and, "What will happen in 48 minutes?"

If they all achieved the concept, then the class was effective.

At this point, Nakamura-sensei asked Kurosawa-sensei to respond to the comments that had been raised.

Facilitator: We have discussed the equation on the board. Now, can we address the function and the presentation of the problem?

Teacher: To tell you the truth, I have had a dilemma regarding the presentation of functions.

We were able to find a variety of variables, but we needed to choose one. The process of focusing on the most important variable is one subject.

The next subject is defining the dependent variable in the problem.

The challenge is effectively addressing these two subjects.

Today's class demonstrated the difficulty but let me explain...

I did not randomly lead the students towards the problem of the number of dots.

The line, distance between dots, size of the "x", and area—all rapidly increasing—were related to the number of dots.

I felt that the students realized the importance of the number of dots, and thus, I started to focus on it.

I do feel the process of narrowing down to a single problem is an important subject.

Next, if we can identify the important variable, then we can focus on the dependent variable.

At that point, another subject that I must carefully consider is how I phrase my question.

Once we identify the variable, should I say, "What is the cause of this change?"

When I use the term, "dependent variable," I didn't think students would understand.

"What will change with it?" does not sound clear.

"To determine this value, what needs to be determined first?" sounds too formal.

So, after finding one variable, I think it is very difficult to ask the right question to find the dependent variable.

As you've mentioned, after defining one variable, I should consider carefully how to treat the dependent variable.

To accomplish what we need, I think what is important is how you present the material.

So, at the beginning, I showed this set of dots, but I wondered what kind of variables the students could identify.

I worried that they would not find one. Therefore, I prepared something like this.

And, at this stage, I used sound effects like "pohn" and "wahn."

By using these sounds, I wanted to evoke images of something changing, like cells.

I was looking for an example familiar to them.

I wanted to draw upon their personal experiences. They may have seen cells increasing under a microscope in science class.

I was looking for an example of something increasing, and the girl over there suggested mice.

She said mice multiply. I wonder why she didn't say it earlier?

I had been struggling to find a good visual example of something increasing.

Therefore I expected the class to depend on what students have seen or experienced.

Facilitator: What do you think? Any opinions? Yes.

Participant: The students understood the concept. Then, it is the teacher's responsibility to wrap up.

A function here is an addition of four dots.

The students placed four dots, and four more dots, and four more dots of the square there.

Therefore by observing the black dots, we see the square is increasing in size.

They understood the change made by each set of four dots.

So, instead of using the sound effect "Pohn! Pohn!" on a daily basis-

We should use the right words regularly so that we can treat functions appropriately...

After this comment, Nakamura-sensei opened the discussion for final thoughts about the lesson as a whole.

Facilitator: We only have about eight minutes.

Sakai-san pointed out the presentation of the math problem and the concept of a function as discussed earlier.

Do you have any opinions, insights, or thoughts about the lesson as a whole?

Participant: In the latter portion... how confidently did students come up with those two answers, and for what reasons?

Did they think so because the rest of the students got the same answer?

Is it correct for them to think that they all got the same answer so it should be right?...

Teacher: Can we show the chart? Is that right?

Participant: The chart is acceptable...

...

Facilitator: Therefore, you are saying that the students were able to formulate equations from their ideas...

But, how they were able to arrive at these equations was never openly discussed.

It might have been written in their notebooks...

But when it is discussed in class, even the students who did not initially understand will benefit.

Therefore, we use charts and graphs.

I think displaying numbers like one, five, nine is a good idea. It remains on the board as a visual aid for the children...

Nakamura-sensei allowed a few minutes for visitors watching the discussion to ask questions and then concluded the session.

POSTLESSON DISCUSSION: QUESTIONS AND RESPONSES

Function Thinking at Sixth Grade

The postlesson discussion between the observers and the teacher—Shunji Kurosawa immediately followed the lesson on Function Thinking. Takashi Nakamura from the University of Yamanashi facilitated the discussion. Nakamura-sensei began the session by having Kurosawa-sensei give his goals for the lesson and describe the degree to which he felt he had achieved them. Nakamura-sensei took seven questions from the Japanese observers, then asked Kurosawa-sensei to address each of them. Nakamura-sensei grouped the questions as he presented them to Kurosawa-sensei for a response. The questions and the responses are summarized below, in the order of the responses.

Observer:	You intended to solve the problem by breaking it into several separate items, right?
Observer:	When you increased the number of the balls at the beginning, you pasted them one by one. Was that intentional? As a result you did not place four balls on the sheet. Was that intentional?
Observer:	Could you tell us about your method for presenting the math problems? For example how to post the sheet, how to provide the sheet, how to present the problem?
Kurowasa-sensei:	I had a dilemma about the method. If I were to post the sheet immediately, I wondered if students could see how it increased. For fourth grade, it would be okay to post one, then another, and so on so that they could see it increasing. But for sixth graders, I wanted just to show the figure and let them discover how the black dots increased. I was not sure they understood it or not when I saw their reactions today. Therefore, I placed the black dots as increasing from one to five and to nine.

Going from five, six, seven, eight, nine, one at a time rather than one, five, nine was not intentional. |
| Observer: | Someone mentioned the number line. Why didn't you use it on the board? |
| Observer: | You did not use graphs or charts. I want to know why. |
| Kurowasa-sensei: | In my class, I let my students judge whether they do multiplication using the number line or not. It is a definition. Therefore, there was no need to use the number line. I used the phrase "four times 48," and the phrase should be enough for them.

And regarding the chart, where it explains the equation, I thought I might need to follow the chart to indicate that it increases four at a time. However, they are sixth graders. They understood that it increases four at a time without filling out the chart. When they fill out the chart, they can see the law of corresponding figures and numbers visually. But, I |

	wanted them to come up with these two equations and compare them today. Therefore, I did not ask them to make a chart.
Observer:	In your opinion, what do you think was the most important aspect of this lesson?
Kurowasa-sensei:	I had a hard time deciding which goal should be number one. When someone asked me why, I would answer that I do not know whether the one I chose will be important in the future or not. I think it is important to grasp the variables in the equation. And I think it is fun seeing a lot of variables. Another important thing was how to read the equation. I wanted some students to grasp it. Finally one of my students, Tatsumi, got it and everyone got it too. I was happy.
Observer:	What percentage of students actually participated in the teacher's prepared lesson? Although I do not have an accurate figure, about 12 or 13 students participated in the process again and again. What percent of the 33 students participated in the process in class?
Kurowasa-sensei	By what standard can we consider whether the students participated or not? Is it a question about whether they came up with answers like 193 or 189 or not. I would say it is 100% because all the students got answers as far as I saw. Nevertheless, if you ask me what percent of my three goals were achieved, because I have to give you a figure, I would say 100 percent.

176

Appendix F:
A Study Lesson:
Large Numbers at Fourth Grade

Background   178

Lesson Plan   183
  Hiroshi Nakano, Teacher, Tokyo Gakugei University, Setagaya Elementary School

Lesson Plan Transcript   191

Blackboard   205

Postlesson Discussion Transcript   207

BACKGROUND

Japanese Counting System

The Japanese counting system is similar to the system used in the United States. The Japanese numbers are written like U.S. numbers and, for numbers ranging from 1-9999, are read with a very similar number-naming scheme. For each place value, there is an indicator of how many in that place. For example, a number like 32 would be read as *san juu ni* which translates literally as three *juu* (i.e., tens) two. This is somewhat like "thirty two" where the word "thirty" is used to refer to three tens, and "two" indicates there are two units or ones.

The number 532 is *go hyaku san juu ni*, or five *hyaku* (hundreds), three *juu* (tens), two—much like our "five hundred thirty two." This similarity continues through the thousands. So a number like 6532 would be read as *rokku sen go hyaku san juu ni*, which is six *sen* (thousands), five *hyaku* (hundreds), three *juu* (tens), two.

The American and Japanese number-naming systems, however, diverge after the number 9999. The U.S. number system goes in blocks of three for unit names: hundreds, thousands, millions, and so on. The Japanese number system, however, uses unit names in blocks of four. Whereas an American would read 16532 as "sixteen thousand, five hundred, thirty two," specifying how many thousands there are (i.e., sixteen), the Japanese specify how many ten thousand there are. The Japanese word for "ten thousand" is "man". Thus, 16532 is read as *ichi man rokku sen go hyaku san juu ni*. This translates as one *man* (ten thousand), six *sen* (thousands), five *hyakyu* (hundreds), three *juu* (tens), two.

Just as in English, rather than saying "thousand thousand" we introduce the word "million". In Japanese, rather than saying *"man man"* (ten thousand ten thousands), the new word *"oku,"* meaning "hundred million" is used. The naming of the next four place values follows the same naming pattern as above, except with the unit *oku* instead of *man*.

Number	Place Value Name (Japanese)	Place Value Name (English)
1	*ichi*	ones
10	*juu*	ten
100	*hyaku*	hundred
1000	*sen*	thousand
10,000	*ichi* (one) *man*	ten thousand
100,000	*juu* (ten) *man*	hundred thousand
1,000,000	*hyaku* (hundred) *man*	one million (new place value name)
10,000,000	*sen* (thousand) *man*	ten million
100,000,000	*ichi* (one) *oku* (new place value name)	one hundred million
1,000,000,000	*juu* (ten) *oku*	one billion (new place value name)
10,000,000,000	*hyaku* (hundred) *oku*	ten billion
100,000,000,000	*sen* (thousand) *oku*	one hundred billion
1,000,000,000,000	*ichi* (one) *cho*	one trillion (new place value name)

Large Numbers at Grade Four: Problems Covered in the Lesson

The mathematics objective in the fourth grade was to have students understand and work with large numbers, beginning in this lesson with a particular focus on the unit, *oku*. In the lesson, students solved four problems that dealt with the quantity or measure of one *oku* objects. Using a "hint" provided by the teacher, students tried to determine how much one *oku* would be.

Problem 1. What is the height of a stack of 1-*oku* (1 hundred million) *yen* if you use 1-man *yen* bills?

> **Hint:**   If you stack 1-*man yen* bills for 100-*man yen*, the height of the bills will be 1 centimeter.
>
> **Answer:** 100-*man* centimeters high.

On the board:

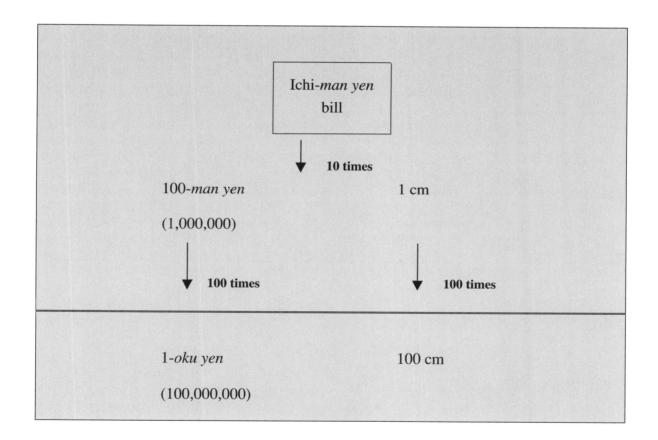

Problem 2. How many classrooms would 1-*oku* (1 hundred million) liters of water fill?

Hint: 10-*man* liters would fill half a classroom.
Answer: 500 classrooms.

On the board:

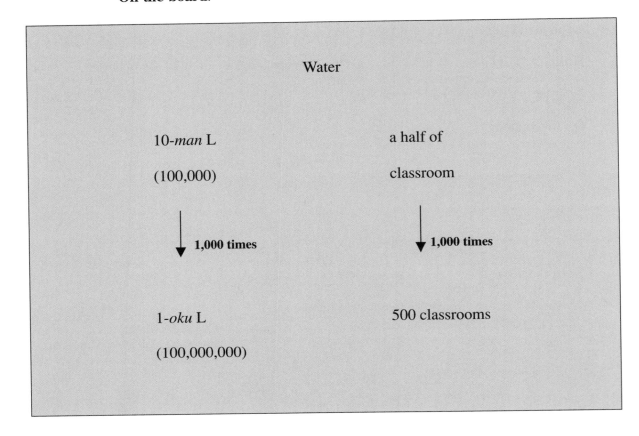

Problem 3. How many Sato-san's (a student named Sato) will it take to make 1-*oku* (1 hundred million) kilograms?

Hint: 500 Sato-sans weigh 1-*man* kilograms.

Answer: 500-*man* people.

On the board:

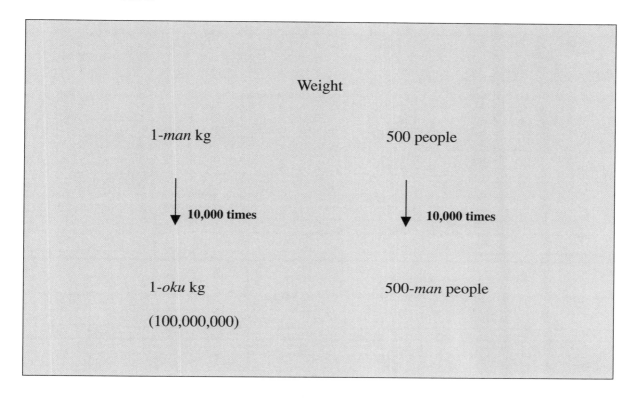

Problem 4. How long is a row of 1-*oku* Daraemon comic books?

Hint: If you line up 1-*man* Daraemon comic books in a row, it will be 150 meters long.

Answer: 100-*man* meters.

On the board:

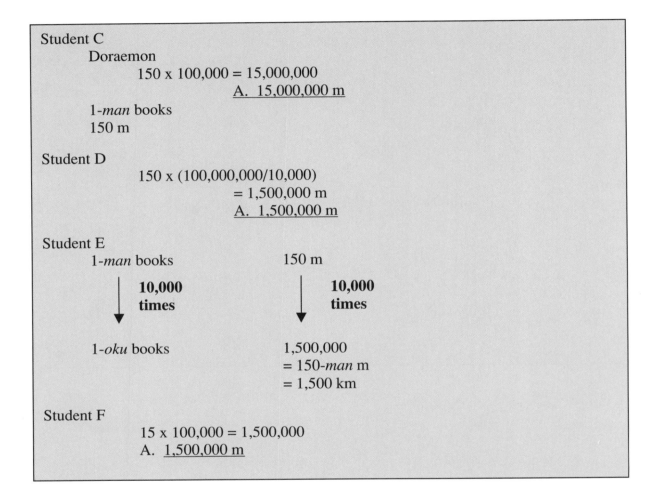

Student C
    Doraemon
          $150 \times 100{,}000 = 15{,}000{,}000$
                  A. 15,000,000 m
    1-*man* books
    150 m

Student D
      $150 \times (100{,}000{,}000 / 10{,}000)$
            $= 1{,}500{,}000$ m
            A. 1,500,000 m

Student E
    1-*man* books   150 m

        10,000   **10,000**
        times   **times**

    1-*oku* books   1,500,000
                    $= 150$-*man* m
                    $= 1{,}500$ km

Student F
      $15 \times 100{,}000 = 1{,}500{,}000$
      A. 1,500,000 m

LESSON PLAN

December 7, 1999 (Tuesday), 5ᵗʰ period
Setagaya Elementary School (a primary school attached to Tokyo Gakugei University Education Department)
Fourth Grade (Class #1) 40 Students (M. 20, F. 20)
Instructor: Hiroshi Nakano

1. Name of the Unit: Large Numbers

2. The Goal of the Unit:

> Understanding the structure, how to read, and how to write the large whole numbers that reach up to "*Oku* (100 million)" and "*Cho* (1 trillion)" and deepening the understanding of the decimal positional notation system.[1]

Interest, Desire, and Attitude
  A. Try to find a better way of thinking (solving) and commonality between two different solutions by presenting own ideas to the class and listening to others' ideas.
  B. Show an interest in large numbers in everyday life and try to use or try to investigate them.

Mathematical Thinking
  C. Using previously learned knowledge of the number system of the numbers up to one thousand, a student can think about the system of large numbers that reach up to "*oku* (100 million)" and "*cho* (1 trillion)."
  D. Understanding the relative size of large numbers based on the system of the unit used for numbering.

Expression and Manipulation
  E. Be able to write and read the numbers up to "*cho* (1 trillion)."

Knowledge and Understanding
  F. Understand the numbers up to "*cho* (1 trillion)", and that the system is based on a decimal positional notation system.

3. About the Unit:

> Up to now, my students learned numbers up to 1 *man* (ten thousand) by counting numbers when they were second grade students. During the third grade, they learned the numbers up to 1000 *man* (10 million) based on previously learned knowledge of the number 1 *man* (10 thousand). In this unit, the

---

[1] (Translator's note) The numeration system for place value in English and Japanese is different. In English, different numerations are used every three place value. For example, thousand, million, billion, and trillion. In Japanese, different numerations are used every four place values. For example, "*Man* (10 thousand)," "*Oku* (100 million)," and "*Cho* (1 trillion)."

study of the size of whole numbers comes to the final stage, and the study range of the large numbers reaches to "*oku* (100 million)" and "*Cho* (1 trillion)." As the study of the size of whole numbers approaches this stage, the most important study points of this unit become the students' understanding of the decimal positional notation system, the Japanese numeration system, and the relative size of large numbers.

The decimal positional notation system has the following main points:

- When numbers reach 10, it is a new unit.
- The quantity of each unit is determined by the place of the numbers.
- The number "0" is used to show that there is no value in the unit (place).

The students were already exposed to these main points when they were in first though third grade. In this unit, the students will learn that all whole numbers are expressed using the numbers 0 though 9 based on the previously learned principles mentioned above.

Japanese numerations were invented for showing a large number using the small number of units. For example, the unit goes up "*ichi* (one)," "*juu* (ten)," "*hyaku* (hundred)," and "*sen* (thousand)." Moreover, the cycle of these units is used to show larger numbers combined with the other units "*man* (10 thousand)", "*oku* (100 million)", and "*cho* (1 trillion)" that are used for every four place values. In this unit the students will understand the merit of the Japanese numerations as well as recognize the necessity for a unit for large numbers like "*oku* (100 million)" and "*cho* (1 trillion)."

In addition, to fostering the students' ability to look at large numbers relatively by thinking about how many 1 *man* (10 thousand), the need to create large numbers like "*oku* (100 million)" and "*cho* (1 trillion)" is an important concept in this unit. The ability to look at numbers relatively means "1 *oku* (100 million) can be shown as 1 *man* (10 thousand) if we look at the number based on 1-*Man* unit." Therefore such ability is very important in order to foster a rich sense of numbers among the students. The ability to look at numbers relatively is important in order to deepen the understanding of the decimal system and eventually becomes useful for estimating numbers and calculating with decimals. Moreover, the image of large numbers such as "*oku* (100 million)" and "*cho* (1 trillion)" will be enriched by looking at numbers relatively.

4. Guidelines for Instruction (6 lessons):

The first lesson (this lesson): (A) Based on the previously learned knowledge of the number system up to 1000 *man* (10 million), the student will learn that there are units like "*oku* (100 million)" and "*cho* (1 trillion)" above the numbers they previously studied and learn about the mechanism of those large numbers. (B) Think about the size of 1 *oku* (100 million).

The second lesson: Understanding how to write and read the numbers more than 1 *oku* (100 million).

The third lesson: Thinking about how to express whole numbers when the numbers were multiplied by 10, 100, and 1/10.

The fourth lesson: Recognizing the merits of the decimal positional notation system through understanding that any size of whole numbers can be expressed using the numbers 0 though 9.

The fifth lesson: Calculating addition and subtraction of large numbers.

The sixth lesson: Doing problems.

5. About the Learning of This Lesson:

The focal point of this lesson is learning about new units like "*oku* (100 million)" and "*cho* (1 trillion)." However these units are often used on TV and in books; therefore, the names of units are not foreign concepts to the students. Particularly the unit "*oku*" is often used in "3 *oku* yen lottery" in everyday life. Thus the unit "*oku*" is not really new to the students. Although the students know the word "*oku*," I suspect that they do not know the fact that the unit is nested in the highly developed Japanese numeration system, and they have not understood the actual quantity of the unit. Therefore I considered these circumstances to develop this lesson. When presented with a number more than 1 *oku* (100 million), students respond as follows: "we cannot read more than 1000 *man* (10 million) (because they have not learned it)." Then the teachers often used the response as a problem that the whole class needs to solve. This was a common way to start this lesson. However, as I described above, the problem like "we cannot read more than 1000 *man* (10 million)" is not a good whole class problem. It may be used individually, but it will be not natural to use it as a whole class problem.

Therefore, at the introduction of this lesson, I decided to check the students' previously learned knowledge. In other words, I decided to check the students' knowledge of the numeration system up to 1000 *man* (10 million).

Sen Man	Hyaku Man	Juu Man	Ichi Man	Sen	Hyaku	Juu	Ichi

By presenting this kind of chart, the students (even the students who do not know the unit "*oku*") can notice the cycle of "*ichi* (one)," "*juu* (ten)," "*hyaku* (100)," and "*sen* (1000)," and the new cycle begins after the number reached "*sen*," and "*ichi*"comes next. In addition, the students can notice that after "*sen man*" a new unit will be needed. In this way, the knowledge that the students learned previously can be used for learning this lesson. By checking the level of understanding of previously learned knowledge and making sure that the students notice the system of the numbers, then we can teach that the new unit that comes after *sen man* is "*oku*" and the units "*ichi*," "*juu*," "*hyaku*," and "*sen*" form a cycle. I believe that this kind of introduction to this lesson will provide for the different kinds of student needs. The students who did not know the new unit "*oku*" will learn the necessity of a new unit in order to make numbers more than 1000 *man*. And the students who already knew the unit "*oku*" will have a chance to deepen their understanding of the Japanese numeration system and recognize the merit of the system.

As I mentioned before, many students today are exposed to the unit "*oku*." However, I have doubts that the students actually have a sense of the quantity of 1 *oku*. (100 million). Therefore, after the students have recognized that the unit "*oku*" comes after "1000 *man*" and that the unit is nested in part of the Japanese numeration system, I decided to prepare an activity that makes the students actively think about the quantity of the number 1 *oku*.

For example:

- How high is a stack of 1 *man yen* bills if we have 1 *oku yen*?
- If we imagine this classroom as a cup to ladle out 1 *oku* liter of water, how many cups would it be?
- How many children do we need in order to have a weight of 1 *oku* kilogram?

These are the kinds of activities that I plan to have. Even these quantities that we will talk about during the activities are often difficult to imagine in reality so we need to imagine in our head. (For example, the quantity of 1 *oku* liter of water is about 500 classroom "cups".) However, because you cannot actually count, it is very hard to imagine how large population numbers and budget numbers are that are presented as examples in the textbooks. Moreover, just practicing reading and writing such numbers represented in the textbooks will not help this situation. Therefore, those numbers may become meaningless numbers that the students will see just on their desks. Even if the students cannot see the actual size of the numbers in front of their eyes, I believe that preparing some activities to help them to see the quantity of 1 *oku* in various ways will help develop the students' interest in the number 1 *oku*.

In addition, I believe that helping the students see the number 1 *oku* in more concrete ways as I proposed above will help foster students' understanding of the relative size of numbers. For example, the height of the stack of 1 *man* yen bills will be 1 centimeter for 100 *man yen*. The height of the stack of 1 *man* yen bills will be 100 centimeter for 1 *oku yen*. In this case, the students can imagine the relationship of the two numbers, 100 *man* and 1 *oku* (100 times of 100 *man* is 1 *oku*) using the example of the thickness of bills. I would like to plan this lesson, incorporating the mentioned activities, to support the students discovering the relative size of numbers on their own.

6. This Lesson:
   (1) The Goal of This Lesson:
       - Based on the previously learned knowledge of the principles of the Japanese numeration system up to 1000 *man* (10 million), the students think about what kind of unit names might be logical to use. And the students will learn that the new units such as "*oku*" and "*cho*" also follow the principles of the Japanese numeration system.

- Understanding the relative size of the number 1 *oku* using various 1 *oku* things and using the knowledge to solve a problem (the length of 1 *oku* comic books).
- Developing interest in thinking about the quantity of 1 *oku*.

Learning Activities[2]

Main Hatsumon (question) and students' anticipated reaction.	* Evaluation
	+ Points to remember
1. Checking the students' previously learned knowledge (concepts)	+ Tell the students that they learned the concepts when they were in third grade.

T:*How can you read the number 12525706?

C: *Sen 2-Hyaku 5-Juu 2-Man 5-Sen 7-Hyaku 6.*

T: Why don't we identify the unit/position of each number?

C:

1	2	5	2	5	7	0	6
Sen Man	*Hyaku Man*	*Juu Man*	*Ichi Man*	*Sen*	*Hyaku*	*Juu*	*Ichi*

T: Did you notice anything from this chart?

C: The units have two cycles of *ichi-juu-hyaku-sen*.

C: The first *ichi-ju-hyaku-sen* cycle does not have anything added but the second *ichi-juu-hyaku-sen* cycle has *man* for each unit.

T: What can we write when we multiply this number by 10?

C: We can write down a "0" at the end of number 12525706.

+ Tell the students that the rule for adding "0" at the end of a number means multiplying the number by 10 was previously learned knowledge.

T: Why don't we clarify the unit/position of each number?

---

[2] T, Teacher; C, children

1	2	5	2	5	7	0	6	0
	Sen Man	*Hyaku Man*	*Juu Man*	*Ichi Man*	*Sen*	*Hyaku*	*Juu*	*Ichi*

2. Think about the new unit

T: Let's think about how we can read the number "1" in the 125257060 based on what we know about the numbers up to 1000 *man*.

C: I think the nest cycle of *ichi-juu hyaku-sen* starts so I think it has *ichi*.

C: I think we will have a different unit name instead of *man*.

T: The next position of the *sen-man* is read as *ichi-oku*.

* Are the students actively thinking about the new large unit based on what they learned before (the number up to 10 million)? (Listen to what students say.)

+ The teacher will help the students think that bigger numbers also follow a similar pattern. Next position of *ichi-oku* is *juu-oku*, then *hyaku-oku*, then *sen-oku*. Finally help the students to think about the unit of "*cho* (1 trillion)."

+ Let the students know that the number 125257060 is the number that represents the population of Japan two years ago.

3. To know what quantity the number 1 *oku* represents

T: The height of a stack of 1 *man yen* bills for 100 *man yen* is 1 centimeter. What is the height of a stack of 1 *oku yen*, if you use 1 *man yen* bills?
C: About 1 meter.
T: If we have 10 *man* (100 thousand) liters of water, we can fill half of this classroom. If we have 1 *oku* liter of water, how many classrooms can we fill? In addition, if a child's weight is 20 kilograms, 1 *man* kilograms would be 500 children. How many children do we need for 1 *oku* kilograms.

+ Ask if any of the students heard the unit "*oku*" in everyday life and relate the conversation to the height of the stack of bills.

+ Ask the students to estimate the answers. Tell the students the answer 500 classrooms and 500 *man* children.

T: Doraemon comic books have sold 1-*oku* up to now. If we lined up 1 *man* (10 thousand) books, the row will be 150 meters long. How long would the row be if we lined up 1 *oku* books?

+ Ask students to think about the answer based on what we discovered through working on the problems before.

---

4. Think about the length of the book on their own

+ Ask students to write down the reasons for their answer.

C: In the case of the bill problem, it was 1 centimeter for 100 *man* yen and 100 centimeters for 1 *oku* yen. So 1 *oku* is 100 times bigger than 100 *man*. Therefore, we can find the answer by calculating $150 \times 100 \times 100$.

* Are the students solving the problem using the relative quantity of 1 *oku*? (Look at students' notebooks.)

C: In the case of the children's weight problem, 1 *man* kilograms is equal to 500 children, and 1 *oku* kilogram is equal to 500 *man* children. So, 1 *oku* is 1 *man* times of 1 *man*. Thus, we can find the answer by 150×10000.

C: 1 *man* comic books equals 150 meters. 10 *man* books is 10 times it so 1500 meters. 100 *man* books is 10 times so it is 15000 meters. Then I continue to do the calculation by multiplying by 10 in each step.

---

5. Presenting the solution

T: Please explain the solution carefully.

T: The length of the comic book will be 1500 kilometers.

+ When the numbers are gathered and form 10, a new unit is formed. So when the position goes up one, then the number was multiplied by 10. Make sure all students understand this concept.

+ Make sure the students understand the relative quantity of 1 *oku* by helping the students to understand each solution method.

* Did the students develop an interest in the number 1 *oku*? (Look at students' notebooks.)

6. Summarizing today's lesson

T: Please write down your thoughts about the number 1 *oku* in your notebook.

C: I understood how large the number 1 *oku* is.

C: I would like to think about the size of 1 *oku* using other things.

7. Evaluation

- Did the students understand the necessity for new units based on the numeration system of the numbers up to 1000 *man*?
- Did the students figure out the length of 1 *oku* comic books using the acquired knowledge of relative quantity for the number 1 *oku*?
- Did the students develop interest in the number 1 *oku*?

LESSON PLAN TRANSCRIPT

A Study Lesson:
Large Numbers in the Fourth Grade
December 7, 1999
Tokyo Gakugei University, Setagaya Elementary School
Teacher: Hiroshi Nakano

Nakano-sensei[3] began the lesson by reviewing what students had learned in earlier grades about place value and large numbers—up to seven places. The students briefly discussed how the Japanese place value system is grouped in sets of four. This is different than the U.S. system in which a new unit name is introduced every three places: hundredths, thousandths, millions, etc. A description of the Japanese counting system is included at the beginning of this appendix.

After about eight minutes, Nakano-sensei was ready to move to the main subject of the lesson, 1-*oku* or 100,000,000.

On the blackboard was written:

$$1\ 2\ 5,\!2\ 5\ 7,\!0\ 6\ 0$$

Teacher: Well, I would like to write the name of units just like we did before:
ichi (ones), *juu* (tens), *hyaku* (hundreds), *sen* (thousands).
Just like Matsumoto-kun said before, this is a (cycle of) units that goes around one more time.
Ichi (ones), *juu* (tens), *hyaku* (hundreds), *sen* (thousands), and these units have the unit *man* (ten-thousands).

---

[3] sensei means teacher

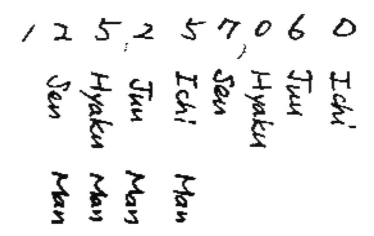

Teacher:	Now, you can see that the number shifted one position so a number sticks out further than the units we studied previously.
	The next step is to think about how we can read the number.
	It is going up like *ichi* (ones), *juu* (tens), *hyaku* (hundreds), *sen* (thousands)-
	Ichi (ones), *juu* (tens), *hyaku* (hundreds), *sen* (thousands) - like what Matsumoto-kun said.
	Tanaka-san was saying the same thing. What do you think the next unit will be?
Students:	Yes, yes.
Teacher:	What is your guess? Yes, please.
Student:	*Ichi* (ones).
Teacher:	Is that right?
Students:	Yes, yes.
Student:	It is "*ichi* (one)-something" number.
Teacher:	That's right.
	I think— maybe—the unit one-something comes next.
	Well, this figure became strange.
Students:	(laughter)
Teacher:	This becomes *ichi* (one)-something.
	If this is *ichi* (one)-something, does that mean you can't put (the label) *man* (ten-thousands) here?
Students:	Yes, yes.
Teacher:	Why?
Student:	We used *man* (ten-thousands) before.
Teacher:	Yes, Otsuka-kun.

Otsuka:	The unit *man* (ten-thousands) is used for the last cycle of numbers so-
Teacher:	Oh, I see. We used it here.
Otsuka:	So the next unit will use a different name.
	It will be next... after 9 *sen man* (9000 man), so it will not be *man* (ten-thousands).
Teacher:	So it is not *man* (ten-thousands). It is not *man*. Yes, Shirai-kun.
Shirai:	In addition to what Otsuka-kun said,
	if you put the unit *man* again here (where the 1 is)-
	Then it will become *ichi-man man* (ten-thousand man). And the position of the unit goes back to the *man* position.
	So it is not *man*.
Teacher:	I see, I think it is okay to call it *ichi-man man* (ten-thousand man)
Student:	That sounds like a name of a food.
Students:	(laughter)
Teacher:	*Ichi man* of *ichi man* and *ichi-man man*. I think it sounds good. But...
	So we need to have a different name for the unit that replaces *man*, don't we?
	I think you already have heard this many times before... that is...
Students:	*Oku* (hundred-millions).
Teacher:	When I asked you a couple of days ago, there were few who had never heard the word *oku*.
	You must have heard the word somewhere before, haven't you?
	But the word *oku* appears in this situation.
	Well, this is the first time for us to learn *oku* formally and—
	because there were two students who did not know *oku* when I asked before...
	this is called *ichi-oku* (1 hundred-million).
	If we write *ichi-oku* (1 hundred-million) using numbers, it becomes... like this and we have...
	One, two, three, four, five, six, seven, eight. Eight zeros.
Students:	Wow, wow... There are a lot of them.
Teacher:	This is something we are going to learn in the fourth grade.

Nakano-sensei spent a few more minutes discussing the new unit, *oku*, then shifted to the problems on which the students would be working.

Teacher:	Well, today, we would like to study the number 1 *oku* (1 hundred-million) further.
	So we will have a quiz competition called, "How much is 1 *oku* (1 hundred-million) quiz competition."
Students:	Yea!
Writing:	How much is 1-*oku* (1 hundred-million) quiz competition.
Teacher:	Oh, somebody said something really good.

	Somebody was talking about 1-*oku* (1 hundred-million) *yen*. I have a 1-*man yen* bill here.
Students:	Wow… I want to have it. I want to have it…
Teacher:	Well this 1-*man yen* bill.
Students:	I want it. I want to have it…
Teacher:	What would be the height of a stack of 1-*oku* (1 hundred-million) *yen* if we used 1-*man yen* bills? This is the first question.
Student:	Yes.
Teacher:	Yes, Shirai-kun please.
Shirai:	I think it reaches up to the height of the blackboard.
Teacher:	I see. It will be from the bottom to the top of this blackboard. Yes, Matsumoto-kun.
Matsumoto:	About 2 meters.
Teacher:	The height 2 meters is a little bit taller than me so about this tall. Okay, I will give you a hint. I wish I can take out 100-*man yen* right now, but I don't have that kind of money.
Students:	(laughter)
Student:	If that's the case, you can sell your house.
Students:	(laughter)
Students:	You can't do that so easily. Where could he live if he sold his house?
Teacher:	A stack of 100-*man yen*. If you stack 1-*man yen* bills for 100-*man yen*, the height of the bills will be 1 centimeter.
Students:	I got it… I got it…
Student:	Why does it become 1 centimeter?
Teacher:	I wish I can take out real bills for 100-*man yen* as evidence. If I stack 1-*man yen* like this, the height will be 1 centimeter. So now, how about 1-*oku* (1 hundred-million) *yen*?
Student:	I can't see the board.
Teacher:	Yes, please.
Student:	I think it is about 10 centimeters.
Teacher:	About 10 centimeters. So it is about this much. Okay, Keita-kun.
Keita:	1 meter.
Teacher:	1 meter. I will tell you the answer. The answer is- For the height of 1-*oku* (1 hundred-million) *yen* is- 100 centimeters.

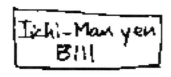

100-Man yen   1 cm
(1000000)

1-Oku yen   100 cm
(100000000)

Students:	Yes, yes !!!
Teacher:	It is 1 meter.
	The height of 1-*oku* (1 hundred-million) *yen* is 1 meter. The height will become about this much.
	Are you okay with this?
	You can talk about the 3-*oku* (3 hundred-million) *yen* lottery later.
	Have you noticed something by looking at this?
	When you move from 100-*man yen* to 1-*oku* (1 hundred-million) *yen*…
Student:	100 times.
Teacher:	I heard somebody say something good.
Student:	100 times.
Teacher:	That's right, isn't it?
	The height is 100 times as big.
Shintaro:	That means the value is also 100 times as big as, isn't it?
Teacher:	You said something really good.
	Shintaro-kun, you are very sharp. So the value is also 100 times bigger.
	Okay, now…
	Okay, we will go on to the second question.
Students:	Yea!
Student:	It is similar to a mathematical principle we learned before.
	If the answer was 100 times the original one, the number that is multiplied is also 100 times.

Teacher: I see. It is one of the principles of calculation.

Student: Yes, we did it long time ago.

Ichi-Man yen Bill

100-Man yen (1000000)   1 cm

↓ 100 times   ↓ 100 time

1-Oku yen   100 cm

(10000 0000)

The class moved on to the next problem: How many classrooms would 1-*oku* (1 *hundred million*) liters of water fill? The students were given the hint that 10-*man* (1 hundred thousand) liters would fill half a classroom.

Students suggested possible answers. After four minutes, Nakano-sensei stated that 500 classrooms filled with water would be approximately 1 *oku* liters—about 1000 times the given hint.

Water

10-Man ℓ   a Half of
(100000)   Classroom

     | 1000 | 1000
     | Times | times
     ↓   ↓

1-oku ℓ   500
           Classrooms
(100000000)

The class proceeded to a third problem: "How many Satoh-sans (a student named Satoh) would it take to make 1-*oku* (1 hundred-million) kilograms?" The students were given the hint that 500 Satoh-sans would weigh 1-*man* kilograms.

After about two and a half minutes, the class decided that 500-*man*—that is, five million—Satoh-sans would weigh 1-*oku* kilograms—about 10,000 times the given hint.

Weight

1-Mankg 500
people

|10000
Times>

|10000
times

1-okukg 500-Man
people

Nakano-sensei recorded the answer on the board, then moved on to the final question.

Teacher: Okay, now we will go on to the last problem.
Students: Yea!
Teacher: Excuse me for changing the subject but,
when I was listening to the radio the other day,
Students: (laughter)
Teacher: the radio said that it has been 30 years since Doraemon was born.
It said that the Doraemon comic book series reached sales of 1-*oku* (1 hundred-million) books.
Students: REALLY!!
Teacher: It is said that 1-*oku* (1 hundred-million) copies of Doraemon books were sold in the last 30 years.
Why don't we solve a problem on Doraemon for the celebration of it's 30th anniversary?
Students: Yea!
Student: Even if it is a Doraemon problem, it is a mathematics problem.

Student:	I don't know what will happen.
Teacher:	Well, a person lined up the Doraemon books like this: 1, 2,... Lined up... If you lined up the books like this for 1-*oku* (1 hundred-million) books, how long will the row of books be?
Student:	It might be 1-*oku* (1 hundred-million) centimeters...
Teacher:	How about you? What did you say?
Student:	It must be about 1-*oku* (1 hundred-million) centimeters.
Teacher:	I see. It is 1-*oku* (1 hundred-million) centimeters. How far can we go if we said 1-*oku* centimeters?
Student:	I think it is about the size of this classroom.
Teacher:	You mean if you line the books this way? I see. Well, I will give you a hint, because if you think about the problem as it is, you may not go forward. Actually, a person actually lined up some books...
Students:	Wow...
Teacher:	It said that the person lined up 1-*man* books.
Student:	Wow, for 1-*man* books...
Teacher:	If 1-*man* books are lined up for 1-man books it is 150 meters.

Doraemon

1-Man books
150 m

Students:	Wow...
Teacher:	It is about the length of this school playground. So it is from here to about Mt. Donguri. Could you wait for a second? Well, how about 1-*oku* (1 hundred-million) books? What kind of length is that going to be? Could Hashimoto-kun wait for a second? Because everybody needs to listen a little bit more. If you use these things, if you use these things, you can figure out what the length for 1-*oku* (1 hundred-million) books would be, can't you? In your notebook, please write down the expression. What would the expression be?

And write down the reasons for the expression.

While thinking about these things, please write out how long the row of *oku* Doraemon books will be.

The students worked independently while Nakano-sensei walked among them, looking at their work and stopping to talk briefly with some about their solutions. The observers from the lesson study team also moved among the students, watching how they approached the problem and taking notes.

After approximately six minutes, Nakano-sensei called the class together.

Teacher:	Who could solve this problem? Well, first... I would like you to tell me the expression. Well, I want somebody to tell me the expression. How about Shirai-kun?
Shirai:	Well, 150 times 10 *man*.
Teacher:	150 times 10 *man*. One, two, three, four, five (counting zeros). So this is good. And what is the answer?
Shirai:	The answer is... Well...
Teacher:	Okay. How many zeros after 15?
Shirai:	There are six zeros.
Teacher:	Six. One, two, three, four, five, six.
Student:	*Ichi* (ones), *juu* (tens), *hyaku* (hundreds), *sen* (thousands), *man* (ten-thousands), *juu-man* (ten man),...
Teacher:	*Ichi* (ones), *juu* (tens), *hyaku* (hundreds), *sen* (thousands), *man* (ten-thousands) *Jyu-man* (ten *man*), *hyaku-man* (hundred *man*), *sen-man* (thousand *man*). 1500 *man*. Is it okay? So the answer is...
Student:	The answer is 1500-*man* meters.

Student C

150 x 100000 = 15000000

A, 15000000 m

Teacher:	Yes. Yes, this is one way to solve this problem. Is there any other way to solve this problem?

Teacher:	Other way...
	Well, who should I ask? How about Matsumoto-kun?
Matsumoto:	I did it a different way, but my answer is a little bit different.
Teacher:	I see your answer is a little different.
Matsumoto:	My answer is different from Shirai-kun's.
Teacher:	Yes.
Matsumoto:	150 times parenthesis 1 *oku* (1 hundred-million) divided by 1 *man*...
Teacher:	150 times 1 *oku* (1 hundred-million)...
	One, two, three, four, five, six, seven, eight, (counting zeros) and divided by...
Matsumoto:	1 *man*.
Teacher:	1 *man*.
	And then?
Matsumoto:	Equals...150 *man*.

Student D

150 × (100000000 ÷ 10000)

= 1500000

A. 1500000 m

Student:	Yes, the answer became the same.
Teacher:	The answer?
Student:	Okay!
Teacher:	Are there any other expressions? Or something you want to add? Yes, well...
	Excuse me. Who are you? Hayashi-kun.
Hayashi:	The answer is...
Teacher:	Could you come to the blackboard? I think it is better to copy your note-book.
	Hayashi-kun's solution is kind of difficult to understand.
	Hayashi-kun's...
	Then... This one became... 150-*man* meters...
	And this became 1500 kilometers.

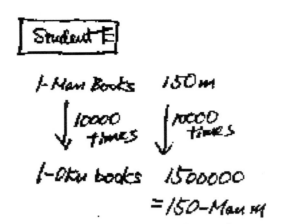

Teacher: Okay.
Are there any other expressions? Yes?

One other student, Maho-san, shared her solution with the class. Nakano-sensei wrote her equation on the board —

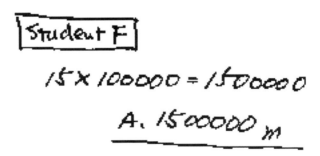

Teacher: Well, now... Matsumoto-kun, Hayashi-kun, and Maho-san got 150 *man*, and only Shirai-kun's was 1500 *man*.
Well, what is going on?
Could Shirai-kun explain in front of the class how you thought about your solution?
Okay, everybody. Please put your pencils down and listen to your friend's explanation.

Shirai: From here, these zeros are increasing one by one.
And this one is also times 10 so...

	150 times 10 *man* equals 1500 *man*. This is how I thought about it. Do you have any questions?
Teacher:	If you don't have any questions, does that mean it's okay with you? Did you understand Shirai-kun's explanation? Okay, you can ask.
Student:	Could you explain it one more time?
Teacher:	Could you explain it slowly?
Shirai:	From here, the number of zeros increased one by one so…
Teacher:	Wait a second, so this one has… So this one has two zeros (times 100).
Shirai & Teacher:	Three zeros.
Shirai & Teacher:	Four zeros.
Teacher:	So you thought that this must have 5 zeros. That's what you thought.
Students:	Oh, I see.
Teacher:	Then…
Shirai:	Then- 150 times 10-man equals… 1500 *man*.
Teacher:	Yes, that is wonderful, isn't it? I see you used the pattern that these zeros increase one by one. I see. So do you think this is a right answer?
Student:	I am trying to read the teacher's face (expression).
Teacher:	How about Tanabe-san?
Tanabe:	But if you look at these, the zeros are decreasing one by one. But 1-man kilograms and 1-man books are both 1 *man* so I think it should be 10,000 times, just like this.
Teacher:	Well, could you explain a little more?
Tanabe:	This is 100 *man* and this one is 10 *man* and this one is 1 *man*. And these zeros are increasing one by one. And 1-*man* kilograms and 1-*man* books both have 1 *man* in it, so I think the number 10,000 times should also be the same.
Teacher:	I see. If we don't say anything addressing what Shirai-kun said, then this lesson will end with Shirai-kun's solution. Shirai-kun. Well, just like Maho-san said… The units used, books and kilograms, are fine because the number is the same. What do you think about this? Shirai-kun, were you convinced with Maho-san's explanation?
Shirai:	Well… The units used for weight and length are different. So I think the 1 *man* times becomes 10 *man* times.
Teacher:	I see, it becomes 1 *man* times to 10 *man* times. I see.
Student:	This is a tricky problem that doesn't have an easy answer.

Although the zeros increase by one, it shouldn't be that easy—like 10 *man*—because it's a continuation of the increase.

Student: I think what Shirai-kun said...the pattern of the increasing zeros...was just speculation.

So I think, the reasons...because of the pattern of the increasing zeros or because the units are different...are not right.

Student: When we started this lesson, nobody told us there is a pattern like that and the increasing pattern is not a rule. So it is his own convenient reason.

Teacher: So what do you think, Shirai-kun?

Some said, "Your own convenient reason" or something like that or it's too much to say "because I see the pattern here."

However, the reason that somebody gave "The numbers are the same even though the units are different."

What do you think about this statement?

Teacher: Well, we are going over the time limit by a lot but...

We will end this lesson with tentative agreement that the answer might be 10 *man* times.

Then during tomorrow's lesson, we will look at Matsumoto-kun, Hayashi-kun, and Maho-san's answers,

and think about how long a row will be if we had 1-oku Doraemon books.

Nakano-sensei ended the class by asking students to write down their thoughts about the lesson in their notebooks and to turn them in.

BLACKBOARD

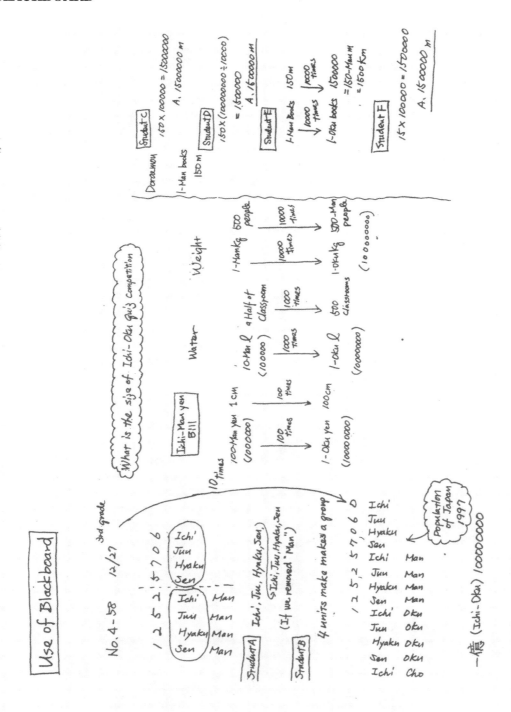

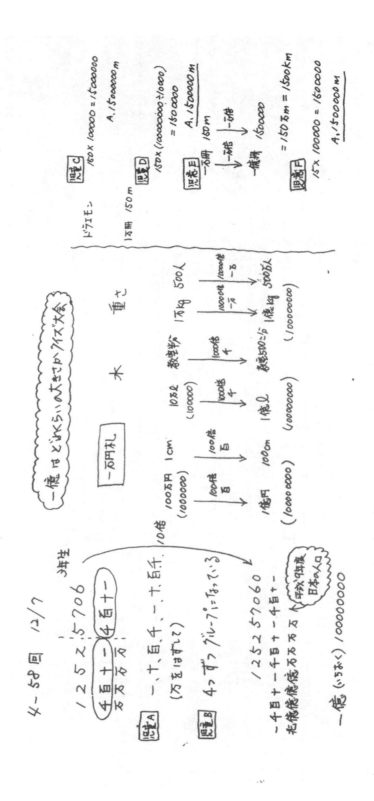

POSTLESSON DISCUSSION TRANSCRIPT

December 7, 1999

Monitor:

Let's start the postlesson discussion with the teacher's (who taught the lesson) self-reflection about the lesson.

Teacher:

In teaching this unit ("Large Numbers"), I wanted to make this lesson help the students foster the image of the size of large numbers like *oku* (100 million)" and "*cho* (1 trillion)." By preparing the lesson in this way, I thought that the students can be interested in a number like "*oku*", and they will have a desire to investigate it on their own.

However, the actual lesson did not go as well as I had thought. By having the students work on several problems to help their thinking about the relative size of the number 1 *oku* (100 million) using a quiz show format, I thought they could use the newly acquired concept (the relative size of numbers) and be able to solve the Doraemon problem (comic book problem). However, in the actual lesson, the students could not see the merit of using the concept of the relative size of the number 1 *oku*. Particularly the concept that 1 *oku* is 1 *man* times 1 *man*.

Monitor:

Please ask questions if you have any.

A:

When did the students learn that, "if you multiply a number by 10 then the number will have "0" at the end of the number (in the one's position)," that is necessary for this lesson?

Teacher:

In our school's curriculum, this unit comes after "Multiplication of Large Numbers." I noticed that some textbooks use the opposite order. In the unit of "Multiplication of Large Numbers" the students learned the multiplication of numbers like "200 x 30" and they learned the concept of adding "0" at the end of the number.

B:

I notice that you did not write down the concept of adding "0" when a number is multiplied by 10 on the blackboard. Do you have any reason for not doing that?

Teacher:

I thought I would write down the concept when one of the students mentioned something like "because the number was multiplied by 1000 we need to add three zeros at the end of the number."

Ito:

Is your definition of "image of 1 *oku*" similar to the definition "1 *oku* is a very large number?"

Teacher:

I was thinking about the definition and the relative size of the number 1 *oku* which is something like 1 *oku* is 1 *man* times 1 *man*.

Monitor:

If you have any opinions please tell us.

C:

I question whether the students deepened their understanding of the concepts of the relative size of large numbers from today's lesson. For example, when the students were working on the Draemon comic book problem, the students did not seem to realize the size difference of 10 *man* times 1 *man* and 1 *man* times 1 *man*. I thought the students were thinking as if one of the numbers has one more "0" than others. I thought they are not really conceptualizing the size of these large numbers. Therefore, the conversation between the teacher and the students was more focused on the "trickiness" of the numbers rather than the actual size. I thought the teacher should have used more visually convincing materials to show the size to the students. For example, the teacher could use something like a number line.

D:

When I teach this lesson, I try to convince the students how large 1 *oku* is by creating materials that will help the students to visualize the size of the number. Thus, I use a 1-millimeter grid for the lesson. I use a 1 millimeter by 1 millimeter square and have students think about how large the figure will be if we have 1-*oku* (100 million) squares. If we do it this way, 1 *oku* becomes a 1 meter by 10 meter rectangle. So while I was watching the lesson, I thought that if the students can not conceptualize the size of 1 *oku*, it is very difficult for the students to know the relative size of 1 *oku*. I know that you cannot bring actual 1-*man* yen bills to show the height differences between 100-*man* yen and 1-*oku* yen, but the teacher needed to show the height of both cases so that the students feel how much these numbers are different.

C:

I understand your suggestion, but I thought showing actual number size differences and letting the students experience it is the content of the third grade curriculum. I think in the fourth grade it is much important to acquire the concept of the relative size of the large numbers, and the focus of the lesson should be on that.

Ito:

The concept of relative size of the large numbers is a really important concept the students need to learn in the fourth grade. However, some aspects of learning large numbers overlap in the third and fourth grades. Therefore, based on the numeration of whole numbers, the students need to see how large the numbers are by using different types of quantities (i.e., length, volume, weight, etc.). If the students do not have an image for how large the large numbers with different units are, I think it is a very dangerous situation. The scenario to have the students acquire such an image of large numbers should not occur by the teacher telling them. Instead, it is better for the students to think about the image.

For example, the teacher can ask the students "please think about the number by using something you can imagine."

In addition, when we use large numbers to show the size of large objects, we usually used a larger measurement unit in order to show its quantity. For example, we use the measurement unit kilometers when we talk about a very long distance instead of meters. When we teach this lesson, we should also think that we need to be consistent, just like teaching units of measurements. When we talk about how far the sun is from the earth, even if we used the unit of kilometers it will be a very large number. I hope that we can make the students understand that the numbers that they are learning now are very large numbers.

Fujii:

I thought if the teacher went over the relationship of numbers such as "1-*oku* liter equals 500 classrooms" and "1-*oku* kilogram equals 500-*man* children" then the students could gain a better image of the number 1 *oku*. They should have a chance to talk about something like "if we have 500 classrooms, we can not fit all the classrooms in our school property." If the teacher and the students could have such conversations and had gone over those problems more carefully, I thought the students could feel that the number 1 *oku* is a very large number.

Shimizu:

I think the students usually do not have a good concept of large numbers like these. I think there is a tendency for students usually to think that 1 *oku* and 10 *oku* are not so different in size. I thought today's lesson had a good exercise for the students in estimating the size of the large numbers by changing the yardstick of the unit (e.g., looking at 1-*oku* kilogram by 20 kilogram of a child).

The lesson went from length, volume, weight, and back to length when the students worked on the Draemaon (comic book) problem. I thought that if the teacher related the two length problems it might be more effective for the students' understanding.

Ito:

I thought the lesson went too fast. I thought the teacher could go over the concept if the number is multiplied by 1000, then the resulting number has three zeros added.

E:

Up to the Draemon problem, the explanation of each problem was something like "because 1 centimeter became 100 centimeters is why it is 100 times; therefore, 1 *oku* is 100 *man's* 100 times." However, when the students needed to work on the Draemon problem, the students needed to think about l *oku* is 1 *man* times 1 *man* first, then multiply the 150 meter by 1 *man*. In other words, the students needed to know how many times 1 *man* is in 1 *oku* in order to solve this problem. Therefore, the teacher needed to guide the students to think 1 *oku* equals how many times for specified numbers.

Fujii:

I noticed the same thing. Up to the Doraemon problem all the explanations for each problem were: "1 centimeter became 100 centimeter so it is 100 times" and "A half of classroom became 500 classrooms so it is 1000 times." I thought the explanation of each problem should be: "Because from 100 *man* to 1 *oku* is 100 times so 1 centimeter is also multiplied by 100 to become 100 centimeters."

Ito:

Because the first three problems were in a quiz show format, I guess the response to the problems were "right" or "wrong," but I think the situation of "1 centimeter became 100 centimeters so it is 100 times" should have been gone over carefully by identifing how many zeros we needed to add and thinking about the relation of 100 *man* and 1 *oku*.

Teacher:

I thought my students could understand 100 times by looking at the relationship between 1 centimeter and 100 centimeters.

Fujii:

The explanation used in the lesson was that way, but actually the 100 times should be found in the relation between 100 *man* and 1 *oku*.

B:

I have a comment on the students' answers for those problems. When the students were working on the second problem that used liters, one of the students said "1-*oku* liters equals 12 classrooms" although the students worked on the first problem, 1 *oku* is 100 times 100 *man*. I thought the student's response was clearly a wrong guess. The teacher mentioned that he wanted to do the first couple of problems in a quiz show style, but does he really think that it is okay for the students to guess the answers. I think guessing without thinking is not good especially after the teacher provided a hint for solving the problem.

Teacher:

In my mind it was more like a guessing quiz show style until the second problem that used liters. I wanted to discuss the problem as a mathematics problem so some of the students start to think about how they can find the answer by calculating.

C:

If I were a student in the classroom, I would like to know the size of 1-*oku* liter by relating to the 1-liter container that the teacher showed in the classroom. The teacher gave a half of the volume of the classroom as a hint to think about the problem, but in my mind I felt like the hint did not come from any relation to the container. I thought the same way for the weight problem. I thought the students wanted to know the relationship between 1 kilogram and 1-*oku* kilograms, and the hint of a child's weight was introduced as a surprise.

Teacher:

Because the focus of the lesson was to have the students foster their ability to look at the relative size of the numbers, the numbers that I prepared for those hints were artificially chosen numbers. I understand what you said, but I think there is a value for looking at the relative size of the numbers—something like "1 *oku* equals 1 *man* 1 *man* times,"—even if the hints were somewhat artificially chosen ones.

Fujii:

I think the students can easily imagine the size of 1-*oku* liters if they are told it is about the size of "500 classrooms" rather than telling them it is "1 *oku* times 1-liter container." In today's lesson, the teacher was helping the students to understand the relative size of numbers by talking about an absolute size comparison of "1-*oku* liters equals the size of 500 classrooms" and relative size comparison of "1- *oku* liters equals 1000 times 10-*man* litters." I thought the teacher was covering these two aspects of the relative size of numbers using "length," "volume," and "weight."

B:

I think it is hard to express a large number like 1 *oku* if we don't use an absolute comparison. I think even you said 1-*oku* liter. It is hard to express the size without using the size of "pools" and "classrooms."

Monitor:

Often people express a large number using the height of the Tokyo Tower.

Ito:

Even in this case I thought the teacher could have asked the students, "What should we use to show how large 1-*oku* liters is? Should we use the size of this classroom which everyone knows very well?" I wanted to have a better flow for the lesson by having the teacher include a conversation like this.

A:

In this lesson, "1 *oku* is 100 *man* times 100 *man*" was talked about as one of the quiz style problems. I think the teacher needed to go over these explanations carefully, using a chart (the chart shows each position (unit) of the number). Using the chart the teacher could explain, "because the numbers moved two positions on the chart, the number was multiplied by 100." I think such clear explanations could help the students be able to solve the problem such as the Draemon problem. Although the students had already learned some parts of concept of the decimal positional notation system using the chart in the third grade, I thought the content that was introduced in today's lesson was a little bit difficult for the students to learn. I thought the content that was taught in today's lesson should have moved to the third lesson of this unit. Learning about the concept that a zero is added because the number was multiplied by 10 should come after the students fully understand the concept of the decimal positioning notation system.

Monitor:

Finally, I would like to ask the advisers to comment on the lesson and close this discussion.

Shimizu:

The lesson style that we often see these days is the problem solving style (*mondai kaiketsu-gata*) that goes through the steps of posing a problem, students solve the problem on their own, student presentation and discussion, etc. However, I think some lessons can be different from the problem solving style just like today's lesson. The focal point of the discussion today was "sense (feeling) of quantity (of large numbers)." In today's lesson the teacher was trying to foster the students' sense of large numbers. Therefore, I thought the teacher needed to go over the decimal positional notation system using the chart that was mentioned by someone before. In addition, the students learned four problems today, but I thought the teacher needed to go over the problems more carefully and unify the relationship in them. I thought the teacher needed to use a visual that shows 1 *oku* as a center of the focus and use some arrows to indicate "1000 times 100 *man*" and "1 *man* times 1 *man*." If the teacher had a chance to use a diagram, that might help the students' understanding of the relation between the numbers.

Fujii:

Because the problems were introduced in a quiz show style, I thought the lesson drew the students' attention well. I thought the students were thrilled waiting to find out the sizes of the number 1-*oku* which were presented in length, volume, and weight. I thought these experiences helped foster students' conception of the quantity of large numbers. The differences between what students learn in the third and fourth grade are that third-grade students learn the number as decimal numbers and the fourth-grade students learn the numeration system (where different numerations are used every four positions). In other words, the second one shows that "1 *man* times 1 *man*" becomes a new unit "*oku*," and if we multiply the number by 1 *man* again, we will get another new unit. I thought today's lesson was carefully planed to cover the concept well. The numbers "1 *man* times 1 *man*" show the characteristic of the number 1 *oku* well. And the teacher mentioned, this relation in the problem of kilograms and Doraemon. However, as some people mentioned the explanation of the relation of the numbers should not be "100 times 1 centimeter equals 100 centimeters," it should be "100 times 100 *man* equals 1 *oku*." If the explanation had been this way, I thought the students could have solved the Doraemon problem.

Ito:

In this unit, the focus of the lesson is usually on learning about the concept of the numeration system, and the lessons tend to be not so interesting. I think the teacher's effort in preparing a thought out lesson that is more attractive for the students can be praised highly. I think these kinds of lessons need to be more fun. However, this unit introduces not only the numeration system but also the decimal positional notation system. The merit of the decimal positional notation system is that the position of a number moves up one, which means the number was multiplied by 10. I thought that if the teacher could go over this in the decimal positional notation system where the number was multiplied by 100 and 1000, the lesson could have been better.

I noticed that there was a student who wanted to show 150 *man* meters using kilometers. I thought the student's effort was important. Moreover, I hope that the teacher also spends some time to help visualize the size of the number used in kilometers. In many cases, students do not know how far apart Tokyo is from Osaka. I think using such numbers for the two cities could provide a clearer image of large numbers. If the teacher could present something that the students could use to 'feel' how large a number is, I thought the lesson would have been better.

Appendix G:
Record of Instruction:
Reasoning About Three Coins at
Third Grade

Homework for Workshop Participants   216

Lesson Plan   217
 Deborah Loewenberg Ball, Professor, University of Michigan

Lesson Plan Transcript   219

Class Description   225

HOMEWORK FOR WORKSHOP PARTICIPANTS

August 7, 2000 (given out at the workshop)

Problem 1

Suppose you have three kinds of coins in your pocket. One is worth 1 cent, one is worth 5 cents, and one is worth 10 cents. If you pull out three coins, what amounts of money might you have?

Problem 2

Again, suppose you have three kinds of coins in your pocket and that one is worth 1 cent, one is worth 5 cents, and one is worth 10 cents. If you pull out two coins, what amounts of money might you have?

Problem 3

Next, suppose you have three kinds of coins in your pocket and that again one is worth 1 cent, one is worth 5 cents, and one is worth 10 cents. What if you pull out four coins? What amounts of money might you have?

Problem 4

Now suppose you have four kinds of coins in your pocket and one is worth 1 cent, one is worth 5 cents, and the last is worth 25 cents. Suppose you pull out three coins. What amounts of money might you have?

Problem 5

Which problem seems harder—problem 3 or problem 4? Why?

LESSON PLAN

Problem:

I have pennies, nickels, and dimes in my pocket. If I pull three coins out, what amount of money could I have?

This is the fourth day of the school year. Three purposes for the class today:
1. (a) To develop students' habits of searching out multiple solutions, establishing whether all solutions have been found.
    (b) To develop students'ability to produce a mathematical explanation. In this case, an explanation for a solution must establish that:
       (1) three coins were used, of these three types;
       (2) the amount of money produced is correct.

2. To communicate to the students what doing mathematics will mean (e.g., explain solutions to the teacher and to one another; listen to, critique, and use other students' ideas; be accountable for their ideas).

3. To begin to learn about the students:
    *   Their addition (multiplication) skills.
    *   Their openness to multiple answers and solutions.
    *   Their strategies for finding solutions.
    *   How they keep track of their solutions.
    *   How skeptical they are that they are done and how they go about determining when they have completed the problem.
    *   How they work with concrete materials.
    *   Their disposition to confer, to consider others' ideas.

Plan:
1. Set up the problem:
    *   Make sure students can read it.
    *   Review coins if necessary.

2. Allow individual work time (10+ minutes)

3. Whole group discussion
    *   Elicit solutions
    *   Ask for explanations/justifications.
    *   Guide the construction of explanations as necessary.
    *   Guide students to attend to and respond to (evaluate) one another's solutions.

4. Conclusion: Did we find all the solutions? How do we know? How can we prove that we have all the solutions?

Strategies they are likely to use:
1. Pull out coins, three at a time, see what you have, if it doesn't repeat something you already have, then write it down. If you keep repeating, you must be done.
2. Think of combinations, make them concretely. Write them down.
3. Think of combinations and write them down.

Different possible approaches to recording:
1. Write down nothing.
2. Write down total amounts of money (e.g. 21, 12) but not the coins used to make them.
3. Write down addition to represent coins (e.g., 5 + 1 + 1 = 7).
4. Write down coins and amounts (e.g., 1 dime and 1 penny and 1 nickel = 16 cents).

LESSON PLAN TRANSCRIPT

Records of Instruction:
The Three-Coin Problem in the Third Grade
September 18, 1989
Spartan Village Elementary School
Teacher: Mrs. Ball

Seating Chart

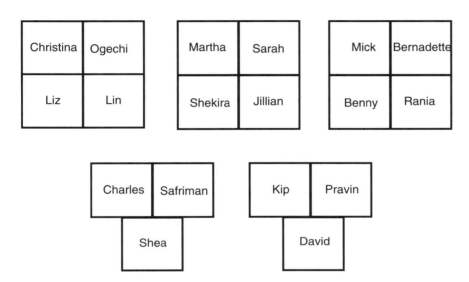

This was the fourth mathematics class of the school year. The class had been working on combination and permutation problems since the first day.

The problem on the board stated: I have pennies, nickels, and dimes in my pocket. If I pull three coins out, what amounts of money could I have?

Ball:	Can I ask somebody to read the problem on the board? David could you read it?
David:	I have pennies... nickels... and dimes... in... my pocket. If... I... pull three... coins... out... what... amount of money (pause) would?
Ball:	Put a C. Could.
David:	...could I have.
Ball:	What problem is this similar to? (pause) Charles?
Charles:	The one with the the coins.
Ball:	What number of coins did we work with last week?
Charles:	Um, two.
Ball:	Two coins...

	Can somebody give one example of amount of money that you could have?
	Shea?
Shea:	Like you, like, you could have um...
Ball:	Could you speak up just a little? I'm not sure that Bernadette can hear you.
Shea:	You could have like, five— you could like, pull out one of each of them and you could like, you could get um, sixteen.
Ball:	Okay, one penny, one nickel, and one dime.
	Is that three coins?
Shea:	Uh huh.
Ball:	And he says that's sixteen cents all together. What do other people think about that?
	Lin?
Lin:	I agree with him.
Ball:	How would you get sixteen cents?
Lin:	Um, one dime would be ten cents, a nickel, a nickel, ten cent...
	Wait, a dime is ten cents and then a nickel is five cents and it's fifteen cents and if it's a penny it will be sixteen cents.
Ball:	Okay.
	I would like you to work on this for a few minutes and see what different combinations you can figure out.
	And use the money if you want, to to help you,
	and then after a little bit we will stop and talk about it together.
	First I would like you to work on it a little bit alone and see what you can come up with by yourself.
	Make sure you have the whole problem copied.
	And then write down whatever you need to write down in your notebook to help you remember what you're figuring out.

The students worked on the problem alone or with the people seated near them.

After they had been working for about 12 minutes, Mrs. Ball called the class together for a brief discussion.

Ball:	I have a question to ask.
	Does anybody have a prediction of how many solutions they think they will find for this problem?
Lin:	I'm not that...
Ball:	Shea?
Shea:	How about around ten.
Ball:	Excuse me just a second. Ogechi and Lin can you hear Shea?
Lin:	Yeah.
Shea:	Around ten.
Ball:	Around ten. Is there a reason why you predicted ten?
Shea:	Because um, I'm not sure.

Ball:	Any, any different predictions? Lin?
Lin:	Nine.
Ball:	Anybody else? Mick?
Mick:	I've found nine.
Ball:	You come up with nine already? Mick has already found nine. How are you going to know when you have all the solutions? (pause) Any ideas? How would you know if you had found them all? Liz?
Liz:	You would start um…
Ball:	Excuse me just a second, Kip and Pravin and Safriman— Right now Liz is talking and I would like you to be able to hear her.
Liz:	You would start doing the ones that you've already done over.
Ball:	Pravin could you hear Liz?
Pravin:	Yes.
Ball:	What did she say?
Pravin:	(shakes head)
Ball:	Excuse me? Can you say it one more time I'm sorry. Pravin listen to Liz, okay? Speak a little louder.
Liz:	Okay. Um, you would start—you would use the, the same ones over again.
Ball:	You would use the same one over again? Anybody have any other ideas of how you would know if you had gotten them all? Is there any other way to tell? (pause) Shekira?
Shekira:	When we confer with somebody and if they have the same answers as you.
Shekira:	If they don't, then you don't have all the answers and you need to write it down, then you have all of them.
Ball:	I have a small concern, right now. I would like everybody to put their coins down and their pens down. I would like everybody to put their coins down and their pens down for a moment. One of the things that's very important is that if one person in the class is talking other people need to listen, because people are saying things that can help you think about the problems. Shekira said some interesting things, and so did Liz, but lots of people were not listening to them. I know it's because you're finding more solutions yourself. But, one of the things that I would really like you to, to see you doing is to listening… …to be listening really hard when someone else has an idea, because it might help you with your thinking.

	I'm sure a lot of people didn't hear Shekira.
	And I had to ask Liz to say, what she said three times.
	Stop for a moment now, and listen hard to Shekira and see what you think about what she is saying.
	Could you say it one more time?
Shekira:	Well, when you think you're done, confer with somebody else at your table and if they have the same answers as you do then...
	Then, you know you have all of them and if you don't then you write it down on your paper.
	Or they write the ones they have that you have.
Ball:	So Liz and Shekira gave us two different ideas.
	Liz said when you start repeating yourself in the ideas you come up with, you think you probably have them all.
	Shekira said...Shekira added something to it. Shekira said when you think you have them all,
	you could confer with somebody else at your table and see if they found any that you haven't found.
	Are there any other ways to know if you have all the answers?
	Mick?
Mick:	It's not about the answers.
Ball:	So, it's another comment?
Mick:	Yeah.
Ball:	What?
Mick:	Um, I think it's ten because I just came up with one more.
Ball:	Okay, well, Mick just came up with one more. He's up to ten possible answers.
	Take a few more minutes to work on it, and then I'd like to spend a few minutes talking about what you've come up with.

The children returned to working on the problem individually and in small groups. After a few minutes, Mrs. Ball called them together again.

Ball:	Let's stop for a moment. Put your coins down.
	It's easy to tell when people have stopped with the coins, because the coins make a lot of noise.
	Put the coins down and put the pens down for a moment. You're going to want your pen though, because while we have...
	while we discuss the problem, if somebody brings up an answer that you didn't find, you might like to record it in your notebook.
	We have one answer recorded on the board, one solution. Who would like to share another solution that they came up with?
	Safriman?
Safriman:	Twelve.
Ball:	Okay, twelve cents. Could somebody tell how Safriman got twelve cents?

	What coins did Safriman use to get twelve cents? Who thinks they know? David?
David:	Um…
	Safriman used dime um, and two pennies.
Ball:	What do other people think about what David said. David said he thinks Safriman used two pennies and one dime.
	What do other people think about that?
	Sarah?
Sarah:	I agree.
Ball:	Can you prove that, that's right?
Sarah:	Yeah, because it's three, three coins.
Ball:	Three coins. How can you prove that that's twelve cents?
Sarah:	Because… ten and two is twelve and that's three coins.
Ball:	Any comments? Liz?
Liz:	I agree with that.
Ball:	Anybody disagree with it?
	Okay, another solution? Another possible way to do this problem? No, I just asked you.
	Somebody different? Bernadette?
Bernadette:	I got seven cents.
Ball:	Who thinks they know how Bernadette got seven cents?
	Kip?
Kip:	One nickel and two pennies.
Ball:	Christina? What do you think about what Kip said?
Christina:	I agree with him.
Ball:	Can you prove that, that's seven cents?
Christina:	Yeah. Because um, a nickel and two pennies is—a nickel is five cents and two pennies will add to seven cents.
Ball:	Comments from anybody else?
	Anybody disagree with this?
	Okay, do we have another solution?
	How about Ogechi, do you have something different in your notebook?
Ogechi:	Thirty cents.
Ball:	How much?
Ogechi:	Thirty
Ball:	Ogechi, do you want to tell us how you got it or should we ask other people to figure it out?
Ogechi:	Three dimes.
Ball:	Okay, three dimes. Jillian, what do you think about what Ogechi said?
Jillian:	I think she's right.
Ball:	Why do you think she's right?
Jillian:	Because… ten plus ten is twenty and plus another ten is thirty.
Ball:	Any comments from anybody else? David?
David:	Twenty five.

Ball:	Oh, you're already giving another one?
David:	Uh huh.
Ball:	Did you agree with Jillian?
David:	Um, yeah.
Ball:	Okay, what is your solution?
David:	Fifteen.
Ball:	Fifteen. Who thinks they know how David got fifteen cents? Sarah?
Sarah:	Um, three nickels.
Ball:	Shea, what do you think about that?
Shea:	I'm not sure.
Ball:	Why are you not sure? What are you figuring out?
Shea:	Oh.
Ball:	Shea, how much is one nickel?
Shea:	Uh, five cents. And two nickels are ten cents, and three nickels are fifteen.
Ball:	So—Do you agree with this then or disagree?
Shea:	Um, agree.
Ball:	We're going to stop. I would like everyone to look over this way for a moment.
	When we start math tomorrow, we're going to continue with this problem a little bit longer.
	I have a question to ask before we stop and a comment to make. I'll make my comment first and then ask my question.
	My comment was, I thought people did a better job just now listening to each other's solutions and giving each other time.
	Did you notice that when somebody was figuring something out people weren't going uh,uh,uh…
	or interrupting. People were listening and thinking about whether it made sense.
	Did you notice that? And did you also notice that people were explaining why it made sense.
	Like people would say it's thirty cents because, Jillian said, because ten plus ten is twenty and ten more is thirty.
	Was that a good explanation?
	It was a good explanation because it helped us understand why that answer made sense.

Mrs. Ball asked the students about a task she had posed to them the day before. After hearing brief reports from several students, she ended the class.

CLASS DESCRIPTION

Name	Gender	Race	Country	English Proficiency	How Long At This School[1]
Benny	M	White	Ethiopia	fluent	3 years
Bernadette	F	White	Canada	native speaker	just started
Charles	M	Asian	Taiwan/Canada	fluent	3 years
Christina	F	African-American	U.S.A.	native speaker	12 months
David	M	Asian	Indonesia	developing	3 years
Ira	F	White	Indonesia	developing	5 months
Jillian	F	White	U.S.A.	native speaker	3 years
Kip	M	African Black	Kenya	fluent	3 years
Lin	F	Asian	Taiwan	fluent	2 years
Liz	F	White	U.S.A.	native speaker	3 years
Marta	F	Latina	Nicaragua	beginning	just started
Mick	M	White	U.S.A.	native speaker	2 years
Ogechi	F	African Black	Nigeria	fair	3 years
Pravin	M	White	Nepal	beginning	5 months
Rania	F	White	Egypt	good	3 years
Safriman	M	Asian	Indonesia	developing	12 months
Sarah	F	White	U.S.A.	native speaker	2 years
Shea	M	White	U.S.A.	native speaker	2 years
Shekira	F	African-American	U.S.A.	native speaker	just started

[1]NOTE: This column reflects the length of time the child had been in this <u>school</u> as of 9/89. No one had been in this <u>class</u> longer than a few days.

Appendix H:
Transcript of Excerpts from
Small Group Discussions

SMALL GROUP DISCUSSIONS

Video highlights of the small group discussions provide further insight into the discussion and issues raised. In particular, the discussions dealt with observations related to two of the questions considered by the small groups:

- Lesson design and teacher knowledge.
  Question 2: How do teachers use mathematics together with other kinds of knowledge and skill in order to connect students with mathematics?

- Language related to the enactment of a lesson.
  Question 3: How do skilled teachers learn about and make use of their students' knowledge and capabilities to help them learn mathematics?

SMALL GROUP DISCUSSION TRANSCRIPT

CLIP 1

Conversation Related to the Use of Mathematical Knowledge

Japanese Participant	Consider what the objective and aim of this lesson is going to be. And also we have to think about before, the children have learned what...beforehand...already? And then we have to predict what the reactions of the children will be. And also what kind of ideas they are going to submit. And if there are different opinions, then how am I going to summarize those? In working on those activities, we utilitize our knowledge in mathematics, and also our pedagogical knowledge as well; so linking those two knowledges, and then creating a lesson plan. So lesson plan preparation is very important.
U.S. Participant	And there's one way to help them begin to realize that there are gaps there, and how to fill in those gaps. That becomes a very useful tool for one, understanding the mathematics themselves, and two, helping their students understand the mathematics. So, I think we in agreement there.

CLIP 2

The Role of the Lesson Plan

U.S. Participant 1	And on the left-hand side of the lesson plan?
Japanese Participant	Yes. That is the more detailed part.
U.S. Participant 1	What is that about? It includes.
Japanese Participant	The lesson part you have aim...of the lesson. That aim could be, could be...your chief focus.
Translator	Should be more in detail.
Japanese Participant	More detail. And accordingly to the plan, you need to have the process of evaluation.
U.S. Participant 1	How will you know when you...
Japanese Participant	If aim comes, evaluation should be consistent. Therefore, if you have aim, you have evaluation. Objective and evaluation.
Japanese Participant 1	Teacher sets the aim. And the teacher evaluates.
U.S. Participant 1	By himself?

Japanese Participant 1	Yeah, I mean...
U.S. Participant 1	Whether the students...
Japanese Participant 1	For instance, this part—I mean—to let them understand, say, for instance...the definition of square.
	And then, evaluation means do they understand, (the definition) properly or not.
	This is a kind of checking point.
U.S. Participant 2	And will it say how the teacher will know that?
	In other words, a student says, "The teacher's goal is for students to understand the definition of square."
	Does a teacher in the evaluation part say how he will know whether they do?
Japanese Participant 2	At this point, very important to take a walk...
U.S. Participant 1	Walk around?
Japanese Participant 2	Between desks.
U.S. Participant 1	Walking among the desks.

CLIP 3

Planning

U.S. Participant	It's about decisions; decisions.
	I mean, if you watch the interaction in Deborah's class...
	that you're constantly making decisions.
	Should I follow this point?
	Should I do this?
	Should I...how far are we going to go?
	And you have to make all these decisions on the fly.
	You may have an idea where you're going, but it is still...
	Whereas I think, for many of our Japanese teachers—my impression is—that they have much more anticipated...
	It isn't that they aren't willing to be spontaneous; they're happy to be spontaneous and so are the students.
	But there's a lot more of it that has a structure in it.

CLIP 4

Role of the Teacher

Translator	N - O - E
Group	N - E (correcting translator)
Translator	R - I - A - G - E
U.S. Participant 1	Got it. Kneading with bread, right?
Japanese Participant 1	Similar to the idea...on the blackboard...
	and teacher try to integrate, compare, and discuss the idea to...get...final...conclusion to lesson.
	So, we have special term for...in summing up

Japanese Participant 2	*Neriage* means…goes up, I mean…
Translator	To raise it.
Group	To raise it up.
Japanese Partcipant 2	Which imply…you can not…stay same level as student…because you are teacher.
	You have to try to level them up.
U.S. Participant 1	This is a different word from the one you just said?
Group	Yes.
U.S. Participant 1	What is the different spelled word?
U.S. participant	N - O - E - R - I - A - G - E (misspelled)
Japanese Participant 1	Try to describe whole class…whole class discussion.
	And a teacher orchestrated. Orchestrate.
	Orchestrate.
Japanese Participant 2	Conduct, conduct.
Japanese Participant 1	Then to…to try them to get higher level, particularly mathematically.
	And they also, I think—*matome* could be a special term.
Group	*Matome. Matome. Matome.*
U.S. Participant 1	M - A
Translator	M - A - T - O - M - E
U.S. Participant 1	Summing up?
Group	Summing up.
U.S. Participant 1	What does it mean?
	Does it literally mean summing?
Japanese Participant 1	Yes, well…I mean, yes.
U.S. Participant 1	What else is it used for in Japanese?
Japanese Participant 2	(*Matome. Matome.*) Wrap up session.
	Wrap up.
	Concluding session, closing.
Japanese Participant 1	**Translation**: So the VCR that Deborah has showed us; has shown us the *neriage* portion. That means the one to one interaction between the teacher and the student. Alright? But I have seen no wrap-up portion.
Group	*Matome? Matome*…that's right, *matome.*
Japanese Participant 1	No, no, no!!
	Translation: So, we have to have a group discussion in class in order to have *neriage*. Okay?
	Translation: But, Japanese teachers tend to avoid a situation, where we have only one to one correspondence and interaction between the teacher and one of the students. We would like to have a group discussion.
Japanese Participant 2	Teacher, student, student, student, student, and teacher.
	Teacher, teacher, student, student, student, teacher.
U.S. Participant	Yeah, we didn't see very much of that.

Appendix I:
A Written Case:
Pattern Trains at Sixth Grade

COMET

Cases of Mathematics Instruction to Enhance Teaching

This case was developed by the collaborative team of Margaret Smith, Edward Silver, Mary Kay Stein, Marjorie Henningsen, and Melissa Boston under the auspices of the COMET Project. COMET, funded by the National Science Foundation, is a project aimed at developing case materials for teacher professional development in mathematics. The project is co-directed by Edward Silver, Margaret Smith, and Mary Kay Stein and is housed at the Learning Research and Development Center at the University of Pittsburgh. For additional information about COMET contact Margaret Smith by phone at (412) 648-7361 or by e-mail at <pegs@pitt.edu>.

OPENING ACTIVITY

Solve

For the pattern shown below, compute the perimeter for the first four trains, determine the perimeter for the tenth train without constructing it, and then write a description that could be used to compute the perimeter of any train in the pattern. (Use the edge length of any pattern block as your unit of measure.)

The first train in this pattern consists of one regular hexagon. For each subsequent train, one additional hexagon is added. The first four trains in the pattern are shown below.

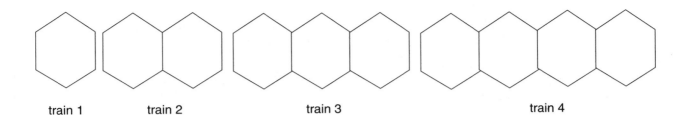

train 1   train 2   train 3   train 4

Consider

Find as many **different** ways as you can to compute (and justify) the perimeter.

THE PATTERN TRAINS

Part 1 — Catherine Evans

Catherine Evans had spent most of her 20-year career teaching in self-contained classrooms (ranging from grades 1-6) where she taught all subjects. Although she taught mathematics nearly every year, she preferred to teach literature, writing, and social studies because, in her view, instruction in these areas allowed for discussions with students and opportunities for creative expression rather than focusing on memorization and procedures.

Catherine viewed teaching mathematics very differently than teaching other subjects. She described her mathematics instruction as following a regular pattern: correcting homework assigned during the previous class by reading answers and having students mark problems as correct or incorrect; presenting new material (either to the whole class or to small groups) by explaining the procedure to be learned and demonstrating a small number of sample problems; monitoring student completion of a few problems; and having students work individually on a larger set of similar problems using the preferred strategy. She saw math as the easiest period of the day,

since it did not require much preparation. In addition, Catherine admitted, "probably during most of my teaching, I never thought of math as being as important as reading and writing."

Catherine Evans had been teaching at Quigley Middle School for three years when the opportunity arose to participate in a new math project. She was intrigued with the approach to mathematics teaching that was being proposed—one that emphasized thinking, reasoning, and communicating ideas—since these were the processes and skills that were central to her teaching in other content areas. Although she did not have any idea what this would mean in mathematics, she was ready for a new challenge and made the commitment to her colleagues to change the way mathematics was taught and learned in her classroom.

Catherine knew this would be hard, but she was confident about her abilities as a teacher. She had always been successful—her students did well on the district standardized tests, teachers in subsequent grades who had her students have always remarked about how well prepared they were, and parents often requested that their children be placed in her classroom. In addition, she had a deep commitment to her students and an enthusiasm for teaching. She saw herself as someone who related well to students and was able to motivate them to learn. She felt that her humor, the ability to laugh at herself and situations, was a valuable asset in the classroom no matter what she was teaching.

Catherine Evans Talks About Her Class

I have been teaching the new curriculum for about six weeks now and I have found that my sixth graders are not always prepared for the challenges presented. The tasks in the curriculum generally can't be solved by just using an algorithm, the solution path is not immediately evident and usually involves exploring and reasoning through alternatives, and most tasks involve providing a written explanation. If my students can't solve a problem immediately, they say, "I don't know," and give up. They have had limited experience in elementary school actually engaging actively with mathematics and expressing their thinking and have found this to be very difficult.

Seeing students give up has caused me great concern. I can't buy the idea that kids don't feel bad starting off with what they perceive to be failure. When they have work they can't do or don't have the confidence to do, then I have to intervene. I decided to help kids do more verbalization in class, get to the kids who didn't volunteer and guarantee them success by asking them to do things they couldn't fail to do right. I can't ignore the fact that success breeds success. Too many are starting out with what I'm sure they perceive to be failure.

In order to ensure student success, I have started to make some modifications in the curriculum, at times putting in an extra step or taking out something that seems too hard; rewriting problem instructions so that they are clearer and at an easier reading level; and creating easier problems for homework. In addition, during classroom instruction I try to break a task into small subtasks so that students can tackle one part of the task at a time.

We have been talking about patterns for a few weeks. The new unit that we started last week uses *trains* of pattern blocks arranged in a geometric sequence. The unit is supposed to help students visualize and describe geometric patterns, make conjectures about the patterns, determine the perimeters of trains they build, and ultimately, to develop a generalization for the perimeter of any train in a pattern. This unit really lays the groundwork for developing the algebraic ideas of generalization, variable, and function that students will explore in grades 6 through 8. Experiences like these lay the foundation for more formal work in algebra in eighth grade.

We spent a lot of time in the beginning of this unit just making observations about the trains—the number of pattern blocks in a train, the geometric shapes that comprise a train, and the properties of a train (e.g., each train has four sides, opposite sides of the train are parallel). Students got pretty good at making observations about specific trains once we had done a few, but I had to keep reminding them that the observations needed to be mathematical. For some patterns I got some really weird responses like "it looks like a squished pop can" or "it looks like a belt buckle." But once I reminded students that the point in making observations was to be able to predict what larger trains were going to look like, they were able to move beyond these fanciful responses.

The Class

Yesterday for the first time we started determining the perimeters of the trains using the side of the square as the unit of measure. Homework last night had been to find the perimeters of the first three trains in the pattern shown below. I also asked students to find the perimeter of the 10th, 20th, and 100th trains in this pattern. My plan for class was to begin by discussing the homework and then having students explore another pattern.

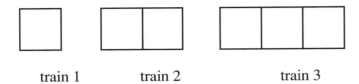

train 1   train 2   train 3

As students entered the classroom and got their papers out, I made a quick trip to the back of the room to check on the video camera. My colleagues and I have decided to videotape some of our classes this year so that we could use the tapes to reflect on how things are going with the new curriculum and to talk about various issues that arise in using the materials. This was my first day of taping, and I was a little nervous about being on film. Students asked about the camera as they entered the classroom but seemed unfazed by the idea of being taped. I just hoped I could forget that it was there.

Discussing the Square Pattern Trains

In order to get things started, I asked students to make observations about the pattern. Shandra said that she had noticed that all of the trains were rectangles. Jake said that he noticed that the perimeter of the first train was 4. I asked him to come up and show us. When he got to the overhead he took a square tile (black) and laid an edge of the square next to each side of the train as he counted the sides.

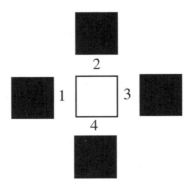

This was the procedure we had established yesterday, and I was pleased to see him use it. I thanked him and he returned to his seat.

Since Jake had started talking about perimeters, I decided that we might as well continue in this direction. I asked Zeke what he found for the perimeter of the second train. Zeke said he thought it was four. I asked him if he would go to the overhead and show us how he got 4. He explained, "the train has four sides — I just counted them 1, 2, 3, and 4." (See the diagram below.)

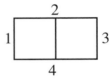

I saw what Zeke was doing. He was counting the number of sides, not the number of units in the perimeter. The number of sides and number of units were the same in the first figure but not in the second figure. I asked Zeke to stay at the overhead and I asked the class if someone could review what perimeter is. David said that it was the sides all the way around. I asked if anyone had another way to say it. David's definition really supported what Zeke had done, and I was looking for a definition that would cause students to question Zeke's solution. Finally Nick said that the perimeter would be six. Nick explained, "I used Jake's way and measured all the way around the outside of the train with the square tile. It's not 4 because the top and bottom each have two units." Although this was not the definition I was looking for, I figured that this explanation would help students see why the perimeter was 6 and not 4.

At this point I decided to ask Desmond to come up and measure the perimeter of the third train for us using the procedure that Nick had just described. I have been trying all year to get him involved. Lately I have been asking him questions that I was sure he could answer. They were not meant to challenge him in any way, just help him feel successful. These experiences have had an immediate positive effect on Desmond—he would actively participate in class following these episodes. So Desmond came up to the overhead, and I gave him the black square and asked him to measure the third train. I really thought that this would be a simple task, but Desmond did not seem to know what to do. Since this experience was supposed to be about experiencing success, I took his hand and helped him move the square along the outside of the train, counting as we proceeded.

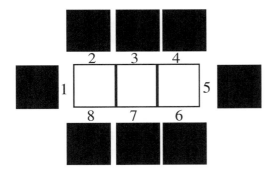

I thanked Desmond for his help. I was sure that this would clear up the confusion. I told Zeke that a lot of people make the same mistake that he did the first time they do perimeter. Just to be sure that Zeke understood the way to find perimeter, I asked him if he could build the fourth train in the pattern. He quickly laid four squares side to side. I then asked him if he could find the perimeter by measuring. He proceeded to count the sides while moving the side of the square

along the perimeter of the train—1, 2, 3, 4, 5, 6, 7, 8, 9, 10. He looked up when he finished and announced, "It will be ten!" I thanked him for hanging in there with us, and he returned to his seat.

Before moving on to the next part of the assignment, I asked if anybody had noticed anything else about perimeter when they did just the first three. Angela had her hand up, and I asked her what she had noticed. She explained, "on the third train there are three on the top and three on the bottom, which makes six, and one on each end." I asked her if she would go to the overhead and show us what she meant. She restated, "See there are three up here (pointing to the top of the train) and three down here (pointing to the bottom of the train) and then one on each end."

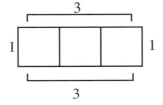

I was surprised by this observation so early on, but knowing that it would be helpful in determining the perimeters of larger trains, I asked Angela if she could use her system to find the perimeter of the fourth train. She quickly said "10." I asked her to explain. She proceeded, "four on the bottom and four on the top and one on each end."

Class can be pretty fast paced sometimes, with individual students, the whole class, and me going back and forth in a rapid exchange. A good example of this happened at this point as I tried to put Angela's observation to the test and see if I could get the whole class involved in using her observation to predict future trains. Once Angela's pattern became obvious to _her_ I wanted to make sure that everyone in the class saw it too. So I proceeded with the following question and answer exchange:

Me: Using your system, do you think you could do any number I say? What would you do for 10? How many on the top and the bottom?

Angela :   10.

Me: How many on the ends?

Angela :   2.

Me: How many all together?

Angela :   22.

Me: Let's do another one. Listen to what she's saying and see if you can do it also. Angela, in train 12, how many will there be on the top and bottom?

Angela :   12.

Me: And then how many will there be on the ends?

Angela :   2.

Me: How many will there be all together?

Angela :   26.

Me: Tamika, what's she doing?

Tamika: She's taking the train number on the top and bottom and adding two.

Me: OK, let's everybody try a few. I can pick any number. Train 50. How many will there be on the top and bottom? Everybody!

CLASS: 50   [with enthusiasm]

Me: How many on the ends?

CLASS: 2.

Me: How much all together?

CLASS: 102.

Me: Train 100, how many on the top and bottom?

CLASS: 100. [louder and with even more enthusiasm]

Me: How many on the ends?

CLASS: 2.

Me: How much all together?

CLASS: 202.

Me: Train 1000, how many on the top and bottom?

CLASS: 1000. [loudest of all]

Me: How many on the ends?

CLASS: 2.

Me: How much all together?

CLASS: 2002.

At this point I asked if they could describe anything I gave them. Another resounding "YES" answered my question. One of the things that I have found is that responding in unison really engages students and helps their confidence. When they respond in unison they feel that they are part of the group. Everyone can participate and feel good about themselves.

Angela's observation had really led us to finding the perimeters for any train, so I decided to continue on this pathway. I asked if anyone had figured out the perimeters using a different way. I looked around the room—no hands were in the air. I wanted them to have at least one other way to think about the pattern so I shared with them a method suggested by one of the students in another class. I explained that she had noticed that the squares on the ends always have three sides—they each lose one on the inside—and that the ones in the middle always have two sides. I used train three (shown in the diagram below) as an example and pointed out the three sides on each end and the two sides on the middle square.

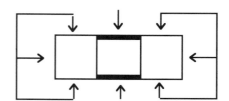

I wanted to see if students understood this so I asked how many squares would be in the middle of train 50 with this system. Nick said that there would be 48. I then added that there would be 48 two's, referring to the number of sides that would be counted in the perimeter, and three on each end. I asked what 48 two's would be. Carmen said it would be 96. I then asked what the perimeter would be. Shawntay said that it would 102. She went on to say that that was the same as what we got from train 50 when we did it Angela's way! I told the class that was right, there isn't just one way to look at it.

Considering a New Pattern

We had spent nearly 20 minutes on the square pattern, and it was time to move on to another pattern. I quickly got out my pattern blocks and built the train shown below on the overhead. I told students that I wanted them to work with their partners and build the first three trains in the pattern, find the perimeters for these three trains, and then to find the perimeters for the 10th, 20th, and 100th trains. I put the pattern of square trains we had just finished back up on the overhead underneath the hexagon pattern and suggested that they might want to see if they could find anything that was the same for the hexagon pattern and the square pattern that would help them. Since the generalizations for the perimeters of these two trains had some similarities, I thought this would help them find the perimeters for the larger trains in the hexagon pattern.

After about 5 minutes students seemed to be getting restless. Since most seemed to have made progress on the task, I decided to call the class together and see what they observed about the pattern. Although this is not exactly what I asked them to do—make observations—I felt that it provided a more open opportunity for all students to have something to say. I asked Tracy what she had noticed. She said that every time you add one. "Add one what?," I asked. "A hexagon," she responded. I then asked about the perimeter. Darrel said that he discovered that it was six. "What was six?," I asked. Darrel clarified that six was the amount around the hexagon—around the edges on the first train. I asked Darrel about the second train. He explained, "the hexagon has six around it and then you take away one for each side in the middle so it is 5 + 5 or 10. Then on the third one you still have 5 + 5 for the end ones and you add four more sides for the new hexagon you added."

I wanted to see if Darrel realized that his observation would lead to a generalization. I asked him if what he had discovered would tell him anything about building another train. Darrel said, "Yeah. On train 4 there would be four hexagons. The end ones would each have five and the two middle ones would each have four." "If you were to build train 10," I asked, "could you tell me how many would have four sides and how many would have five sides?" Darrel appeared to think about it for a few seconds and

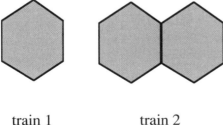

train 1   train 2

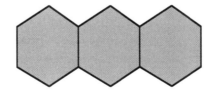

train 3

then responded that eight hexagons would have four sides and two hexagons would have five sides. I wanted to make sure that students understood what Darrel was saying so I asked him where the two with the five sides would be. He looked at me as though I were crazy and said, "Mrs. Evans, they would have to be on the ends!"

Again, I wanted to see if students could use Darrel's method on any train. I asked Tommy if he could describe the 20th train. Tommy explained, "For train 20 you'd count the sides and count the ends. You subtract 2 from 20 and that would be 18 and then you multiply 18 by 4, because all the hexagons in the middle have four and then you would add 10 from the ends." I was impressed with his explanation, and he seemed to be pretty proud of himself too. I wanted to make sure that everyone had all the steps that Tommy had so nicely explained.

I then asked Jeremy if he could do the 30th train. He said that he didn't know. I felt that he could probably do this if I provided a little structure for him. I asked him how many hexagons would have five sides. He said in a questioning tone, "two?" I nodded and said that this was correct. I then asked how many hexagons would be in the middle. He wrote something down on paper that I could not see and indicated that there would be 28. I then asked him how many sides each of the 28 hexagons would have on the perimeter. He responded more confidently this time with four.

I then asked the class how we could write 2 five's and 28 four's. No hands shot up immediately and I glanced at the clock. Where had the time gone—the bell was going to ring any minute. I told the students that for homework I wanted them to come up with a way to calculate the perimeter of the 30th train and any

other train we could come up with. I thought that this would push us toward more formal ways of recording calculations and, ultimately, generalizations.

Reflecting on Class Later That Day

The lesson was all I could have asked from the kids! They found the perimeters of the trains and were even making progress on finding generalizations. I have had this kind of a lesson about five times this year, and it is very exciting. I want to see the tape as soon as possible to find other things I could have done. The kids were very proud of themselves I think and so was I!

Reflecting on Class Several Weeks Later

A few weeks after this class I had the opportunity to share a 10-minute segment of a videotaped lesson with my colleagues at one of our staff development sessions. I decided to show a segment from the pattern block lesson since I thought it had gone so well. Although they didn't say so directly, I think they felt that I was too leading. Maybe they were right. It is easy to be too leading and feel OK about it because the kids seem happy. After all, many kids are happy with drill and practice.

I decided to go back and watch the entire tape again and see if I could look at it objectively. The lesson contained too much whole group teacher questioning and students explaining and not enough time for students to stretch and discover independently/collaboratively. I wondered, in particular, what most students really understood about Angela's method. Sure many of them answered my questions, but were they just mindlessly applying a procedure that they had rehearsed? Did it mean anything to them? Although choral response might make kids feel good, it really masks what individual students are really thinking and what it is they understand. Just because they could come up with answers to my questions doesn't mean that they really understand or that they have any idea how to apply it. I am now left wondering what they really learned from this experience.

Reflecting at the End of the School Year

In early June, at the end of the year retreat, my colleagues and I were asked to make a 10-minute presentation regarding the areas which we thought had changed most over the year. I began by showing a clip of one of my fall lessons—the one in which Desmond went to the overhead to measure the perimeter of the pattern train and in which I assumed control, even moving his hands. I told my colleagues, "I'd like to start with the first clip because I feel it pretty much sums up how I taught at the beginning of the year, and I'd like to show you that I really have become less directive than this tape." I showed the clip without sound. Attention was drawn to two pairs of hands on the overhead, the large pair (mine) which seemed to be moving the smaller pair (Desmond's). I explained, "You'll see Desmond comes up and I am very helpful—very directive and move the lesson along. That was a big thing with me—to move these lessons and if they didn't get it, I'd kinda help them do so." I added that I asked many yes/no questions very quickly and did not provide time for students to think. In contrast, I then showed video clips from the spring, in which I walked around the room, asking groups of students questions that would help them focus their efforts rather than telling or showing them what to do. For me, the differences in my actions and interactions with students on these two occasions provided evidence that I had changed.

Transition

Catherine Evans and her colleagues continued their efforts to improve the mathematics teaching and learning at Quigley Middle School. They met frequently to talk about their work and attended professional development sessions once a month and during the summers to support their growth and development. And their efforts were paying off—students were showing growth not only in basic skills but also in their ability to think, reason, and communicate mathematically.

At the beginning of the third year of the math project a new teacher joined the faculty at Quigley—David Young. Catherine and her colleagues welcomed David into their community. From their own experiences they knew how hard it was to teach math "in this way." But David had something that Catherine and her colleagues did not have initially—the opportunity to work beside teachers who had experience with the curriculum.

The case of David Young picks up at the beginning of David's second year at Quigley. He has been working with Catherine and others and has had one year's experience teaching "this new way." Catherine is now beginning her fourth year of the math project.

THE PATTERN TRAINS

Part 2 — David Young

David Young has just started his second year at Quigley Middle School. The job at Quigley was at first overwhelming for David. His mathematics teacher colleagues were implementing an instructional program based on a constructivist view of learning. Although such approaches had been foundational to his teacher preparation program, his teaching up to this point had been fairly traditional. The schools he had been in for student teaching and his first year teaching did not support innovation. But at Quigley the students were not passive recipients of what the teacher dished out, and drill and practice seemed to have a fairly limited role in instruction. Students were actually doing mathematics—exploring, making conjectures, arguing, and justifying their conclusions.

The enthusiasm and energy he saw in his colleagues was invigorating but also scary. His colleagues all had lots of experience, but he had almost none. He worried about his ability to be a contributing member of the community and whether or not he would be able to teach in a new way. David's fears were put to rest early in his first year. His colleagues were very supportive and understanding. They told him "war stories" about their initial experiences in teaching "this way" and how they had helped each other through the tough times. They would see him at lunch, in the morning before school, or just in the hall way and ask "What are you doing today?" and "How is it going?" They would give him some suggestions based on what had worked well for them, but they never told him what to do or harshly judged the decisions he made. Mostly they listened and asked a lot of questions. Over time David felt that he could ask or tell them anything. It was, he decided, the perfect place to teach.

During his tenure at Quigley, David had been working hard to help students develop confidence in their ability to do mathematics which he in turn felt would influence their interest and performance in the subject. Far too many students, he thought, hated math in large measure because they had not been successful in it. He had talked a lot with Catherine Evans about his concerns. Catherine had been quite open about her early experiences in teaching math the new way (just three years ago)

and her misstarts in trying to help students feel successful. David came to believe that developing confidence as a mathematics doer resulted from facing challenges and persevering in the face of them. The key, Catherine had often said, was trying to find a way to support students in solve a challenging task— not creating less challenging tasks for students to solve.

David Young Talks About His Class

This is the beginning of my second year teaching sixth grade with this new curriculum. The first year was rough—both for me and kids—as we tried to settle into our new roles in the classroom. Me as the facilitator and my students as constructors of knowledge. When things did not go well, my colleague Catherine was always there with a sympathetic ear and a word of encouragement. She is such a wonderful teacher—everything in her classroom seems to always go so well. (She is right next door, and we have a connecting door between our rooms. Sometimes during my free period I leave the door open and listen in on what is happening over there.) Although she has repeatedly said that it was a long and painful trip from where she started to where she is today, it is hard to believe. I guess it is comforting though to know that if she made it, I can too.

Catherine and I are both teaching sixth grade this year, so we touch base nearly everyday about what we are doing. We are only a month into the school year, and so far we have been working with patterns. Up to this point we have focused primarily on numerical patterns. The new unit that we started yesterday uses *trains* of pattern blocks arranged in some geometric sequence. The unit is supposed to help students visualize and describe geometric patterns, make conjectures about the patterns, determine the perimeters of trains they build, and ultimately, to develop a generalization for the perimeter of any train in a pattern.

Last year this unit did not go well. It was too much teacher talk and too little time for students to think. I moved them through the entire set of exercises in one period. I felt great because I had really "covered" the material, but a week later it was clear that the students hadn't gained much from the experience. When I talked with Catherine about it she told me about her first time through this unit three years ago. She said that one thing she learned is that kids need time to think, to struggle, and to make sense of things for themselves. If you make it too easy for them they will never learn to figure things out for themselves. This made sense to me, but it was hard not to step in and tell them what to do. I was determined, however, to do a better job this time around.

The Class

Yesterday my sixth grade class spent some time getting familiar with the pattern blocks—identifying the shapes and determining the perimeters of the blocks. Today they are going to make observations about trains of pattern blocks and determine the perimeters for the trains. Basically I am just going to follow the curriculum here. It suggests giving students a pattern sequence and having them compute the perimeter for the first three or four trains and then to determine the perimeter of a larger train like 10 or 20. Ultimately the curriculum suggests asking students to imagine that they are constructing the 100th train and to look for ways to find the perimeter. I will see how things go, but I hope to be able to follow this suggestion and use large numbers like 1000 so there is no way they can build or draw the trains and count the number of sides.

Getting Started: The Square Tile Pattern

I started by building the pattern of squares shown below on the overhead and asking students to work with their partners to find the perimeters of the first four trains in the sequence. Emily immediately asked for pattern blocks so she could actually build the trains. This of course started a series of requests to use the blocks. I hadn't anticipated this, but I had no problem with it either. I grabbed a few bags of blocks and dropped them off at the tables of students who had requested them.

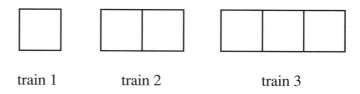

train 1   train 2   train 3

Students started building the trains and quickly seemed to realize that the fourth train would have four squares. They then began to determine the perimeter and record their findings. This initial activity seemed to be pretty easy for students. After about five minutes I asked Derek to go to the overhead and show us how he found the perimeter for the first three trains. Using a technique that we had used yesterday when we began exploring the perimeter of the blocks, Derek drew line segments parallel to the side of the square as he counted (as shown below), in order to show that he had counted a particular segment. Once he had completed the count, he recorded the perimeter on top of the train. I asked Derek what the numbers "4," "6," and "8" represented. He responded that "these are the distance around the outside of the train in units." I asked what a unit was, and he explained that he had used the side of the square as the unit. (The previous day we

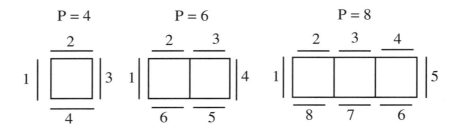

P = 4   P = 6   P = 8

had discussed that fact that we were going to be measuring using the side of the square as our unit. That way we could talk about the number of units without worrying about the actual measurement.)

I then asked the class what they thought the perimeter of the fourth train would be. Crystal said that she thought it would be 10. I asked her how she found it. She explained, "I just built the fourth one and counted the way Derek did." Jamal said that he got 10 too, but that he just added two more to the third train. I asked him to explain. He said, "When you add on one more block to the train the perimeter only gets bigger by two more units cause only the new piece on the top and bottom add to the perimeter." I asked the class if they had any questions for Jamal. Kirsten said that there were four sides in every square, so how could the perimeter only increase by two? Jamal went to the overhead and explained, "See if you look at the second train there are two units on the top and bottom, and one on each side. When to go to train three and add one more square (as shown below) you still only have one unit on each side cause the sides of the new square are on the inside not on the perimeter."

I then asked students to take a few minutes and think about what the tenth train would look like. I wanted to be sure that all students had time to consider this larger train. I know that sometimes I move too quickly and don't allow enough wait time for students to think about things. This tends to work against the students who have good ideas but work at a slower pace. Since I have been waiting longer, more students have been involved.

I started by asking Michele what she thought the perimeter would be. She said she got 22. I asked her if she could explain to us how she got this answer. She indicated that she had built the tenth train and then counted. Although this was a perfectly good approach for the tenth figure, it was going to be less helpful when we started considering larger trains. I asked if anyone did it another way. Travis said that he got 22 too, but that he just took ten plus ten plus 2. Although his answer was correct, it was not immediately obvious why he added this set of numbers. I asked him why he did this. He explained, "See when I looked at the first four trains I saw that the number of units on the top and bottom were the same as the number of the train. So in

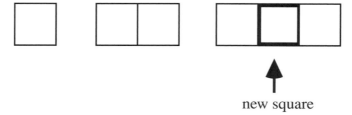

new square

train one there was one unit on the top and one on the bottom. In train two there were two units on the top and on the bottom. In train three there were three units on the top and the bottom. So I figured that this would keep going so the tenth train would have 10 units on the top and the bottom. Then for all the trains you have to add on the two sides because they never change."

I thanked Travis for sharing his strategy and asked if anyone had thought about it another way. Joseph said that he multiplied the number of squares in the train by 4, then subtracted the sides that were in the inside. I indicated that this was an interesting way to think about it and asked him if he would explain. He began, "Well, each square has 4 sides, so in the tenth train there would be 4×10 or 40 sides. But some of these are in the inside, so you have to subtract." "How did he know how many would be on the inside?" I asked. He explained, "Well, there are eight squares in the inside of the train, and each of those squares had two sides that didn't count and that gives you 16. Then there are two squares on the outside of the train and that each of those had one side that didn't count, so that gave you 18. So 40 – 18 gives you 22 and that's the answer."

As he finished his explanation a few hands shot up around the room. I asked the class if they had any questions for Joseph. Kendra asked how he knew that there were eight squares on the inside of the train. Joseph said that he had looked at the first four trains and noticed that the number of squares on the inside was two less than the train number—the second train had zero squares on the inside, the third train had one on the inside, and the fourth had two on the inside. I thanked Joseph for sharing his thinking about the problem with the class. I was really

pleased with the two different generalizations that had been offered and decided to ask one more question before moving on to a new pattern to see if the class could apply these noncounting approaches to a larger train.

I asked the class it they could tell me the perimeter of the 100th train. After waiting about 2 minutes for students to consider the question, I asked if anyone had a solution. Katherine said that she thought it would be 202. I asked her how she figured it out. She said she needed to draw and came up to the overhead. She drew a rectangle on the overhead and asked us to pretend that it was 100 squares. She then continued, "Like Travis said the number of units on the top and bottom is the train number, and then there are the two on the side. So for the 100 train, it would be 100 + 100 + 1 +1."

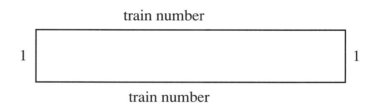

I commented that this seemed like a really fast way to do the problem. Rather than ask for additional ways to think about this pattern, I decided to move on. I passed out a sheet of four patterns (see attached) and asked students to work with their partners on pattern 1 on the sheet. In particular I wanted them to sketch the fourth train in the pattern, find the perimeter of each of the four trains, and then to see if they could find the perimeter of the tenth train without building the train. I knew the last condition would be a challenge for some, but I wanted them to think harder to find another way.

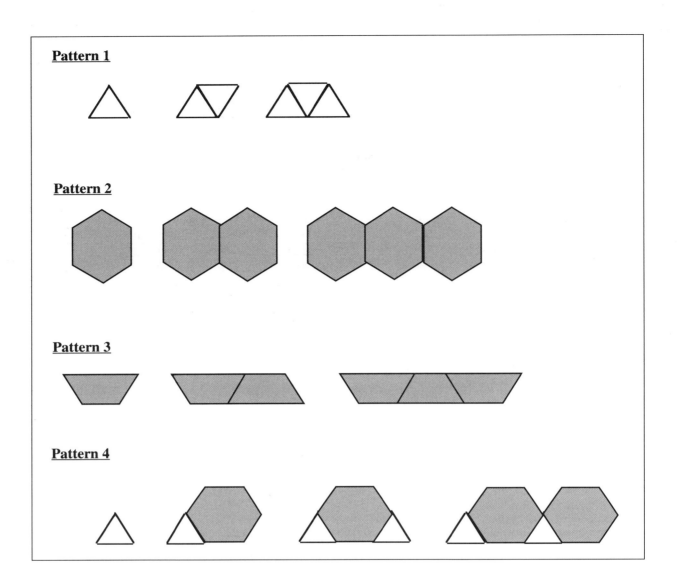

Pattern 1

Pattern 2

Pattern 3

Pattern 4

Continuing Work: The Triangle Pattern

I walked around visiting the pairs as they worked on the new train. Again students seem to quickly see the pattern—add one more triangle—and count the sides to find the perimeter. I observed several pairs starting to build the tenth train and asked them to try to find another way. I suggested that they look at the four trains they had built and see if they could find any patterns that would help them predict the tenth train. In a few cases where the students were really stuck I suggested that they try to see if they could find a connection between the train number and the perimeter as a few students had done in the last pattern.

Once it appeared that most pairs had made progress on this task, I asked James to come up and build the fourth train and describe the pattern. James quickly assembled the triangles, changing the orientation each time he added one. He explained, "you just add one more triangle each time and every new one is turned the opposite way of the last one." I then asked Catherine what she found for the perimeter of each train. She said that the first one was 3, the second one was 4, the third one was 5, and the fourth one was 6. I asked her what the fifth one would be. She quickly said "7." I asked her how she did it so fast, and she responded, "After the first one you just add one every time. The fourth train is 6 so the fifth train would be one more."

I then asked if anyone could tell me what the perimeter of the 10th train would be. Janelle said she thought it would be 12. I asked her how she found it. She said she made a table and looked for a pattern. Since this was the first time anyone had mentioned making a table, I thought it would be worth having her explain this strategy to the class. She came up and constructed the table shown below. She explained, "I looked in the table and I saw that the perimeter kept going up by one, but that the perimeter was always two more than the train number. So that for train number 10 the perimeter would be two more or 12."

Train #	Perimeter
1	3
2	4
3	5
4	6

Before I could even ask if anyone had done it another way, Joseph was waving his hand. He announced that he got 12 too, but that he did it another way. He said that the train number was the same as the number of triangles, just like the squares. He went on, "Since each triangle has three sides, I multiplied the number of

triangles by 3. So $3 \times 10 = 30$. But then you have to subtract the sides that are in the inside. It's like the square. You take the number of triangles on the inside. For the tenth train that would be 8. Each of those triangles has two sides that don't count and that give you 16. Then there are two triangles on the outside of the train and that each of those had one side that didn't count, so that makes 18. $30 - 8 = 12$."

"Wow," I said, "there are lots of different ways to look at these trains aren't there?" I was ready to move on, but Darrell was trying to get my attention. He said, "Aren't you gonna ask us to find the 100th?" That hadn't been my plan, but if he wanted to find the 100th I was happy to oblige. I asked Darrell if he wanted to tell us what the perimeter of the 100th train would be. He said, "It'll be 102. Cause like Janelle said, it will always be two more." I asked the class if they agreed with Darrell. I saw lots of nodding heads that convinced me that we were indeed making progress.

Exploring Three New Patterns

I told the class that they would have 15 minutes to work with their partners on patterns 2, 3, and 4. For each pattern they needed to sketch the next train, find the perimeter for all trains, and determine the perimeter for the 10th train without building the train. I wanted students to have a longer period of time for exploring the patterns without interruption. I figured that in 15 minutes everyone would at least get the first one done, and pattern four would be a challenge for those who got that far since it was less straight-forward than the previous patterns and that the odd and even trains would be described differently.

As students worked on the patterns, I again walked around the room observing what they were doing, listening in on their conversations, occasionally asking a question, and reminding them that they would need to be able to justify their methods to the rest of the class. The most challenging aspect of the task for most students was finding the perimeter to the tenth train without drawing it. For pattern 2, I encouraged them to try to find a way to talk about the perimeter of a figure in terms of the train number. "How are those two numbers related?," I asked as I moved from group to group.

Discussing the Hexagon Pattern

After 15 minutes all students had completed patterns 2 and 3. Since there were only 10 minutes left in class I thought I would have them talk about pattern 2 before the bell rang. I started by asking Jungsen to describe the pattern and give the perimeter for the first four. She explained that each train had the same number of hexagons as the train number and that the perimeters were 6, 10, 14, and 18. "What would the perimeter of the next one be?," I asked. James said

he thought it would be 24 because the hexagon had six sides and it would be six more. Michelle said that she thought it would 23, because it would only be 5 more because all sides didn't count. I asked if anyone had a different guess. Derek said that he thought it would be 22. A number of students chimed in with "I agree!" I asked Derek to tell us how he got 22. He said that every time you added a new hexagon, you only added on four more sides. "The perimeters were 6, 10, 14, and 18. You just keep adding four."

I asked if anyone could explain it another way. Kirsten said that she thought she could. "Every time you add another hex", she explained, "you just add two sides on the top and two on the bottom." She pointed to the trains on the overhead and continued, "If you look at train two, you have four sides on the top, four on the bottom, and the two on the ends. If you look at train three you added one more hex which gives you two more sides on the top and the bottom. That gives you just four more."

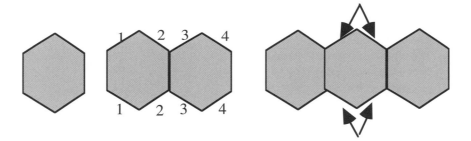

I asked if anyone had found the perimeter of the tenth train. Carmen said that she thought it would be 42. I asked how she got this. She said that the tenth train would have 20 sides on the top, 20 sides on the bottom, and one on each end. I asked how she knew it would be 20. She went on to explain, "The number on top is double the train number. See, the second train has four, the third train has six, so the tenth train would have 20."

I thanked Carmen for sharing her solution and asked if anyone had another way. Joseph was again waving his hand. I asked Joseph if he used his method on this problem too. He said he did and explained that since each hexagon had six sides you needed to multiply the train number by 6 to get 60. Then you needed to subtract the inside sides which would be 18. So it would be 60 – 18 which was 42. Kirsten asked Joseph if you always subtracted 18 for the tenth train. Joseph said that so far that seemed to work for the squares and the hexagons, but he wasn't sure if it always worked. Kirsten's question was a good one. I made a note to be sure to include a pattern for which it would not work, just to push Joseph to consider what was generalizable about his approach and what wasn't.

I finally asked about the perimeter of the 100th train. It seemed as though everyone thought they had it this time. I took a quick look at the clock. The bell was going to ring any minute. I told students for homework to write down what they thought the perimeter of the 100th one would be and to explain how they figured it out. We would start there the next day and then jump right in and try pattern 4.

Appendix J:
To Become a Mathematics Teacher

SOURCE:
-Prepared by Waseda University
-Focused on lower secondary and upper secondary school in Japan

INTRODUCTION

In Japan, in order to become a teacher, one must obtain a teacher's certificate by completing the subjects in a university course, in accordance with the provisions of the Education Personnel Certification Law. This paper describes the process by which undergraduate students get a first class certificate of mathematics as a way to be a lower secondary and upper secondary school mathematics teacher.

Types of Ordinary Teacher Certificate

As Table 1 shows, there is a variety of certificates, according to the degree students will get and the school level of certificate. In addition, there are also several kinds of certificates for lower or upper secondary school teachers by subject areas in which prospective teachers intend to specialize.

SOURCE:
Those who want to become a special school teacher (for handicapped students) also have to take units to be such a teacher as well as units for getting the ordinary teacher certificate.

What You Need to Be a Mathematics Teacher

Students who want to be a math teacher are supposed to take the lessons described below (see Table 2). There are two kinds of lessons; the former consists of subjects about mathematics and the latter of ones on *kyoushoku*[1], which are subjects that students are to have before they become a teacher.

(1) Subjects about mathematics. Students have to take at least 20 units of lecture on mathematics. For example, in Waseda University, they are to register and pass several areas in mathematics such as algebra, geometry, analysis, statistics, and computer.

---

[1] *Kyoushoku* generally means the whole things of working as a teacher in school as well as subjects in university that students are to register and pass before becoming a teacher.

TABLE 1 Types of Ordinary Teacher Certificate

Classification	Completion of a Master's Course	Completion of an Undergraduate Course	Completion of a Junior College Course
Elementary school teachers	First-class certificate	First-class certificate	Second-class certificate
Lower secondary school teachers	First-class certificate	First-class certificate	Second-class certificate
Upper secondary school teachers	First-class certificate	First-class certificate	
Kindergarten teachers	First-class certificate	First-class certificate	
Nursery school teachers	First-class certificate	First-class certificate	Second-class certificate

TABLE 2 The Condition of Getting a Certificate in Waseda University

Classification	First Class (lower)	Advanced (lower)	First Class (upper)	Advanced (upper)
Qualification of certificate	Bachelor	Master	Bachelor	Master
Number of units needed (at least)				
Constitution	2	2	2	2
Physical education	2	2	2	2
Oral communication by foreign language	2	2	2	2
Operation of information technology	2	2	2	2
Subjects to get advanced certificate		24		24
Subjects on mathematics	20	20	20	20
Subjects on *kyoushoku*	31	31	25	25

There are also subjects on mathematics and *kyoushoku*.

(2) Subjects on *kyoushoku*. If we take Waseda University as an example, there are many subjects on kyoushoku as follows.

- *kyoushoku-gairon*: This subject deals with general things of *kyoushoku*, for example, the value of school education, the role of teacher, the essence of their work, and so on.
- *kyouiku-genri*: In this subject, students study the concept, history, and thought of education, including social, institutional, and managerial problems in education.
- *kyouiku-sinrigaku*: This literally means educational psychology. In this subject, the theme is primarily focused on developmental psychology and the process of learning. In other words, *kyouiku-sinrigaku* deals with the psychological development of children and how they learn a way of thinking as well as respective knowledge.
- *kyouiku-rinshouron*: The theme of this subject is the theory and method of *kyouiku-soudan*[2], including basic elements of counseling.
- *seitosidou-seikatusidouron*: In this subject, students are supposed to learn the theory and method of matters about moral discipline and consultation with children about the selection of courses for their future.
- *suugakuka-kyouikuhou*[3]: This subject is focused on the method of teaching mathematics. It includes general and fundamental matters such as the aim of mathematics teaching, educational value of substance, evaluation, and so

on. Through their topics, students are expected to understand not only mathematics well. They also have to appreciate the tight "hierarchy" of mathematics and the importance of building desirable ability and attitude through teaching mathematics.

- *kyquiku-iia-shuu kiso-enshuu*: Those who want to get a teacher's certificate have to take this subject. It is composed of a preliminary lecture and a reflection about *kyouiku-jisshuu*. In the former, students are supposed to learn the value, substance, method, and general things of *kyouiku-jisshuu*. In the latter, they have to overview and evaluate their experience by themselves.
- *kyouiku-jisshuu*: During *kyouiku-jisshuu* (usually for several weeks), they are to have classes in schools and teach mathematics practically as well as to join homeroom and club activities. To prepare for the classes with the teacher who is in charge, they have to make a *shidou-an* (or *kyou-an*) with detailed information and flow chart of the class. They also need to write down in a diary notes on what happened and what they learned or thought during *kyouiku-jisshuu*. Then after it is over, they are supposed to hand in the notes to the university they attend.

OVERVIEW

What follows are some typical comments from students who took part in *kyouiku-jisshuu*.

- There is a big difference between knowing and understanding. I needed to prepare myself for the classes I had every day, so I was exhausted from such work at the end of *kyouiku-jisshuu*. Preparation is never perfect.

---

[2] *Kyouiku-soudan* is the entire things of counseling with children in school.

[3] To be an upper secondary school mathematics teacher, students need to take four units at least, but those who want to be a lower secondary school math teacher are required to take six units in total.

- We have to have flexibility during class. We always need to do things from a student's point of view.
- I think the most important thing is to have a good relationship with the students. For example, to memorize a student's name was very good for classes as well as personal relationships.

We can summarize their comments as follows: It is true that working as a teacher in school was very hard, but it was also one of the most exciting experiences they had, so that they cannot forget about it.

Appendix K: Glossary

GLOSSARY OF TERMS

lesson study – *jugyokenkyu*: A general term for a collaborate professional development process that involves joint lesson planning under a common goal. Lesson study includes planning, implementing, observing, and reflecting on the lesson. Lesson study takes many forms and has many variations depending on the purpose and site: intraschool lesson study, intercity lesson study, a lesson study that includes a demonstration lesson that is open for everybody. Usually, in any type of lesson study, the lesson study group designs the "theme" of the study, and the details are left to one or a few teachers. Some lesson study groups or "circles" may plan a lesson together, mainly by examining a lesson plan. A postlesson discussion takes place in all of these cases.

study lesson – *kenkyu jugyou*: The lesson that is produced as part of the lesson study process, the product of lesson study.

demonstration lesson: A lesson publicly taught and discussed.

JAPANESE VOCABULARY RELATED TO LESSON STUDY

bansho: Blackboard writing, the design of how records of the lesson are placed on the board.

hatusumon: A thought provoking question.

konaikenshu: In-school professional development. Lesson study may be chosen by teachers for their professional development (*konaikenshu*) activity.

kikan-shido: Purposeful walking among the students' desks, looking at their work, giving some feedback, hints, questions for evaluation, deciding an order of responses for discussion, selecting students for the whole class discussion.

kokaijugyo: Open-house study lesson.

kyoushoku: Generally means the whole of working as a teacher in school as well as subjects in university that students are to register and pass before becoming a teacher.

matome: The summing up or wrap-up of the lesson. Teachers must do *matome* for students to learn the lesson with a depth of mathematical understanding.

neriage: Comparing ideas among students and "kneading them up" to bring out the mathematics. Integrating and discussing the ideas leading toward the final conclusion. The teacher is not at the same level as the students but functions as the conductor, orchestrating the lesson to raise the level of mathematics.

shu hatusumon: The main critical question. As part of the preplanning, teachers should consider anticipated student solutions, "cautious points" where students might be mistaken in their thinking, and evaluation points to use to assess student understanding.

yamaba: The highlight or climax of the lesson. A lesson should have a highlight in order to be interesting.

Appendix L: Workshop Reading List

PREWORKSHOP READINGS

Ball, D. L., and Bass, H. (2000). Interweaving content and pedagogy in teaching and learning to teach: Knowing and using mathematics. In J. Boaler (Ed.), *Multiple perspectives on the teaching and learning of mathematics*. Westport, CT: Ablex.

Ball, D. L., and Cohen, D. (1999). Developing practice, developing practitioners. In L. Darling-Hammond, and G. Sykes (Eds.), *Teaching as the learning profession: Handbook of policy and practice*. San Francisco, CA: Jossey-Bass.

Dossey, J., and Usiskin, Z. (2000). *Mathematics education in the United States 2000*. Reston, VA: National Council of Teachers of Mathematics.

Lewis, C. (2000). *Lesson study: The core of Japanese professional development*. Paper Prepared for the American Educational Research Association Meeting, New Orleans, LA.

National Research Council. (1996). *The preparation of teachers of mathematics: Considerations and challenges*. Mathematical Sciences Education Board. Washington, DC: National Academy Press.

National Science Foundation. (2000). *Observations on science and mathematics teacher education in Japan*. Tokyo, Japan: National Science Foundation Tokyo Regional Office.

Sawada, D. (1996). Mathematics as connection making in Japanese elementary schools. *School Science and Mathematics, 96(5)*, 258-262.

Shimizu, Y. (1999). Aspects of mathematics teacher education in Japan: Focusing on teachers' roles. *Journal of Mathematics Teacher Education, 2*, 107-116.

Shimizu, Y. (1999). Studying sample lessons rather than one excellent lesson: A Japanese perspective on the Third, International Mathematics and Science Study videotape classroom study. *Zentralblatt fuer Didaktik der Mathematik, 31(6)*, 191-195.

Shimizu, Y. (2000, August). *Discussing multiple solutions for a problem: How do Japanese teachers capitalize on the diversity of students' thinking in their lessons?* Paper presented at the meeting of The Study of Teaching Practice as a Medium for Professional Development United States - Japan Teacher Preparation Workshop, Makuhari, Japan.

Yoshida, M. (1999). *Lesson study (jugyokenkyu) in elementary school mathematics in Japan: A case study*. Prepared for the American Educational Research Association, Montreal, Canada.

Appendix M: References

American Federation of Teachers (2000). *Salary data of the 100 largest U.S. cities.* Available: www.aft.org/research/tables/tableV-1.html [January 26, 2001].

American Federation of Teachers. (1992, rev. 1997) *Thinking mathematics I: Foundations, thinking mathematics.* Washington, DC: Author.

Ball, D. L. (1990). The mathematical understandings that prospective teachers bring to teacher education. *Elementary School Journal, 90,* 449-466.

Ball, D. L. (1991). Research on teaching mathematics: Making subject matter knowledge part of the equation. In J. Brophy (Ed.), *Advances in research on teaching, Volume 2: Teachers' knowledge of subject matter as it relates to their teaching practice* (pp. 1-48). Greenwich, CT: JAI Press.

Ball, D. L., and Bass, H. (2000). Interweaving content and pedagogy in teaching and learning to teach: Knowing and using mathematics. In J. Boaler (Ed.), *Multiple perspectives on the teaching and learning of mathematics.* Westport, CT: Ablex.

Ball, D. L. and Cohen, D. K. (1999). Developing practice, developing practitioners: Toward a practice-based theory of professional education. In G. Sykes and L. Darling-Hammond (Eds.), *Teaching as the learning profession: Handbook of policy and practice* (pp. 3-32). San Francisco, CA: Jossey Bass.

Ball, D. L. and Wilson, S. M. (1990). *Knowing the subject and learning to teach it: Examining assumptions about becoming a mathematics teacher* (Research Report 90-7). East Lansing, MI: Michigan State University, National Center for Research on Teacher Learning.

Battista, M. T. (1999, February). The mathematical miseducation of America's youth: Ignoring research and scientific study in education. *Phi Delta Kappan,* 424-433.

Bauersfeld, H. (1996). *Social constructivism, classroom cultures, and other concepts – What can they mean for teachers?* Plenary Lecture of Psychology of Mathematics Education-North American Chapter-18, Panama City, FL.

Beaton, A. E., Mullis, I., Martin, M., Gonzalez, E., Kelly, D., and Smith, T. (1996). *Mathematics achievement in the middle school years: IEA's third international mathematics and science study.* Chestnut Hill, MA: TIMSS International Study Center Boston College.

Becker, J. P., and Jacob B. (2000). The politics of California school mathematics: The anti-reform of 1997-99. *Phi Delta Kappan, 81(2),* 529-537

Blank, R., and Langesen, D. (1999). *State indicators of science and mathematic education: 1999.* Washington, DC: Council of Chief State School Officers.

Briars, D. J., and Resnick, L. B. (2000). *Standards, assessments—and what else? The essential elements of standards-based school improvement.* CSE Technical Report 528. Los Angeles, CA: University of California, Center for the Study of Evaluation, National Center for Research on Evaluation, Standards, and Student Testing.

Campbell, J., Voelkl, K., and Donahue, P. (1997). *NAEP 1996 trends in academic progress.* Washington, DC: National Center for Education Statistics.

Council of Chief State School Officers. (1998). *Standards, graduation, assessment, teacher licensure, time and attendance: A 50-state report August 1998.* Washington DC: Author

Dossey, J. (2000). The state of NAEP mathematics findings: 1996. In E. Silver and P. A. Kenney (Eds.), *Results from the seventh mathematics assessment.* Reston, VA: National Council of Teachers of Mathematics.

Dossey, J., and Usiskin, Z. (2000, July-August). *Mathematics education in the United States 2000.* Capsule summary written for The Ninth International Congress on Mathematics Education, Tokyo/Makuhari, Japan.

Fried, S. N., Loucks-Horsley S., and Sneider, C. I. (Eds.). (1998). *Designing professional development for teachers of science and mathematics.* Thousand Oaks, CA: Corwin Press.

Grossman, P. L., and Stodolsky, S. S. (1995). Content as context: The role of school subjects in secondary school teaching. *Educational Researcher, 24,* 5-11.

Hashimoto, Y. (1999). The latest thinking in Japanese mathematics education: Creating mathematics curricula for all students. In Z. Usiskin (Ed.), *Developments in school mathematics education around the world,* vol. 4 (pp. 50-57). Reston, VA: National Council of Teachers of Mathematics.

Hirabayashi, I. (2000, August). *Lesson as drama and lessons as another form of thesis presentation.* Paper presented at the U.S. - Japan Teacher Preparation Workshop, Makuhari, Japan.

Husen, T. (1967). *International study of achievement in mathematics: A comparison of twelve countries.* New York: John Wiley.

Ingersoll, R. (1998). The problem of out-of-field teaching. *Phi Delta Kappan, 79*(10), 773-776.

Japan Society of Mathematical Education, Research Section. (2000). *School mathematics in Japan.* Tokyo: Author.

Kimmelman, P., Kroeze, D., Schmidt, W., von der Ploeg, A., McNeely, M., and Tea, A. (1999). *A first look at what we can learn from high performing school districts: An analysis of TIMSS data from the first in the world consortium.* Jessup, MD: U.S. Department of Education.

Lewis, C. (2000, April). *Lesson study: The core of Japanese professional development.* Paper presented at the American Education Research Association 1999 Annual Meeting, New Orleans, LA.

Lewis, C., and Tsuchida, I. (1997). Planned educational change in Japan: The shift to student-centered elementary science. *Journal of Education Policy, 12(5),* 313-331.

Lewis, C., and Tsuchida, I. (1998 Winter). A lesson is like a swiftly flowing river: Research lessons and the improvement of Japanese education. *American Educator,* 14-17, 50-52.

Ma, L. (1999). *Knowing and teaching elementary mathematics: Teachers' understanding of fundamental mathematics in China and the United States.* Mahwah, NJ: Erlbaum.

McKnight, C., Crosswhite, R., Dossey, J., Kifer, E., Swafford, J., Travers, E., and Cooney, T. (1987*).* *The underachieving curriculum: Assessing U.S. school mathematics from an international perspective.* Champaign, IL: Stipes.

McLaughlin, M.W. (1993). What matters most in teachers' workplace context? In J.W. Little and M.W. McLaughlin (Eds.). *Teachers work: Individuals, colleagues, and contexts.* New York: Teachers College Press.

National Advisory Committee on Mathematical Education. (1975). *Overview and analysis of school mathematics: Grades K-12.* Reston, VA: National Council of Teachers of Mathematics.

National Center for Education Statistics. (1995). *Teacher supply, teacher qualifications, and teacher turnover, aspects of teacher supply and demand in the U.S., 1990-91.* Washington, DC: U.S. Department of Education.

National Center for Education Statistics. (1996). *Pursuing excellence: A study of U.S. eighth-grade mathematics and science teaching, learning, curriculum, and achievement in international context.* Washington, DC: U.S. Department of Education.

National Center for Education Statistics. (2000). *The condition of education 2000.* Washington, DC: U.S. Department of Education.

National Council of Teachers of Mathematics. (1989). *Curriculum and evaluation standards for teaching school mathematics.* Reston, VA: Author.

National Council of Teachers of Mathematics. (1991). *Professional standards for teaching mathematics.* Reston, VA: Author.

National Council of Teachers of Mathematics. (1995). *Assessment standards for school mathematics.* Reston, VA: Author.

National Council of Teachers of Mathematics. (2000). *Principles and standards for school mathematics.* Reston, VA: Author.

National Research Council. (1996). *From analysis to action: Undergraduate education in science, mathematics, engineering, and technology.* Center for Science, Mathematics, and Engineering Education. Washington, DC: National Academy Press.

National Research Council. (2001). *Knowing and learning mathematics for teaching.* Mathematics Teacher Preparation Content Workshop Steering Committee, Center for Education, Division of Behavioral and Social Sciences and Education. Washington, DC: National Academy Press.

National Science Foundation. (1998). *Shaping the future.* Arlington, VA: Author.

National Science Foundation. (2000). *Observations on science and mathematics teacher education in Japan.* Tokyo, Japan: National Science Foundation Tokyo Regional Office.

Okabe, T. (1999). *The university student who can't do fractions.* Tokyo, Japan: Toyo Keizai Shinpo Sha.

Okabe, T. (2000). *The university student who can't do decimals.* Tokyo, Japan: Toyo Keizai Shinpo Sha.

Pólya, G. (1952). *How to solve it.* Princeton, NJ: Princeton University Press.

Pólya, G. (1963). On learning, teaching, and learning teaching. *American Mathematical Monthly, 70,* 605-619.

Porter, R., Desimone, L., Herman, R., and Yoon, K.S. (1999). *Designing effective professional development: Lessons from the Eisenhower Program.* Washington, DC: U.S. Department of Education.

Post, T. R., Harel, G., Behr, M. J., and Lesh, R. (1991). Intermediate teachers' knowledge of rational number concepts. In E. Fennema, T. P. Carpenter, and S. J. Lamon (Eds.), *Integrating research on teaching and learning mathematics* (pp. 194-217). New York: SUNY Press.

Riley, R. W. (2000, February). *Setting new expectations.* Paper presented at the Seventh Annual State of American Education address, Southern High School, Durham, NC.

Schifter, D. (1998). Learning mathematics for teaching: From a teachers' seminar to the classroom. *Journal of Mathematics Teacher Education, 1(1)* 55-87.

Schifter, D., Bastable, V., and Russell, S. J. (with Yaffe, L., Lester, J. B., and Cohen, S.) (1999). *Developing mathematical ideas, number and operations part 2: Making meaning for operations casebook.* Parsippany, NJ: Dale Seymour.

Shields, P.M., Esch, C.E., Humphrey, D.C., Young, V.M., Gaston, M., and Hunt, H. (1999). *The status of the teaching profession: Research findings and policy recommendations.* Santa Cruz, CA: The Center for the Future of Teaching and Learning.

Shimahara, N., and Sakai, A. (1995). *Learning to teach in two cultures.* New York: Garland.

Shimizu, Y. (2000, August). *Discussing multiple solutions for a problem: How do Japanese teachers capitalize on the diversity of students' thinking in their lessons?* Paper presented at the meeting of The Study of Teaching Practice as a Medium for Professional Development U.S. - Japan Teacher Preparation Workshop, Maruhari, Japan.

Shulman, J. (1992). *Case methods in teacher education.* New York: Teachers College Press.

Shulman, L. (1986). Those who understand: Knowledge growth in teaching. *Educational Researcher, 15(2)*, 4-14.

Stein, M. K., Smith, M. S., Henningsen, M. A., and Silver, E. A. (2000). *Implementing standards-based mathematics instruction: A casebook for professional development.* New York: Teachers College Press.

Stevenson, H., Lee, S., and Stigler, J. (1986). Mathematics achievement of Chinese, Japanese, and American children. *Science, 231*, 693-699.

Stevenson, H., and Stigler, J. (1992). *The learning gap: Why our schools are failing and what we can learn from Japanese and Chinese education.* New York: Simon and Schuster.

Stigler, J., Gonzales, P., Kawanaka T., Knoll, S., and Serrano, A. (1999). *The TIMSS videotape classroom study: Methods and findings from an exploratory research project on eighth grade mathematics instruction in Germany, Japan, and the United States.* Washington, DC: National Center for Education Statistics.

Stigler, J., and Hiebert, J. (1999). *The teaching gap: Best ideas from the world's teachers for improving education in the classroom.* New York: Free Press.

U.S. Department of Education. (2000). *Progress through the teacher pipeline: 1992-93 college graduates and elementary/secondary school teaching as of 1997.* Washington, DC: Author

Weiss, I.R., Matti, M.C., and Smith, P. S. (1994). *Report of the 1993 national survey of science and mathematics education.* Chapel Hill, NC: Horizon Research, Inc.

World Almanac. (2000). *The world almanac and book of facts.* New York: World Almanac Books.

Yoshida, M. (1999, April). *Lesson study [Jugyokenkyu] in elementary school mathematics in Japan: A case study.* Paper presented at the American Education Research Association 1999 Annual Meeting, Montreal, Canada. Available from Myoshida1@earthlink.net.

SUPPLEMENTAL READING LIST

Curcio, F. R. (2001). *Japanese lesson study: Ideas for improving mathematics teaching (videotape and user's guide).* Reston, VA: National Council of Teachers of Mathematics.

Fernandez, C., Chokshi, S., Cannon, J., and Yoshida, M. (2001). Learning about lesson study in the United States. In E. Beauchamp, Ed.*, New and old voices on Japanese education.* Armonk, NY: M.E. Sharpe.

Lewis, C. (April 2000). *Lesson study: The heart of Japanese professional development.* AERA Mathematics Education Special Interest Group Invitational Address, New Orleans.

Linn, M., Lewis, C., Tsuchida, I., and Songer, N. B. (2000). Beyond fourth grade science: Why do US and Japanese students diverge? *Educational Researcher, 29(3)*, 4-14.

National Institute on Student Achievement, Curriculum, and Assessment (1998). *The educational system in Japan: Case study findings.* Washington, DC: Office of Educational Research and Improvement, U.S. Department of Education.

Wang-Iverson, P., Liptak, L, and Jackson, W. (2000, May) *Journey beyond TIMSS: Rethinking professional development.* Paper presented at ICME II in Hangzhou, China. Available from wang@rbs.org.

Yoshida, M. (1999). *Lesson study: A case study of a Japanese approach to improving instruction through school-based teacher development.* Doctoral dissertation, University of Chicago.